HAWK
INVESTIGATIONS

hawkeye

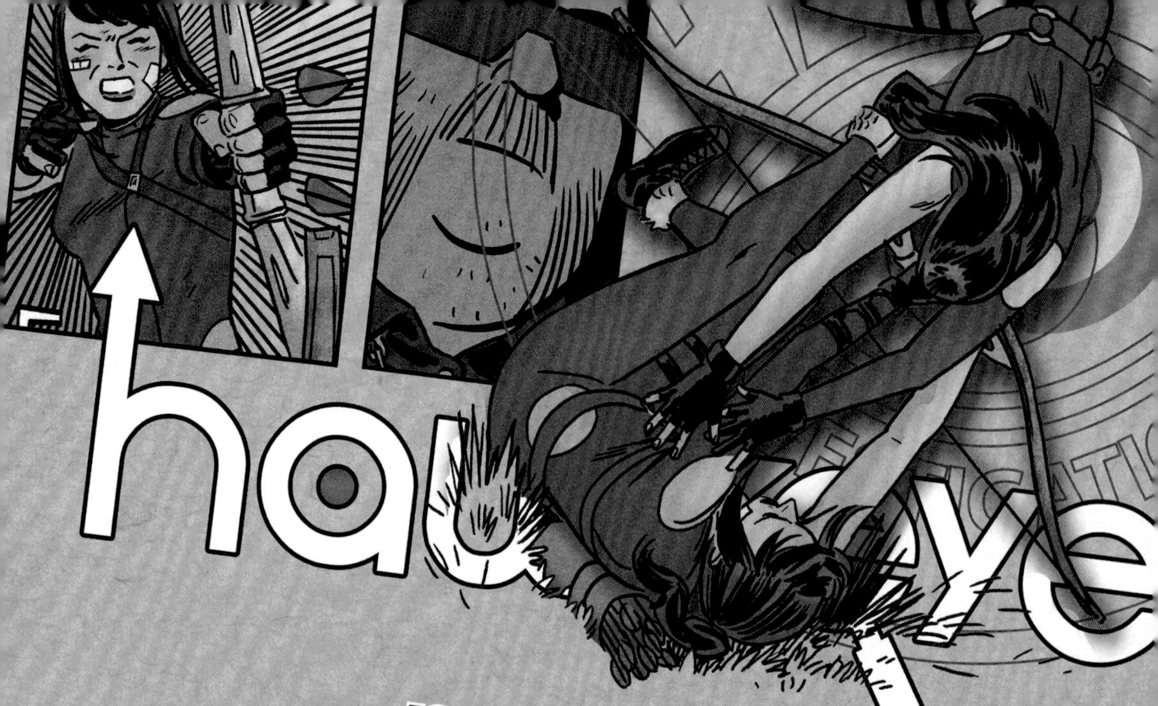

masks

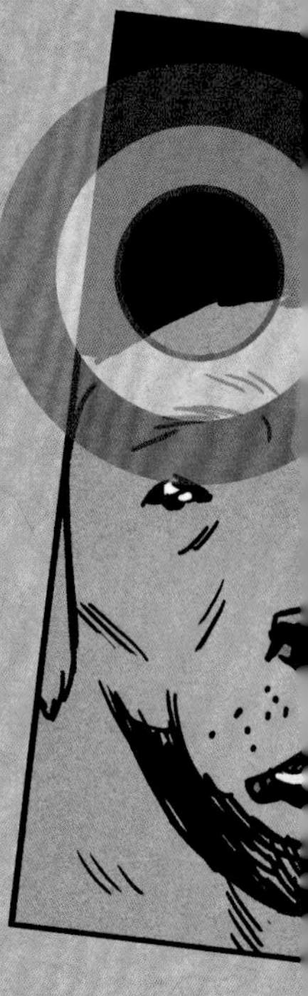

Kelly Thompson
writer

Leonardo Romero (#7-11)
& **Michael Walsh** (#12)
artists

Jordie Bellaire
color artist

VC's Joe Sabino
letterer

Julian Totino Tedesco
cover art

Charles Beacham
& **Alanna Smith**
editors

Sana Amanat
supervising editor

collection editor **Jennifer Grünwald** • assistant editor **Caitlin O'Connell**
associate managing editor **Kateri Woody** • editor, special projects **Mark D. Beazley**
vp production & special projects **Jeff Youngquist** • svp print, sales & marketing **David Gabriel**
book designer **Jay Bowen**

editor in chief **Axel Alonso** • chief creative officer **Joe Quesada**
president **Dan Buckley** • executive producer **Alan Fine**

HAWKEYE: KATE BISHOP VOL. 2 — MASKS. Contains material originally published in magazine form as HAWKEYE #7-12. First printing 2017. ISBN# 978-1-302-90515-6. Published by MARVEL WORLDWIDE, INC., a subsidiary of MARVEL ENTERTAINMENT, LLC. OFFICE OF PUBLICATION: 135 West 50th Street, New York, NY 10020. **Printed in Canada.** DAN BUCKLEY, President, Marvel Entertainment; JOE QUESADA, Chief Creative Officer; TOM BREVOORT, SVP of Publishing; DAVID BOGART, SVP of Business Affairs & Operations, Publishing & Partnership; C.B. CEBULSKI, VP of Brand Management & Development, Asia; DAVID GABRIEL, SVP of Sales & Marketing, Publishing; JEFF YOUNGQUIST, VP of Production & Special Projects; DAN CARR, Executive Director of Publishing Technology; ALEX MORALES, Director of Publishing Operations; SUSAN CRESPI, Production Manager; STAN LEE, Chairman Emeritus. For information regarding advertising in Marvel Comics or on Marvel.com, please contact Jonathan Parkhideh, VP of Digital Media & Marketing Solutions, at jparkhideh@marvel.com. For Marvel subscription inquiries, please call 888-511-5480. **Manufactured between 10/27/2017 and 11/28/2017 by SOLISCO PRINTERS, SCOTT, QC, CANADA.**

10 9 8 7 6 5 4 3 2 1

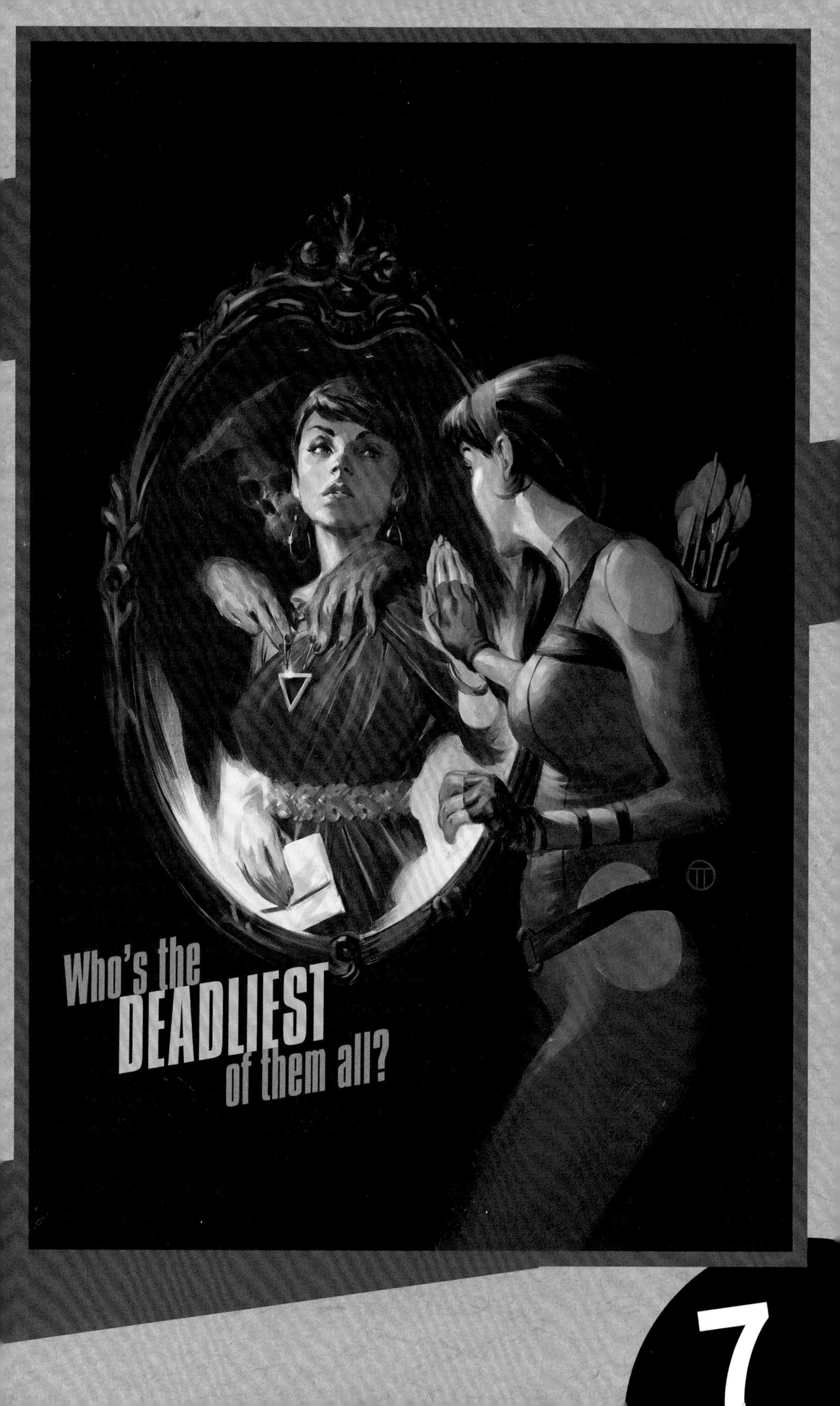
Who's the
DEADLIEST
of them all?
7

**SUPER POWERED
HATEMONGER**

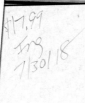

$17.99
Ing
7/30/18

HAWK
INVESTIGATIONS

22 1
Ven

MY NEW FRIENDS

CASE NO.: 016003
INVESTIGATOR: KATE BISHOP, A.K.A. HAWKEYE
CLIENT: Kate Bishop, A.K.A. ME

CASE OVERVIEW:

I know I've made quite a splash as Private Detective in L.A. (I took down a
crazy hatemonger with supernatural empath powers and saved a girl
who transforms into a dragon from eating her admittedly incompetent
boyfriend.) But the fact is, I came here to find answers about my past.
It's quickly becoming clear, though, that my past might be chasing me...

**GIRL WHO TURNS
A DRAGON**

DETAIL OF EVENTS:

After I wrapped up the aforementioned case involving the girl with
the dragon body, I dropped my friend and mentor Jessica Jones off
at the airport, picked up my buddy Lucky Dog and headed home for
some much need R & R (I mean. I live in SoCal now. Am I NOT
supposed to enjoy that?). Rest was not had--I was jumped by
people inside my own house.

ACTION TAKEN:

First I'm going to ice my face. Then I'm trackdown whoever's
responsible for this and teach them a lesson.

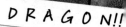
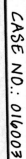
DRAGON!!

ADDITIONAL NOTES:

The jerks who attacked me left a box. I have my
suspicions as to who it's from and I'm more than
slightly nervous to find out if I'm right.

STATUS:

OPEN

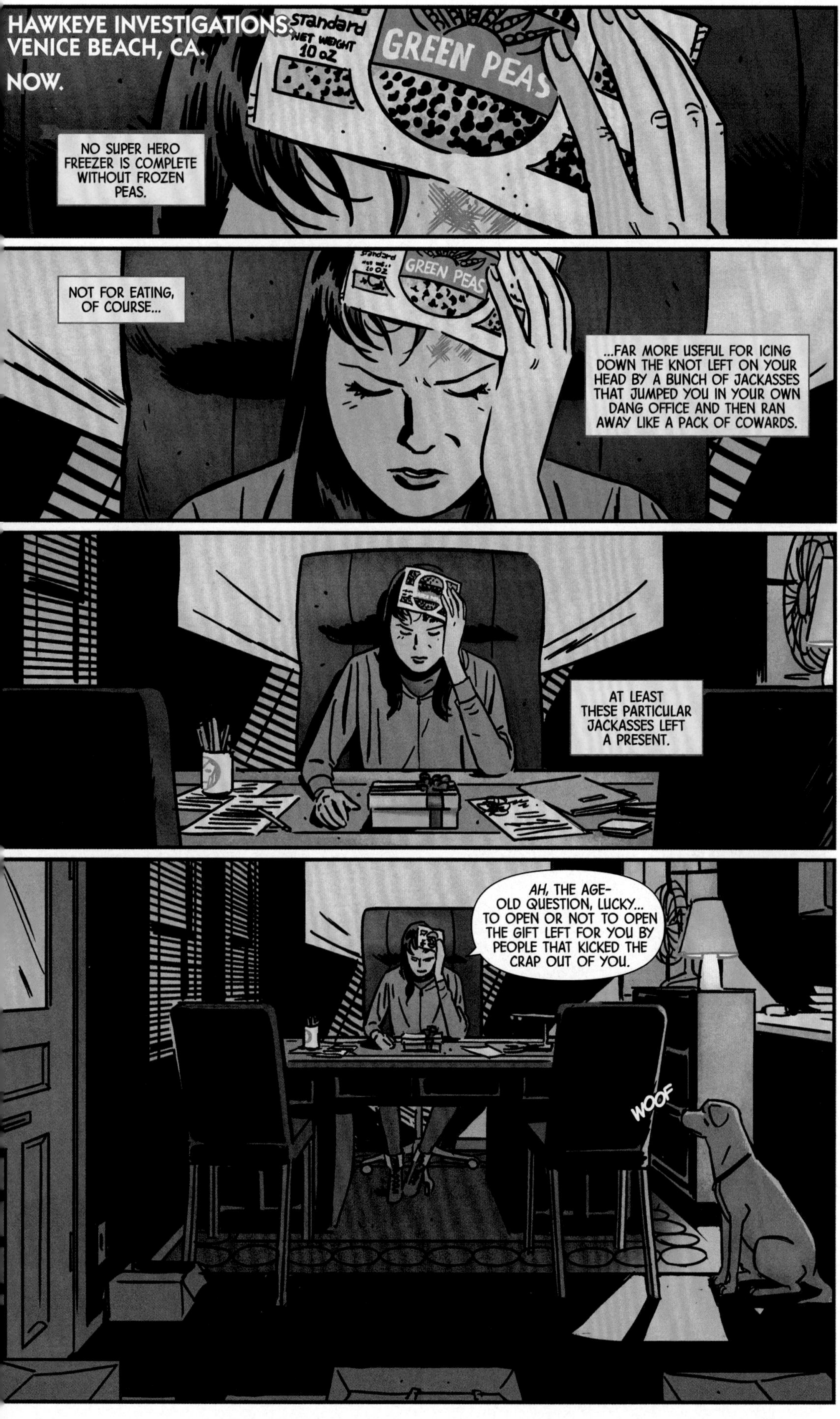
HAWKEYE INVESTIGATIONS: VENICE BEACH, CA.
NOW.
standard NET WEIGHT 10 oZ
GREEN PEAS
NO SUPER HERO FREEZER IS COMPLETE WITHOUT FROZEN PEAS.
NOT FOR EATING, OF COURSE...
...FAR MORE USEFUL FOR ICING DOWN THE KNOT LEFT ON YOUR HEAD BY A BUNCH OF JACKASSES THAT JUMPED YOU IN YOUR OWN DANG OFFICE AND THEN RAN AWAY LIKE A PACK OF COWARDS.
AT LEAST THESE PARTICULAR JACKASSES LEFT A PRESENT.
AH, THE AGE-OLD QUESTION, LUCKY... TO OPEN OR NOT TO OPEN THE GIFT LEFT FOR YOU BY PEOPLE THAT KICKED THE CRAP OUT OF YOU.
WOOF

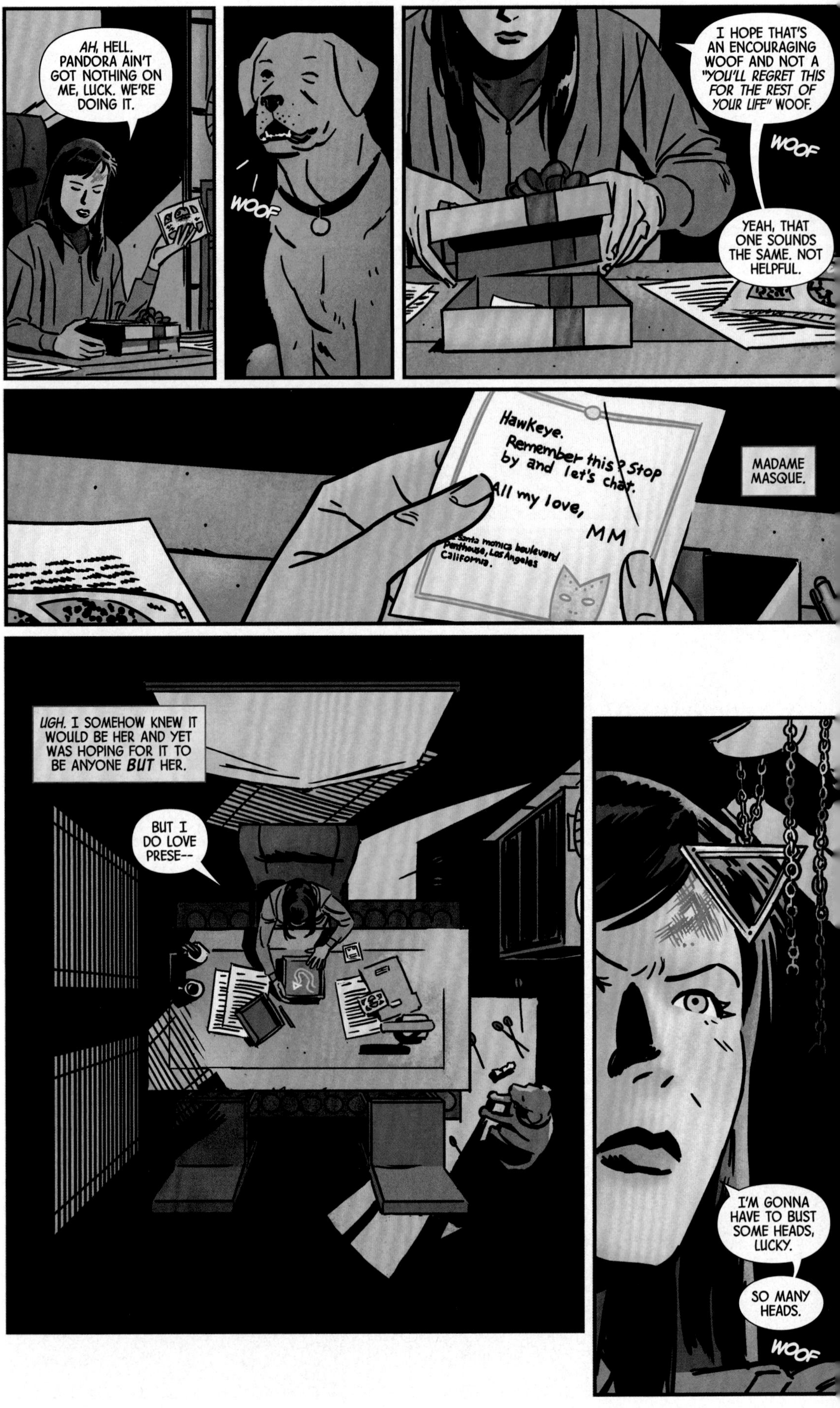

AH, HELL. PANDORA AIN'T GOT NOTHING ON ME, LUCK. WE'RE DOING IT.
WOOF
I HOPE THAT'S AN ENCOURAGING WOOF AND NOT A "YOU'LL REGRET THIS FOR THE REST OF YOUR LIFE" WOOF.
WOOF
YEAH, THAT ONE SOUNDS THE SAME. NOT HELPFUL.
Hawkeye. Remember this? Stop by and let's chat.
All my love, MM
Santa monica boulevard Penthouse, Los Angeles California.
MADAME MASQUE.
UGH. I SOMEHOW KNEW IT WOULD BE HER AND YET WAS HOPING FOR IT TO BE ANYONE BUT HER.
BUT I DO LOVE PRESE--
I'M GONNA HAVE TO BUST SOME HEADS, LUCKY.
SO MANY HEADS.
WOOF

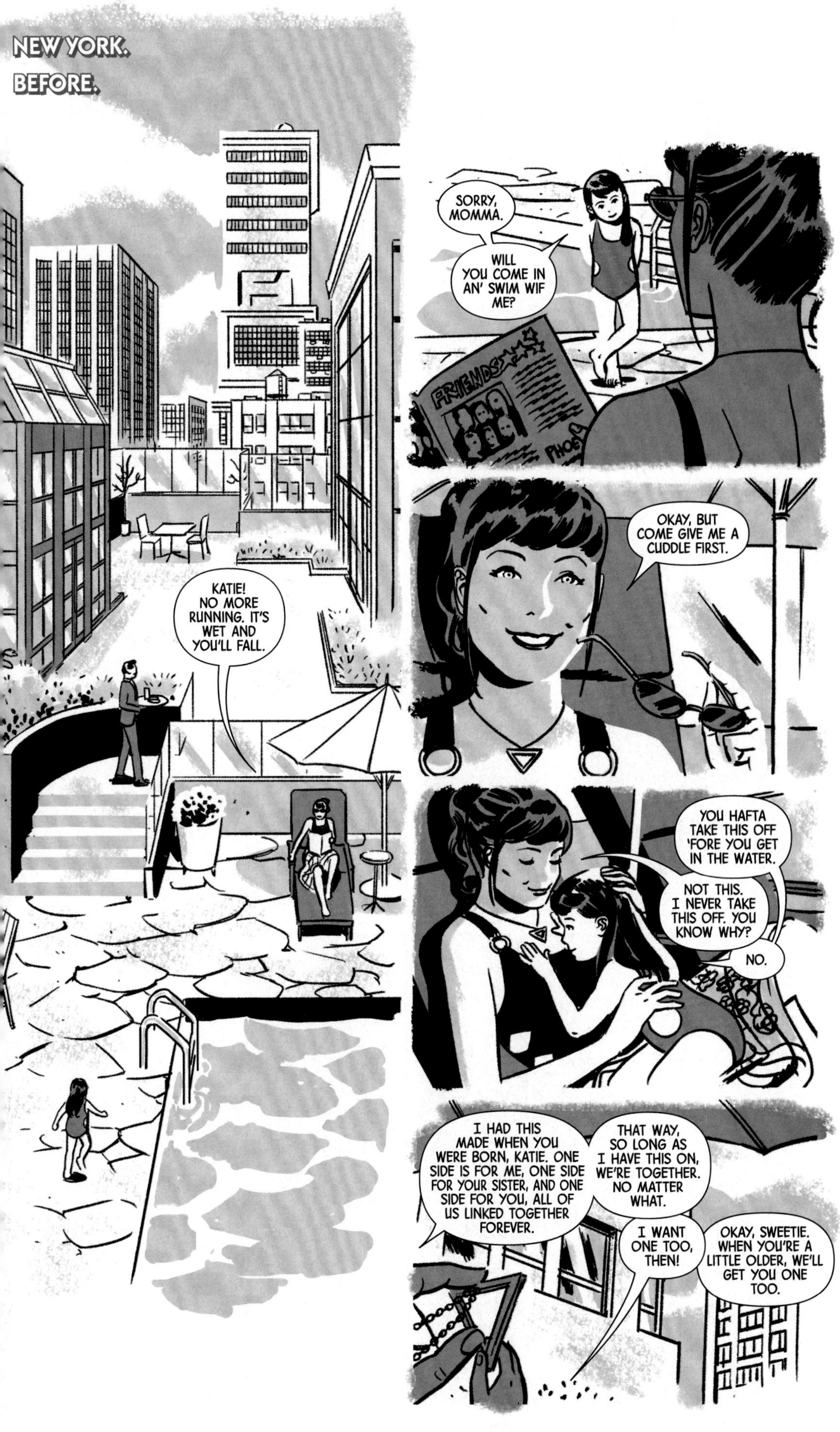

NEW YORK.
BEFORE.
KATIE! NO MORE RUNNING. IT'S WET AND YOU'LL FALL.
SORRY, MOMMA.
WILL YOU COME IN AN' SWIM WIF ME?
FRIENDS
OKAY, BUT COME GIVE ME A CUDDLE FIRST.
YOU HAFTA TAKE THIS OFF 'FORE YOU GET IN THE WATER.
NOT THIS. I NEVER TAKE THIS OFF. YOU KNOW WHY?
NO.
I HAD THIS MADE WHEN YOU WERE BORN, KATIE. ONE SIDE IS FOR ME, ONE SIDE FOR YOUR SISTER, AND ONE SIDE FOR YOU, ALL OF US LINKED TOGETHER FOREVER.
THAT WAY, SO LONG AS I HAVE THIS ON, WE'RE TOGETHER. NO MATTER WHAT.
I WANT ONE TOO, THEN!
OKAY, SWEETIE. WHEN YOU'RE A LITTLE OLDER, WE'LL GET YOU ONE TOO.

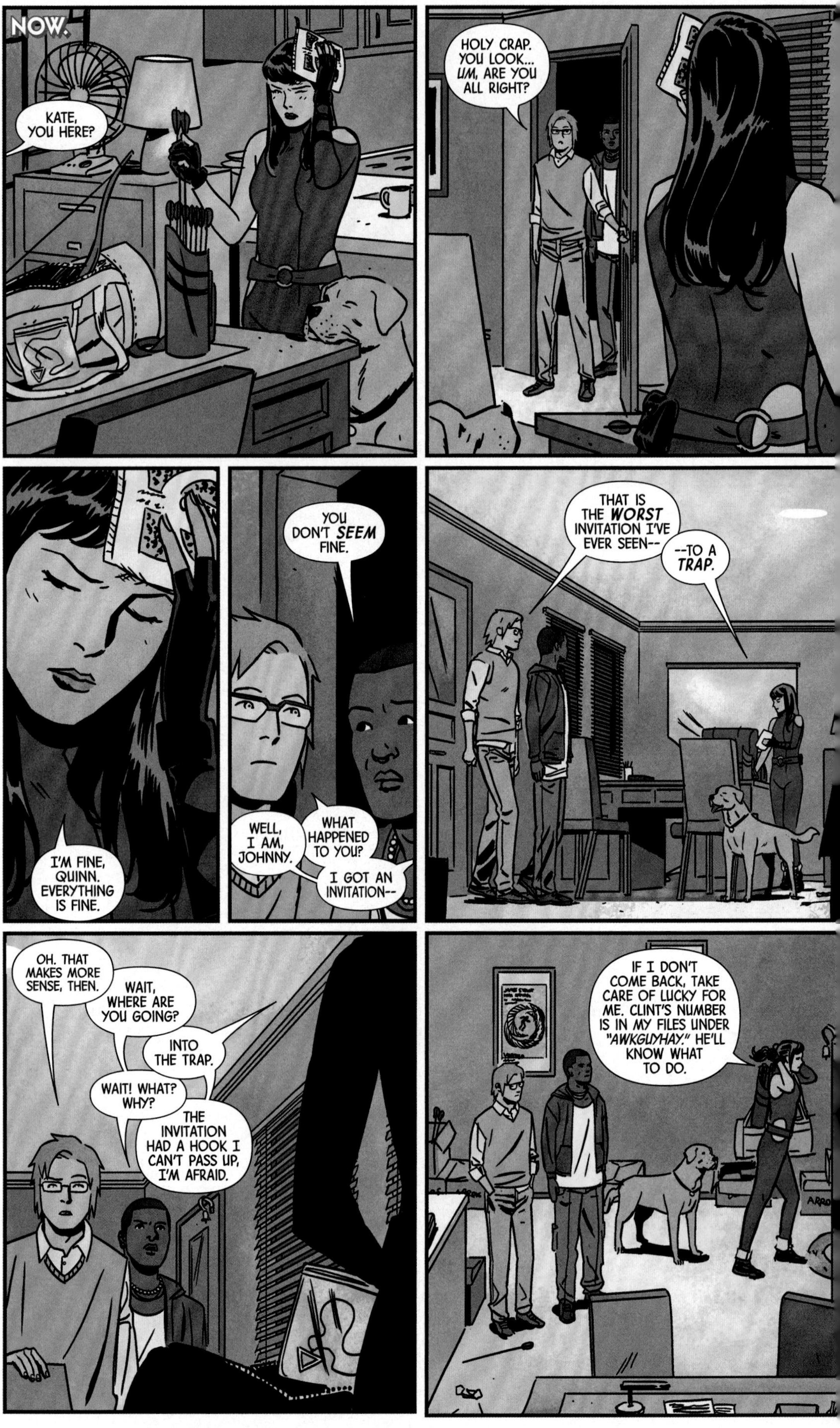
NOW.
KATE, YOU HERE?
HOLY CRAP. YOU LOOK... UM, ARE YOU ALL RIGHT?
I'M FINE, QUINN. EVERYTHING IS FINE.
YOU DON'T SEEM FINE.
WELL, I AM, JOHNNY.
WHAT HAPPENED TO YOU?
I GOT AN INVITATION--
THAT IS THE WORST INVITATION I'VE EVER SEEN--
--TO A TRAP.
OH. THAT MAKES MORE SENSE, THEN.
WAIT, WHERE ARE YOU GOING?
INTO THE TRAP.
WAIT! WHAT? WHY?
THE INVITATION HAD A HOOK I CAN'T PASS UP, I'M AFRAID.
IF I DON'T COME BACK, TAKE CARE OF LUCKY FOR ME. CLINT'S NUMBER IS IN MY FILES UNDER "AWKGUYHAY." HE'LL KNOW WHAT TO DO.

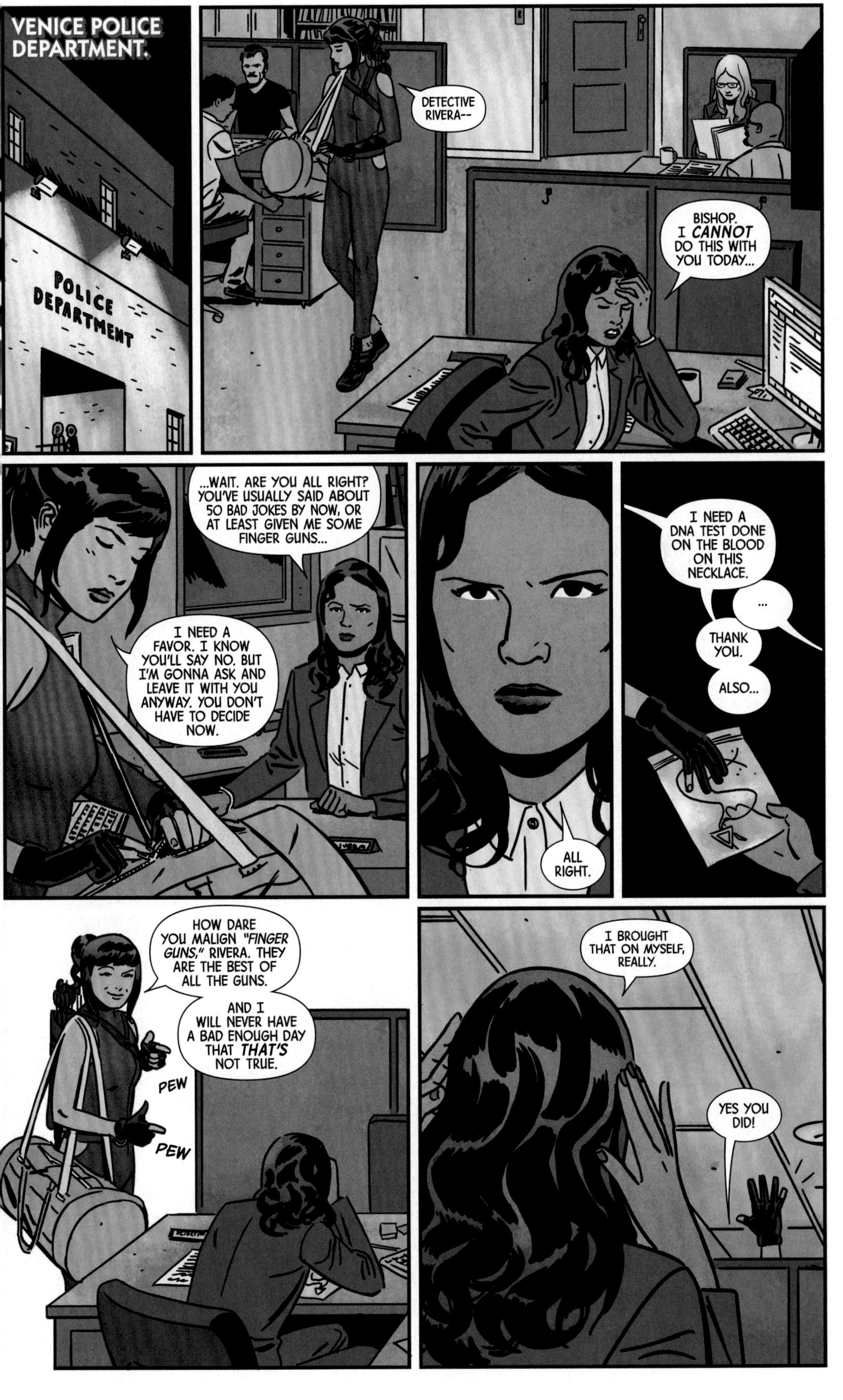

VENICE POLICE DEPARTMENT.
POLICE DEPARTMENT
DETECTIVE RIVERA--
BISHOP. I *CANNOT* DO THIS WITH YOU TODAY...
...WAIT. ARE YOU ALL RIGHT? YOU'VE USUALLY SAID ABOUT 50 BAD JOKES BY NOW, OR AT LEAST GIVEN ME SOME FINGER GUNS...
I NEED A FAVOR. I KNOW YOU'LL SAY NO. BUT I'M GONNA ASK AND LEAVE IT WITH YOU ANYWAY. YOU DON'T HAVE TO DECIDE NOW.
ALL RIGHT.
I NEED A DNA TEST DONE ON THE BLOOD ON THIS NECKLACE.
...
THANK YOU.
ALSO...
HOW DARE YOU MALIGN *"FINGER GUNS,"* RIVERA. THEY ARE THE BEST OF ALL THE GUNS.
AND I WILL NEVER HAVE A BAD ENOUGH DAY THAT *THAT'S* NOT TRUE.
PEW
PEW
I BROUGHT THAT ON MYSELF, REALLY.
YES YOU DID!

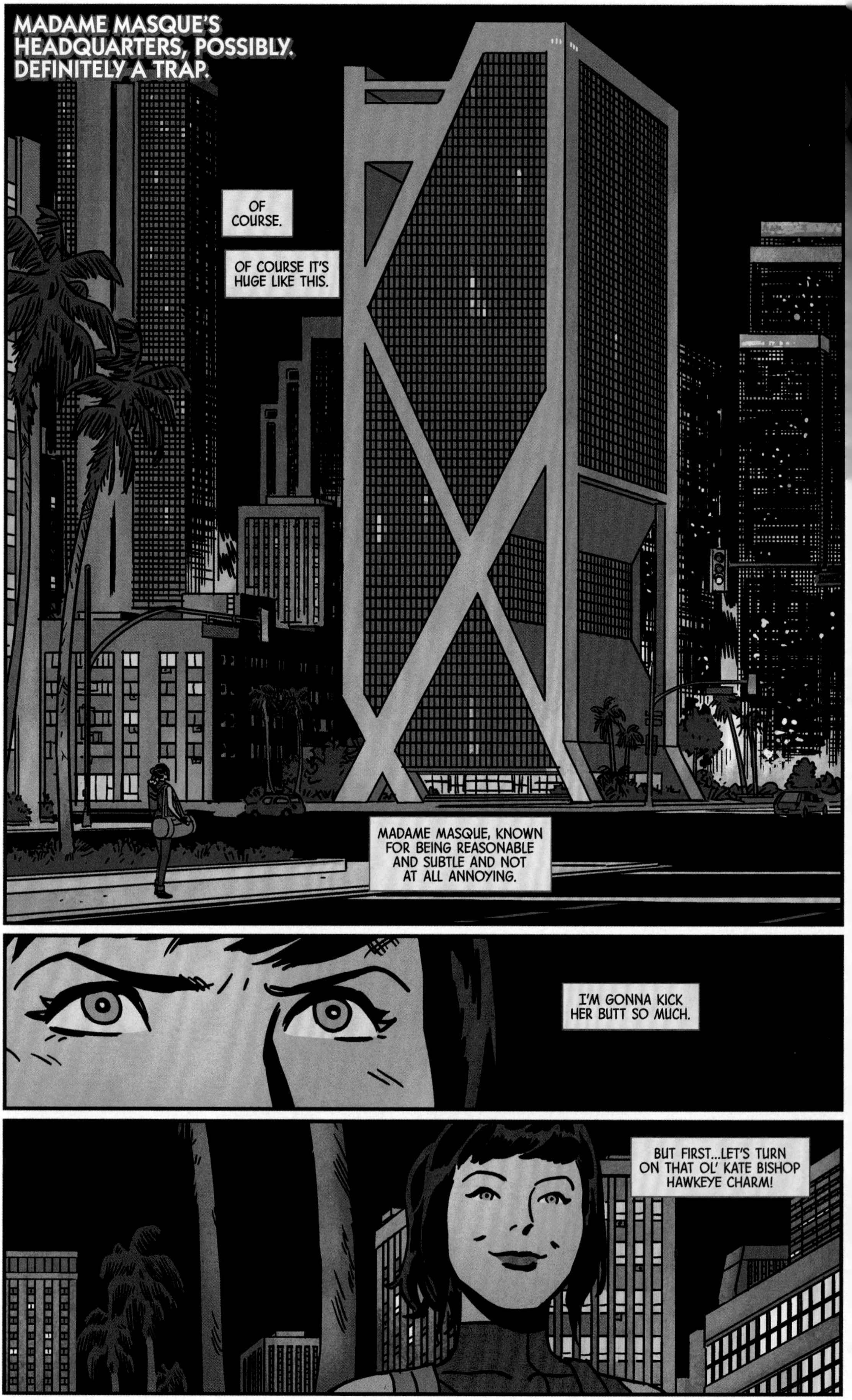
MADAME MASQUE'S HEADQUARTERS, POSSIBLY. DEFINITELY A TRAP.
OF COURSE.
OF COURSE IT'S HUGE LIKE THIS.
MADAME MASQUE, KNOWN FOR BEING REASONABLE AND SUBTLE AND NOT AT ALL ANNOYING.
I'M GONNA KICK HER BUTT SO MUCH.
BUT FIRST...LET'S TURN ON THAT OL' KATE BISHOP HAWKEYE CHARM!

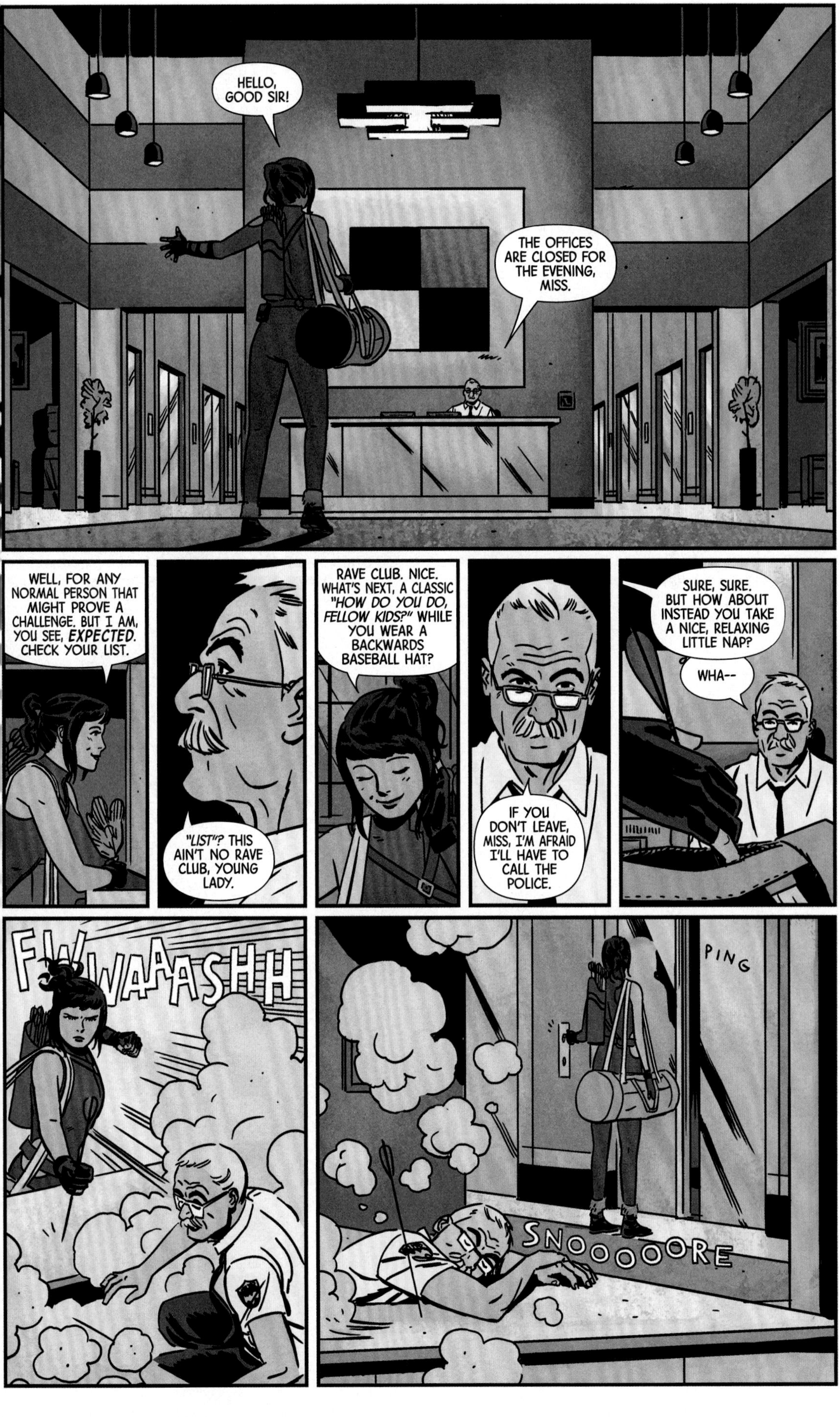
HELLO, GOOD SIR!
THE OFFICES ARE CLOSED FOR THE EVENING, MISS.
WELL, FOR ANY NORMAL PERSON THAT MIGHT PROVE A CHALLENGE. BUT I AM, YOU SEE, *EXPECTED*. CHECK YOUR LIST.
"*LIST*"? THIS AIN'T NO RAVE CLUB, YOUNG LADY.
RAVE CLUB. NICE. WHAT'S NEXT, A CLASSIC "*HOW DO YOU DO, FELLOW KIDS?*" WHILE YOU WEAR A BACKWARDS BASEBALL HAT?
IF YOU DON'T LEAVE, MISS, I'M AFRAID I'LL HAVE TO CALL THE POLICE.
SURE, SURE. BUT HOW ABOUT INSTEAD YOU TAKE A NICE, RELAXING LITTLE NAP?
WHA--
FWWAAAASHH
PING
SNOOOOOORE

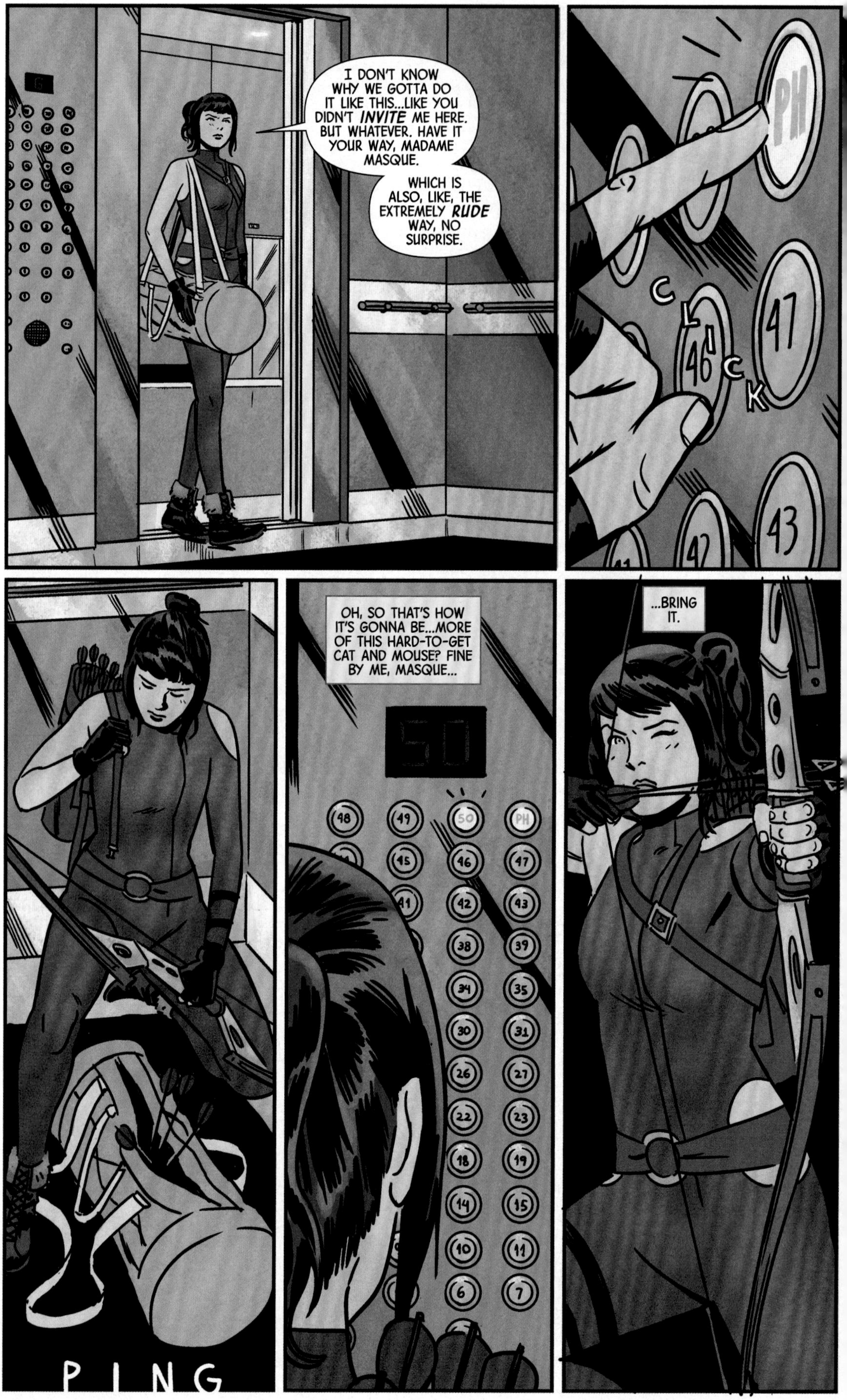
I DON'T KNOW WHY WE GOTTA DO IT LIKE THIS...LIKE YOU DIDN'T *INVITE* ME HERE. BUT WHATEVER. HAVE IT YOUR WAY, MADAME MASQUE.
WHICH IS ALSO, LIKE, THE EXTREMELY *RUDE* WAY, NO SURPRISE.
CLICK
PING
OH, SO THAT'S HOW IT'S GONNA BE...MORE OF THIS HARD-TO-GET CAT AND MOUSE? FINE BY ME, MASQUE...
...BRING IT.

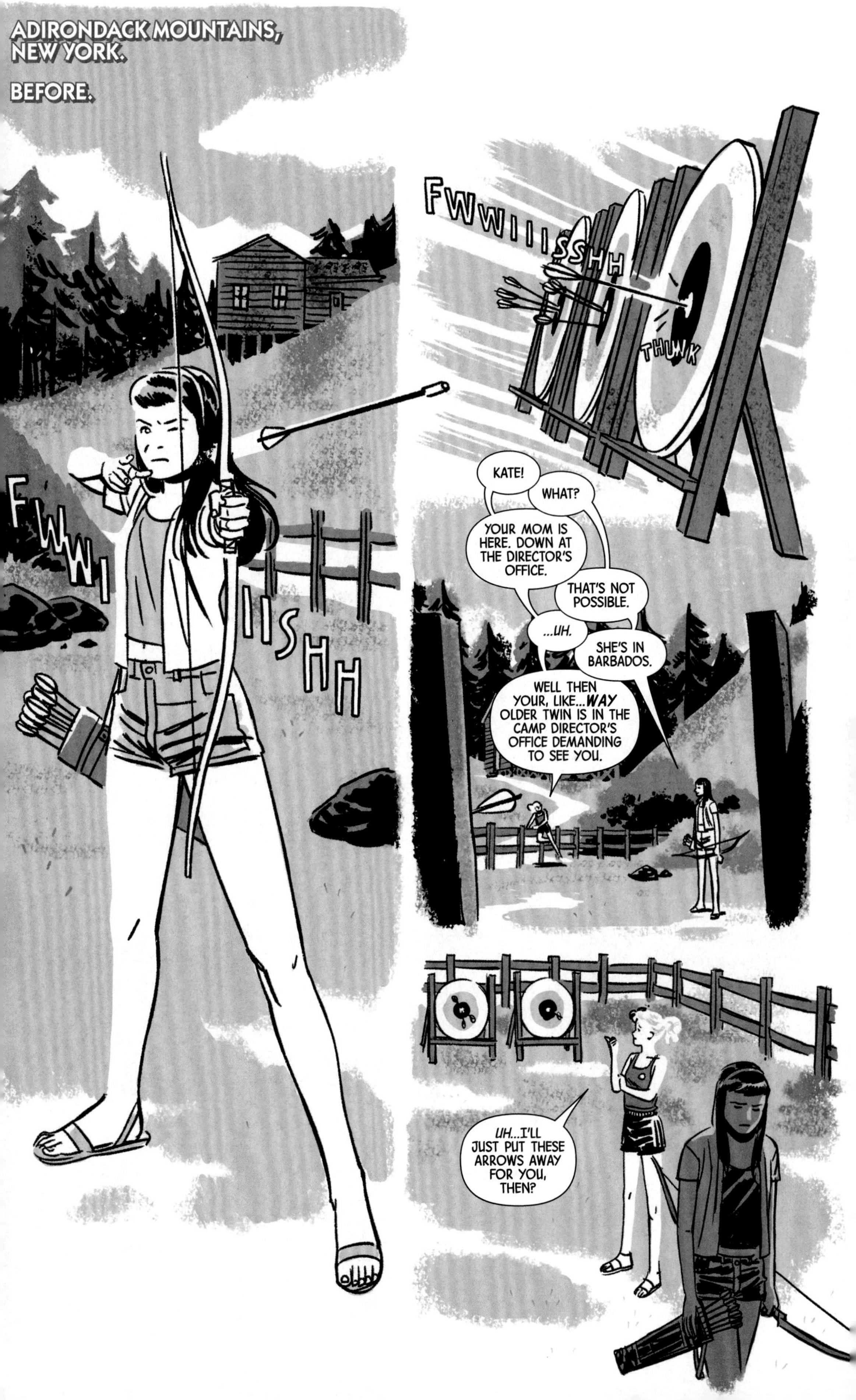
ADIRONDACK MOUNTAINS, NEW YORK.
BEFORE.
FWWIIIISHH
FWWIIIISSHH
THUNK
KATE!
WHAT?
YOUR MOM IS HERE. DOWN AT THE DIRECTOR'S OFFICE.
THAT'S NOT POSSIBLE.
...UH.
SHE'S IN BARBADOS.
WELL THEN YOUR, LIKE...WAY OLDER TWIN IS IN THE CAMP DIRECTOR'S OFFICE DEMANDING TO SEE YOU.
UH...I'LL JUST PUT THESE ARROWS AWAY FOR YOU, THEN?

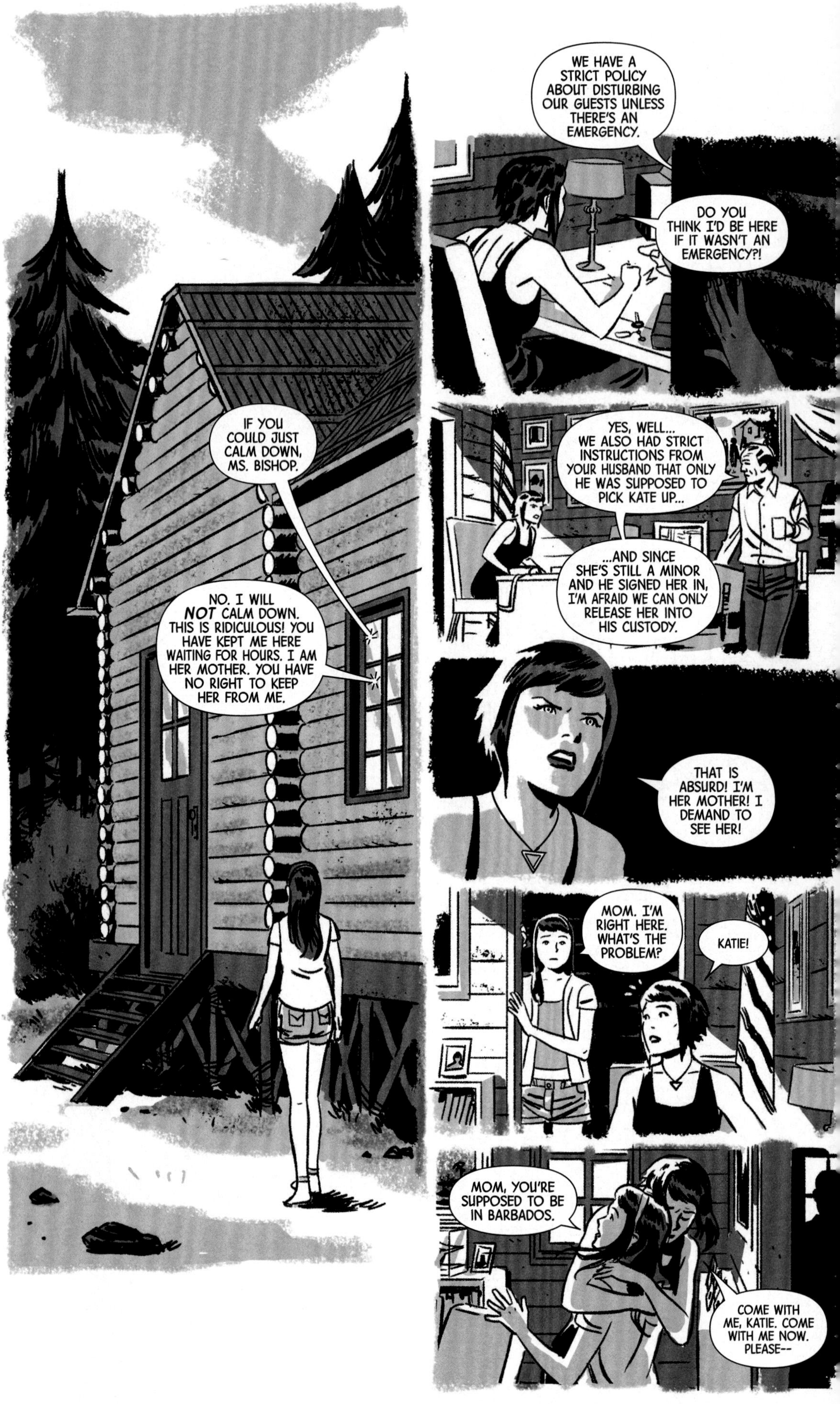

IF YOU COULD JUST CALM DOWN, MS. BISHOP.
NO. I WILL *NOT* CALM DOWN. THIS IS RIDICULOUS! YOU HAVE KEPT ME HERE WAITING FOR HOURS. I AM HER MOTHER. YOU HAVE NO RIGHT TO KEEP HER FROM ME.
WE HAVE A STRICT POLICY ABOUT DISTURBING OUR GUESTS UNLESS THERE'S AN EMERGENCY.
DO YOU THINK I'D BE HERE IF IT WASN'T AN EMERGENCY?!
YES, WELL... WE ALSO HAD STRICT INSTRUCTIONS FROM YOUR HUSBAND THAT ONLY HE WAS SUPPOSED TO PICK KATE UP...
...AND SINCE SHE'S STILL A MINOR AND HE SIGNED HER IN, I'M AFRAID WE CAN ONLY RELEASE HER INTO HIS CUSTODY.
THAT IS ABSURD! I'M HER MOTHER! I DEMAND TO SEE HER!
MOM. I'M RIGHT HERE. WHAT'S THE PROBLEM?
KATIE!
MOM, YOU'RE SUPPOSED TO BE IN BARBADOS.
COME WITH ME, KATIE. COME WITH ME NOW. PLEASE--

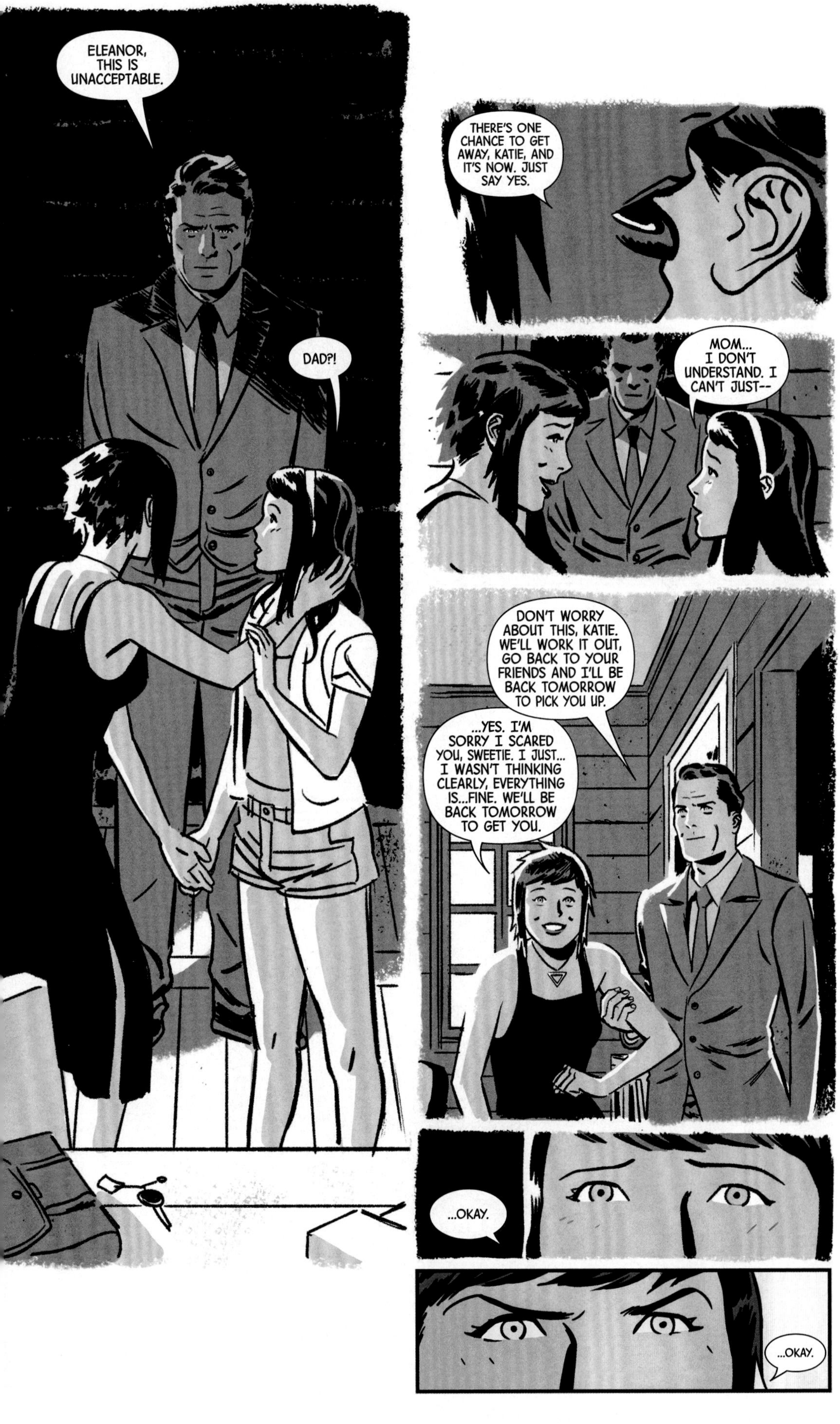
ELEANOR, THIS IS UNACCEPTABLE.
DAD?!
THERE'S ONE CHANCE TO GET AWAY, KATIE, AND IT'S NOW. JUST SAY YES.
MOM... I DON'T UNDERSTAND. I CAN'T JUST--
DON'T WORRY ABOUT THIS, KATIE. WE'LL WORK IT OUT, GO BACK TO YOUR FRIENDS AND I'LL BE BACK TOMORROW TO PICK YOU UP.
...YES. I'M SORRY I SCARED YOU, SWEETIE. I JUST... I WASN'T THINKING CLEARLY, EVERYTHING IS...FINE. WE'LL BE BACK TOMORROW TO GET YOU.
...OKAY.
...OKAY.

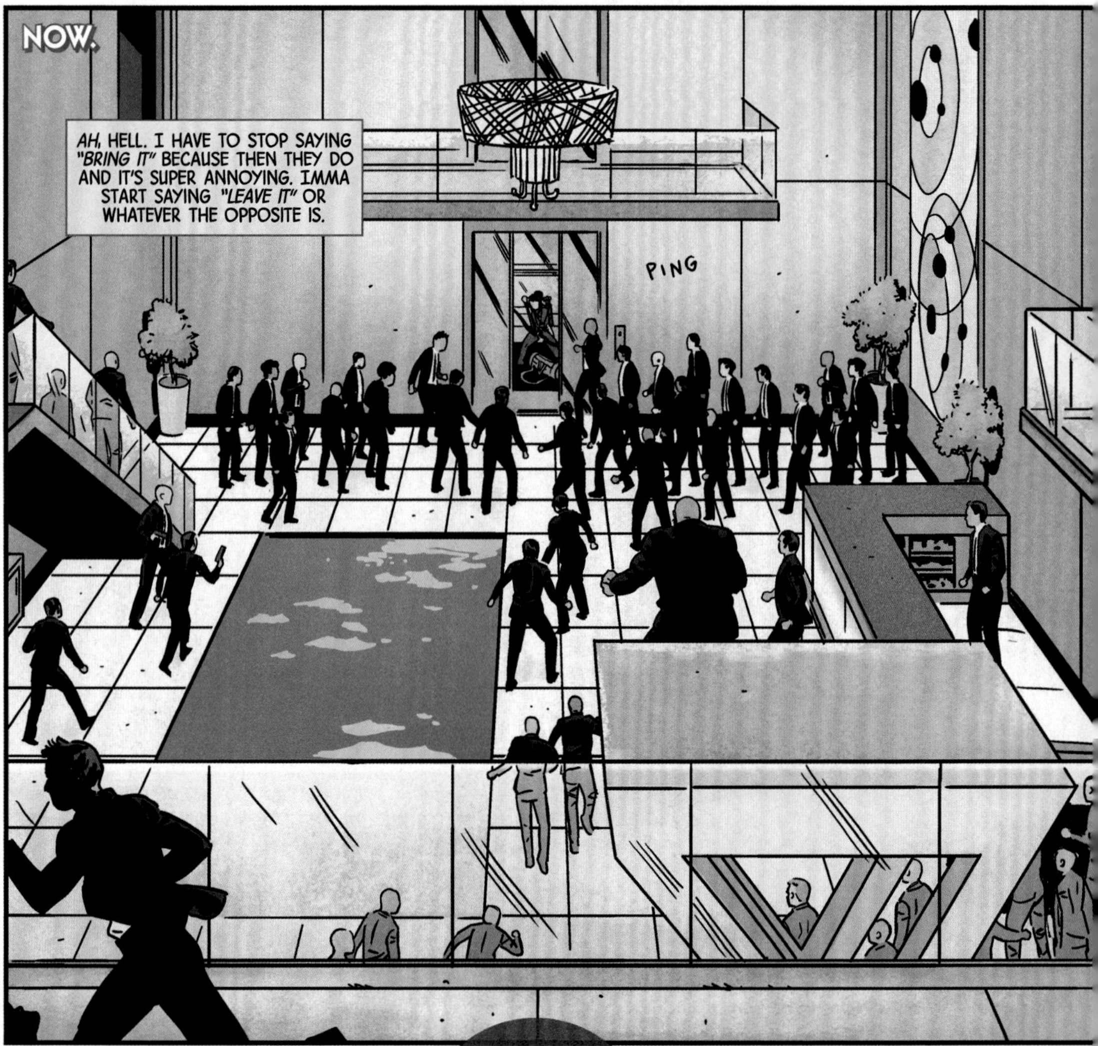
NOW.
AH, HELL. I HAVE TO STOP SAYING "BRING IT" BECAUSE THEN THEY DO AND IT'S SUPER ANNOYING. IMMA START SAYING "LEAVE IT" OR WHATEVER THE OPPOSITE IS.
PING

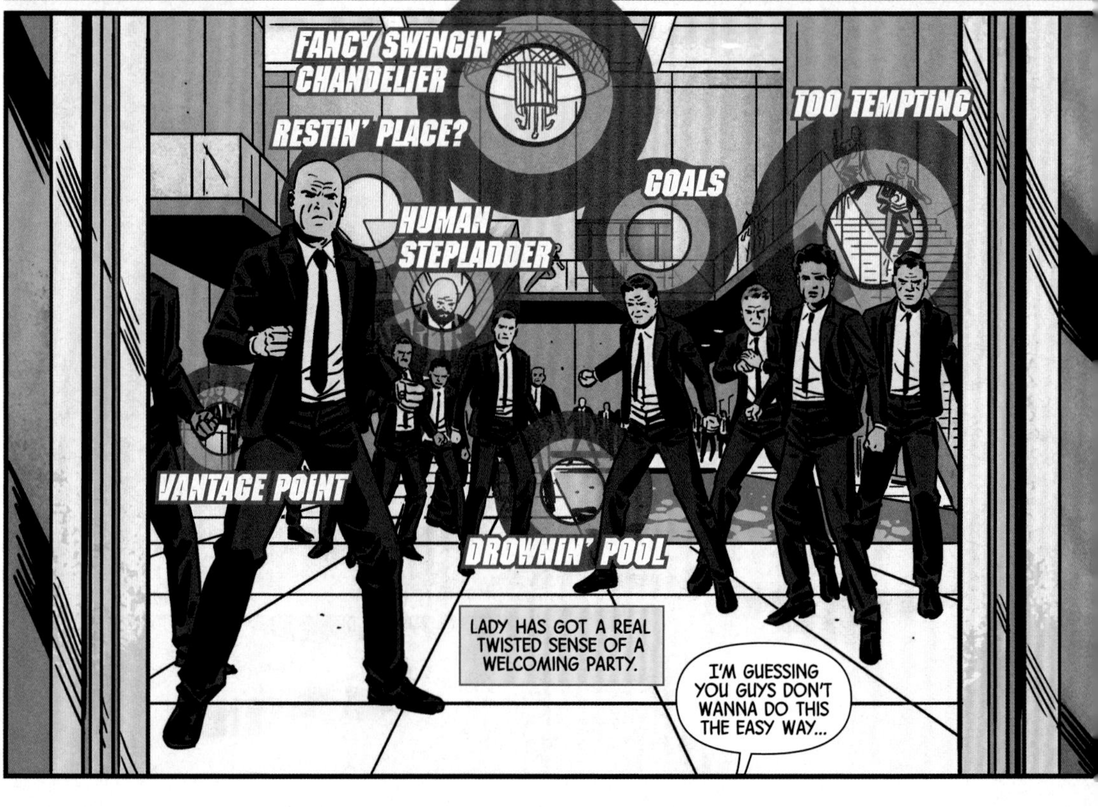
FANCY SWINGIN' CHANDELIER
RESTIN' PLACE?
TOO TEMPTING
GOALS
HUMAN STEPLADDER
VANTAGE POINT
DROWNIN' POOL
LADY HAS GOT A REAL TWISTED SENSE OF A WELCOMING PARTY.
I'M GUESSING YOU GUYS DON'T WANNA DO THIS THE EASY WAY...

...HARD WAY IT IS.

FWOOOSHHHHH

BAMF

SWICK
SWICK

FWOOOOOOOSHHHHHH

SMASH

SORRY, THIS IS WHAT THE HARD WAY LOOKS LIKE, DUMMY!

GAAAAAH.

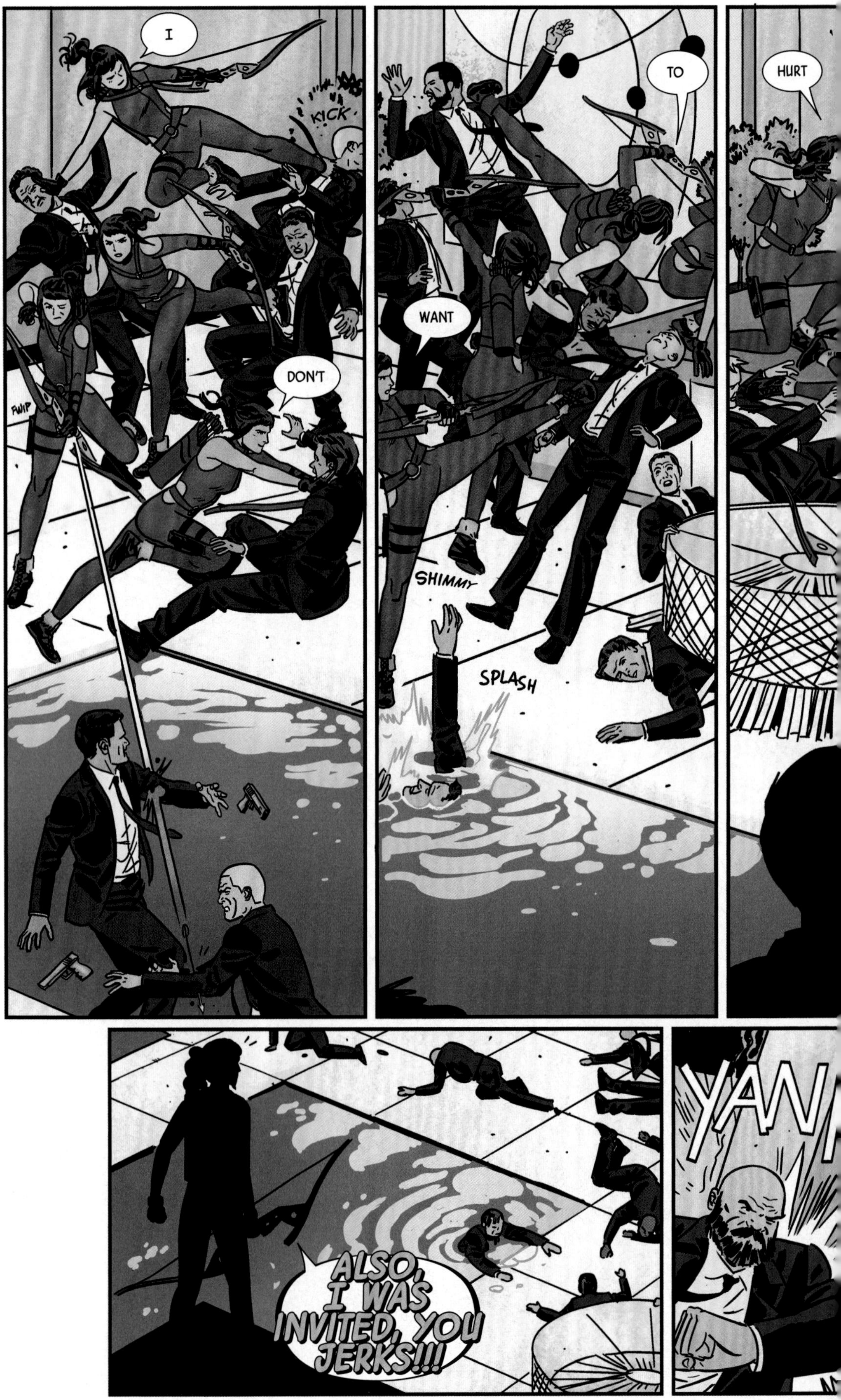

I
KICK
FWIP
DON'T
WANT
TO
SHIMMY
SPLASH
HURT
ALSO, I WAS INVITED, YOU JERKS!!!

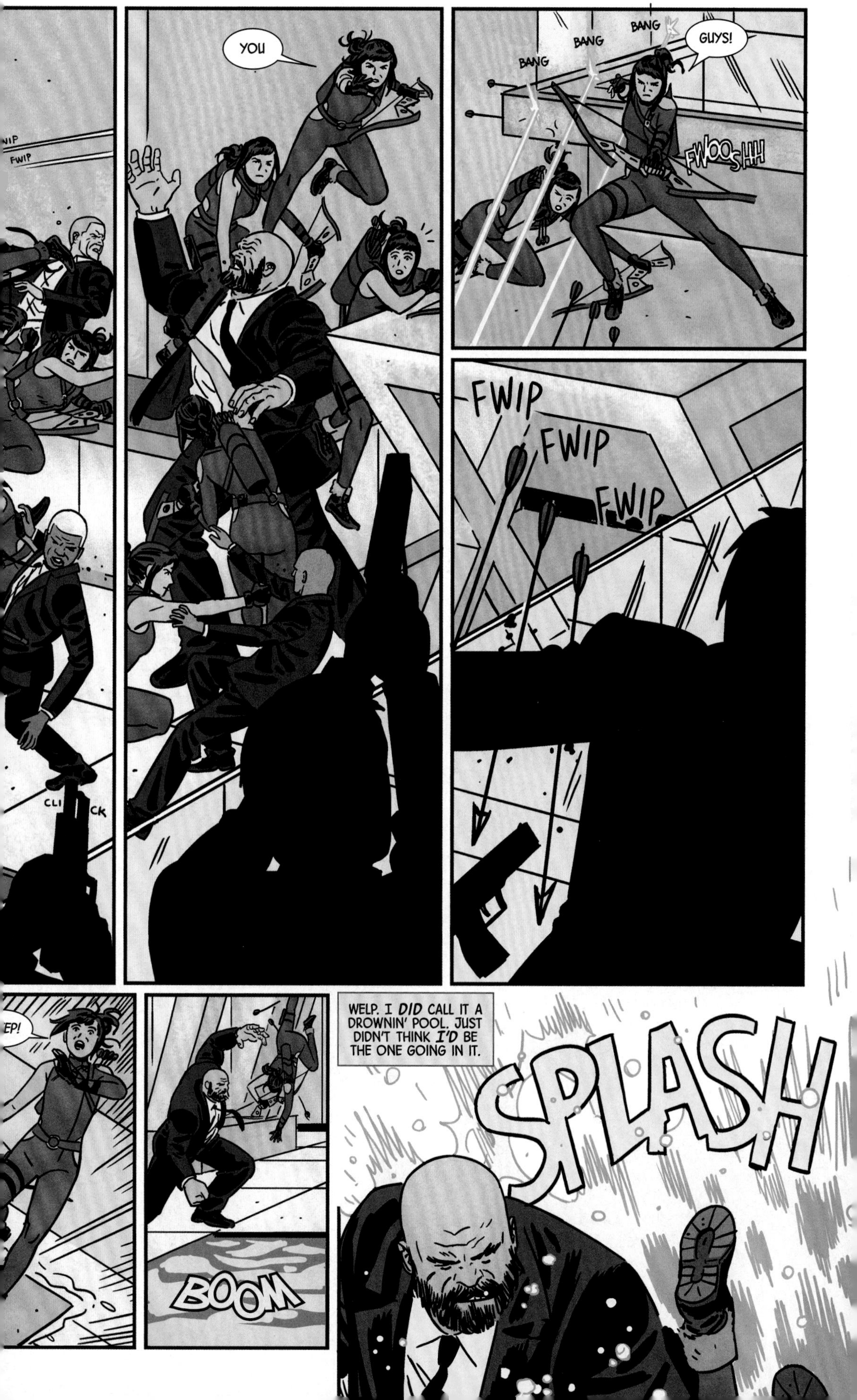
NIP
FWIP
CLI
CK
YOU
BANG
BANG
BANG
GUYS!
FWOOSHH
FWIP
FWIP
FWIP
EP!
BOOM
WELP. I *DID* CALL IT A DROWNIN' POOL. JUST DIDN'T THINK *I'D* BE THE ONE GOING IN IT.
SPLASH

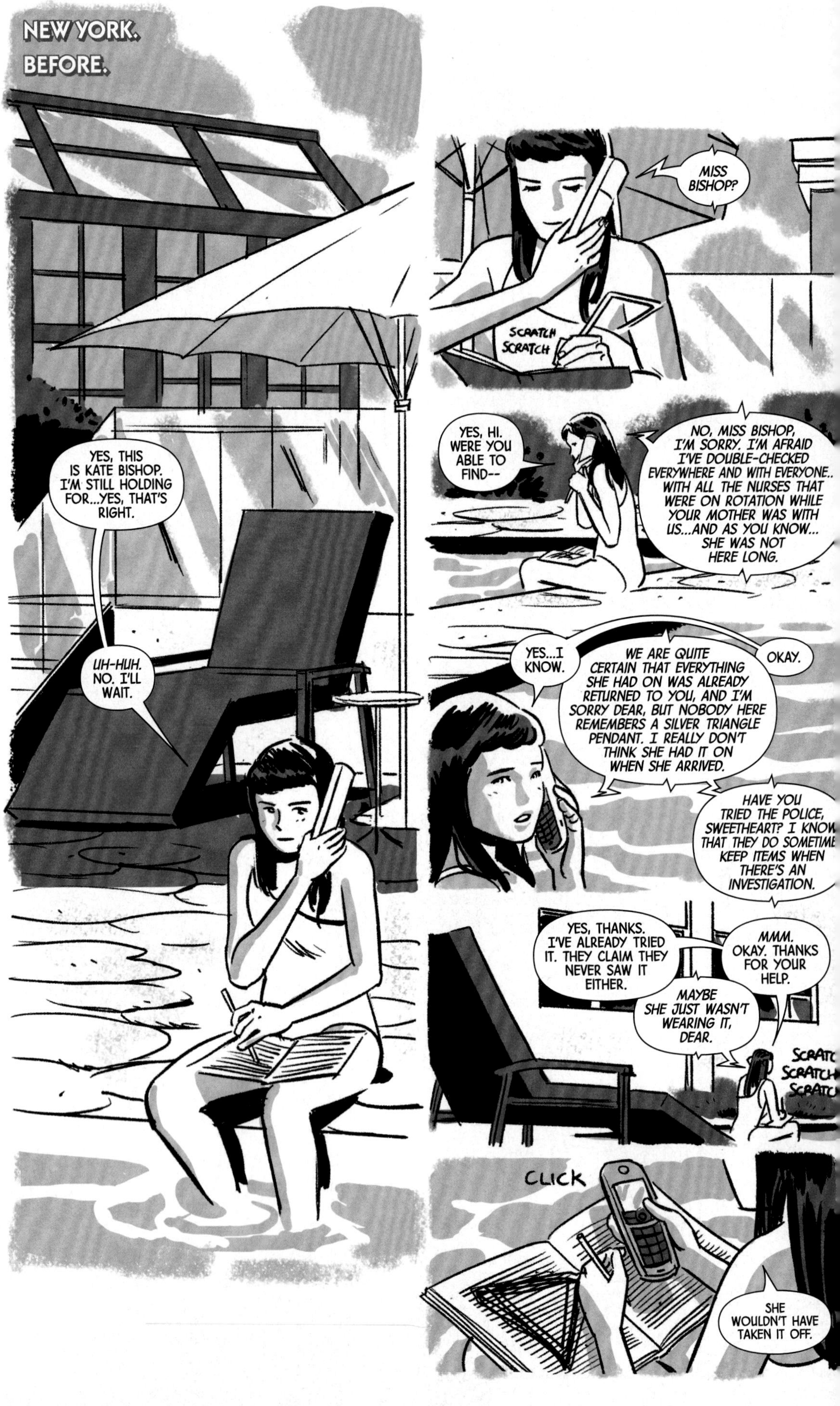

NEW YORK.
BEFORE.
YES, THIS IS KATE BISHOP. I'M STILL HOLDING FOR...YES, THAT'S RIGHT.
UH-HUH. NO. I'LL WAIT.
MISS BISHOP?
SCRATCH SCRATCH
YES, HI. WERE YOU ABLE TO FIND--
NO, MISS BISHOP, I'M SORRY. I'M AFRAID I'VE DOUBLE-CHECKED EVERYWHERE AND WITH EVERYONE.. WITH ALL THE NURSES THAT WERE ON ROTATION WHILE YOUR MOTHER WAS WITH US...AND AS YOU KNOW... SHE WAS NOT HERE LONG.
YES...I KNOW.
WE ARE QUITE CERTAIN THAT EVERYTHING SHE HAD ON WAS ALREADY RETURNED TO YOU, AND I'M SORRY DEAR, BUT NOBODY HERE REMEMBERS A SILVER TRIANGLE PENDANT. I REALLY DON'T THINK SHE HAD IT ON WHEN SHE ARRIVED.
OKAY.
HAVE YOU TRIED THE POLICE, SWEETHEART? I KNOW THAT THEY DO SOMETIME KEEP ITEMS WHEN THERE'S AN INVESTIGATION.
YES, THANKS. I'VE ALREADY TRIED IT. THEY CLAIM THEY NEVER SAW IT EITHER.
MMM. OKAY. THANKS FOR YOUR HELP.
MAYBE SHE JUST WASN'T WEARING IT, DEAR.
CLICK
SHE WOULDN'T HAVE TAKEN IT OFF.

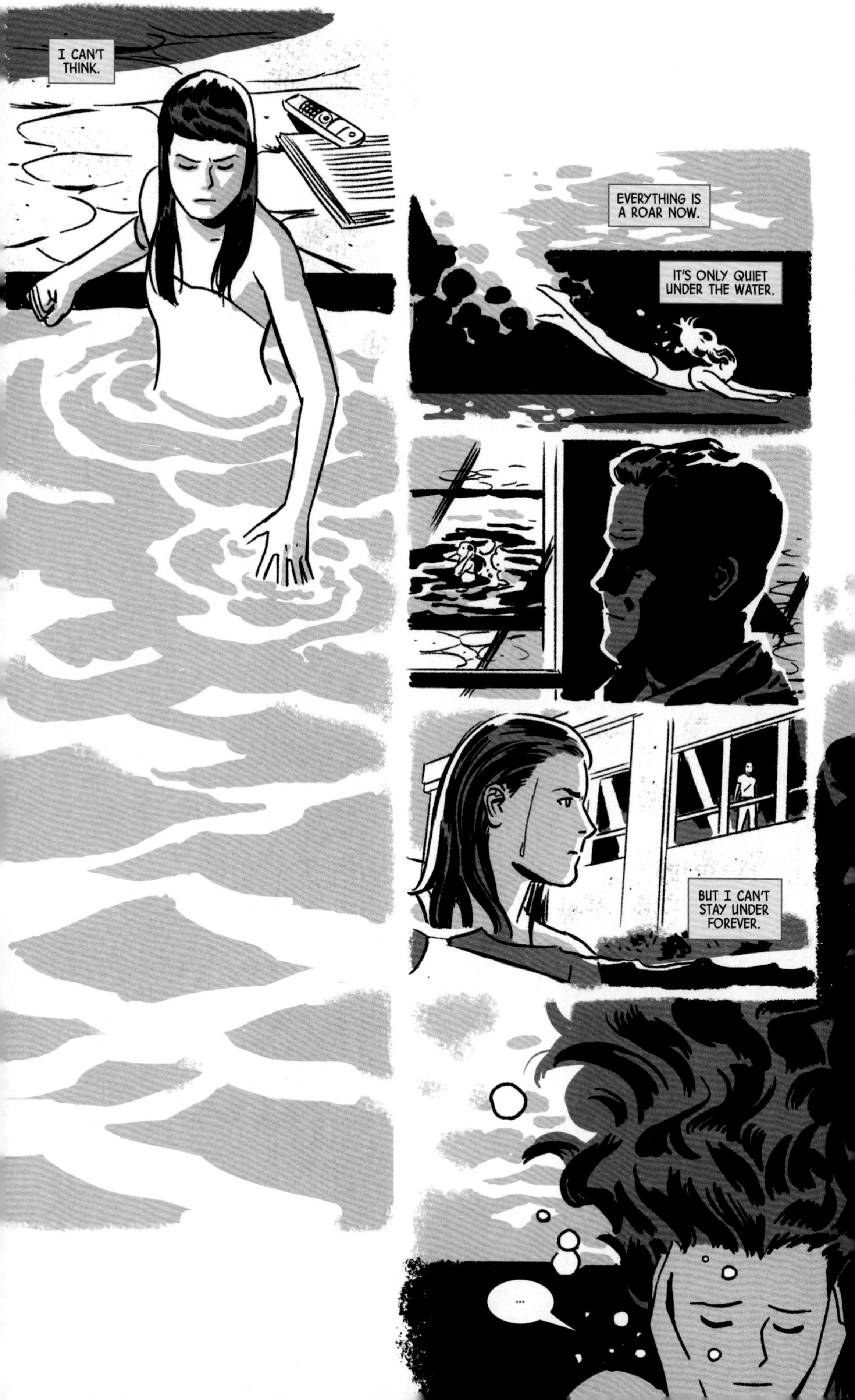
I CAN'T THINK.
EVERYTHING IS A ROAR NOW.
IT'S ONLY QUIET UNDER THE WATER.
BUT I CAN'T STAY UNDER FOREVER.
...

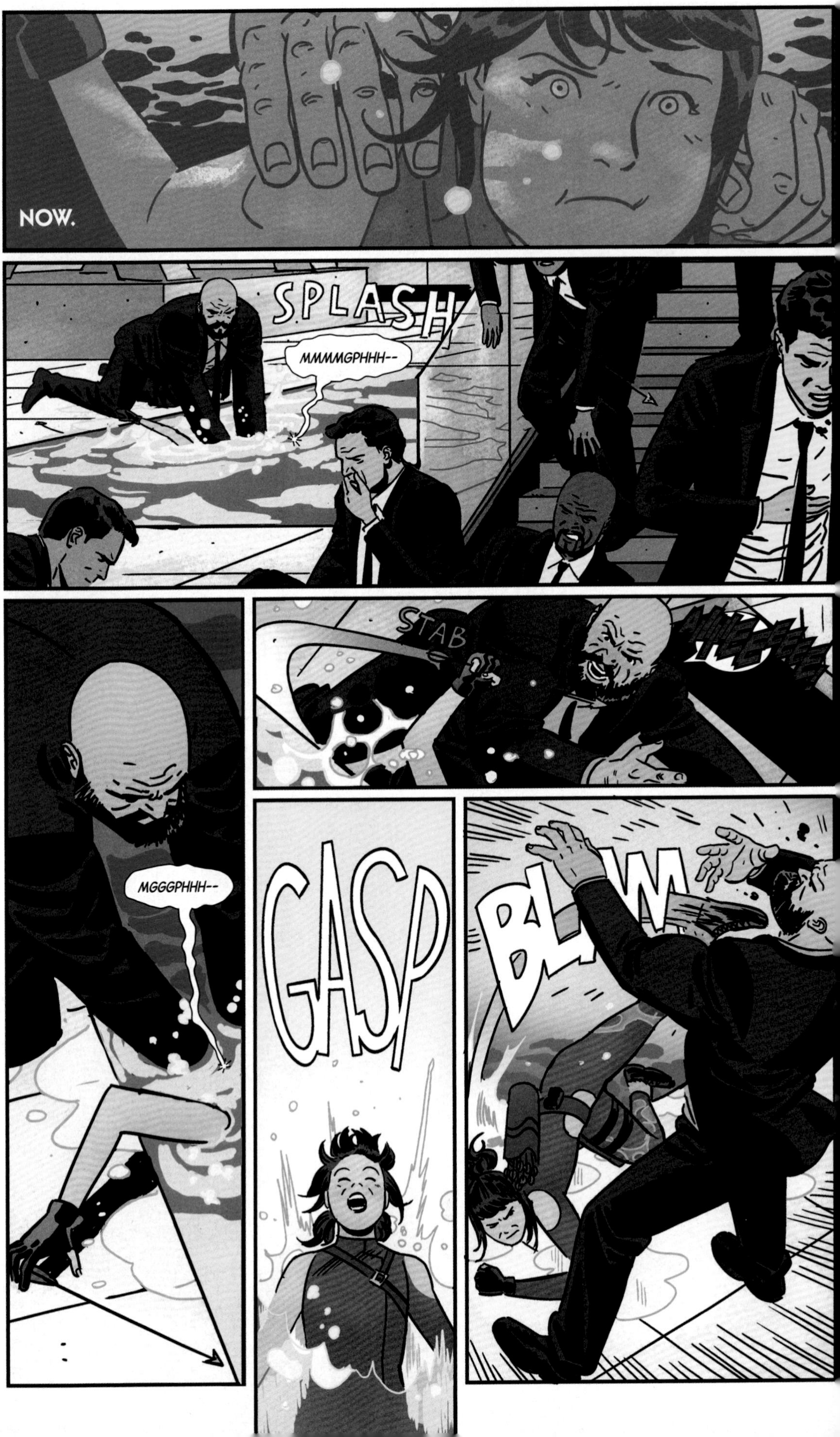
NOW.
SPLASH
MMMMGPHHH--
MGGGPHHH--
STAB
GASP
BLAM

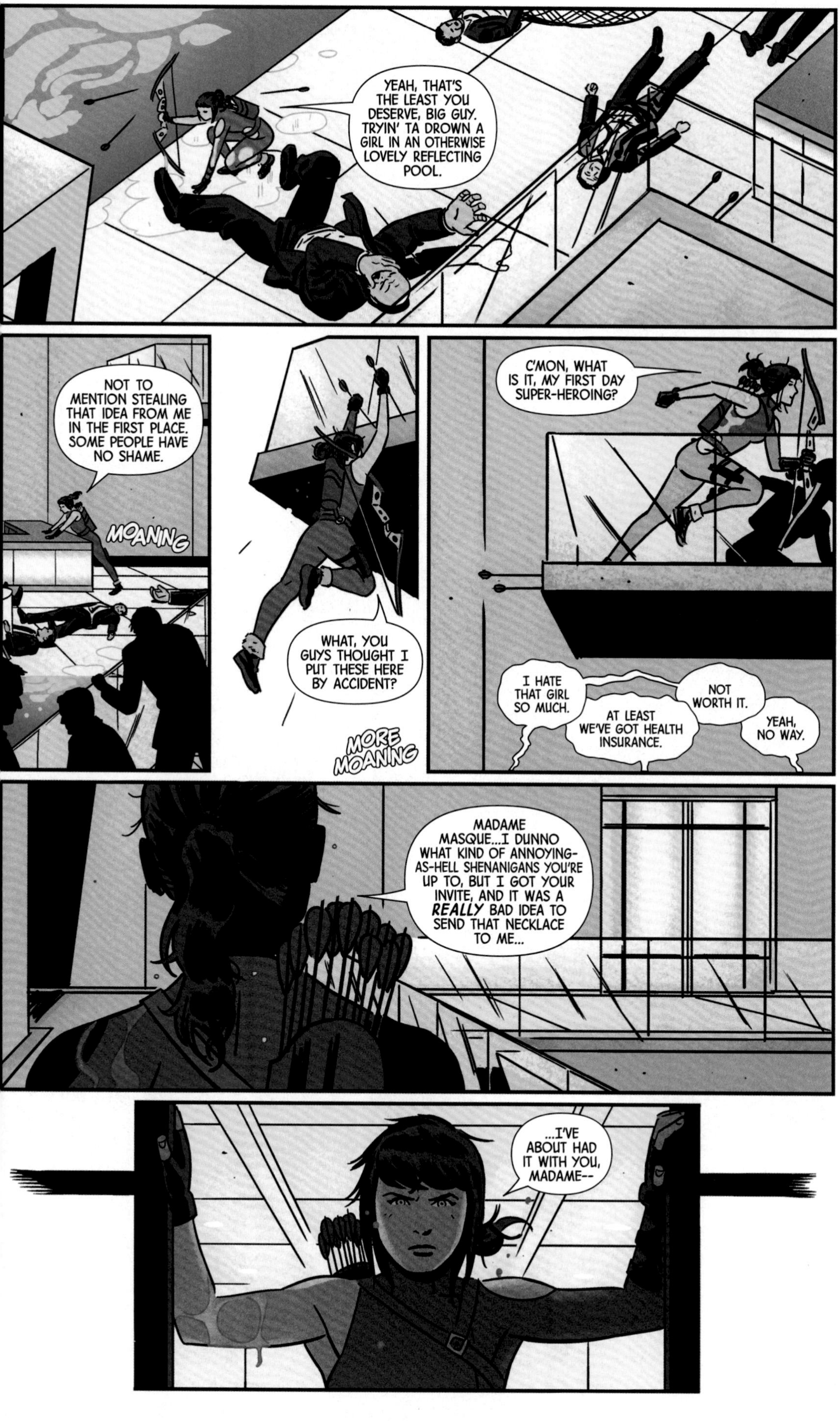
YEAH, THAT'S THE LEAST YOU DESERVE, BIG GUY. TRYIN' TA DROWN A GIRL IN AN OTHERWISE LOVELY REFLECTING POOL.
NOT TO MENTION STEALING THAT IDEA FROM ME IN THE FIRST PLACE. SOME PEOPLE HAVE NO SHAME.
MOANING
WHAT, YOU GUYS THOUGHT I PUT THESE HERE BY ACCIDENT?
MORE MOANING
C'MON, WHAT IS IT, MY FIRST DAY SUPER-HEROING?
I HATE THAT GIRL SO MUCH.
AT LEAST WE'VE GOT HEALTH INSURANCE.
NOT WORTH IT.
YEAH, NO WAY.
MADAME MASQUE...I DUNNO WHAT KIND OF ANNOYING-AS-HELL SHENANIGANS YOU'RE UP TO, BUT I GOT YOUR INVITE, AND IT WAS A REALLY BAD IDEA TO SEND THAT NECKLACE TO ME...
...I'VE ABOUT HAD IT WITH YOU, MADAME--

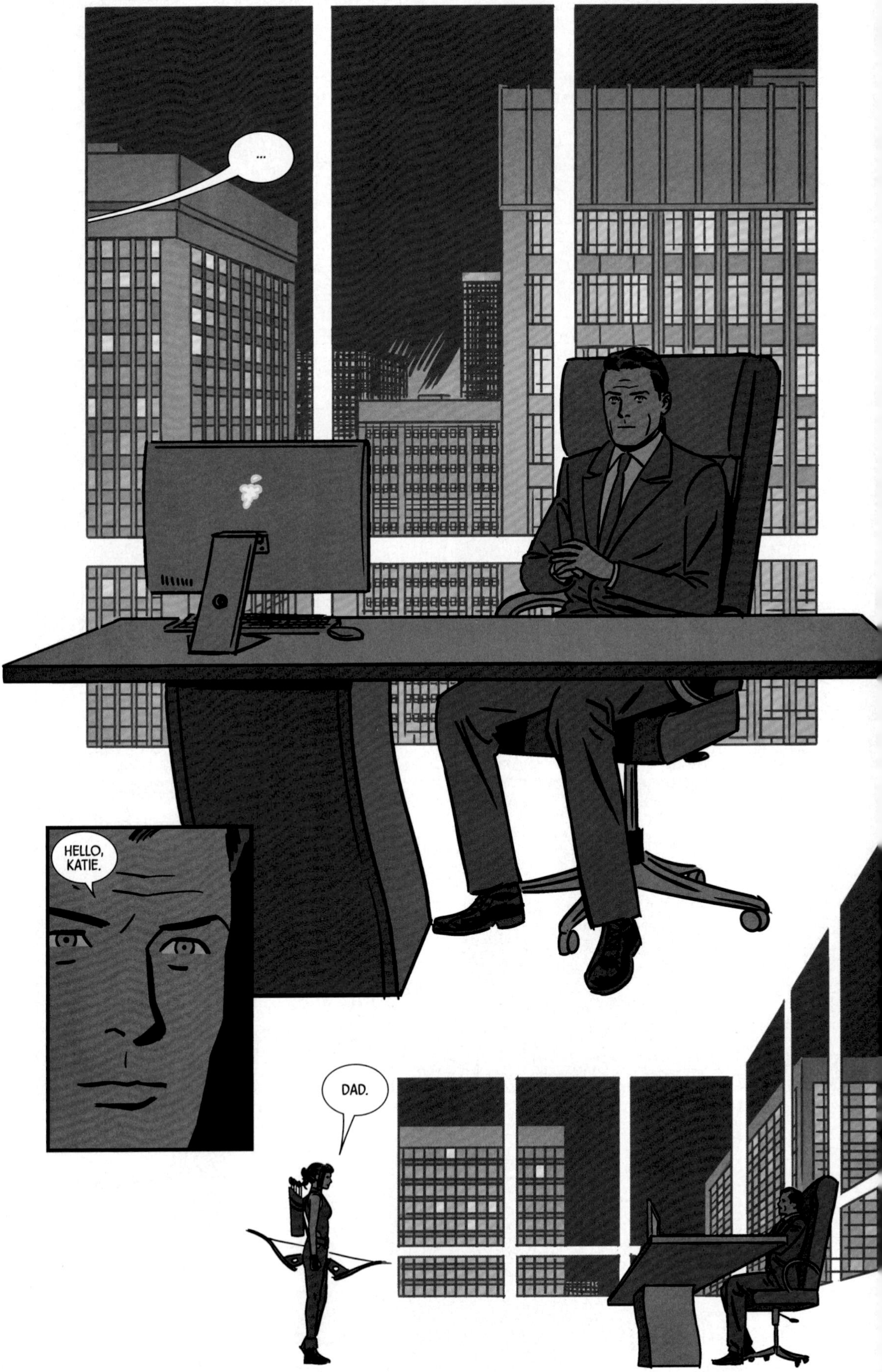
...
HELLO, KATIE.
DAD.

HAWK

INVESTIGATIONS

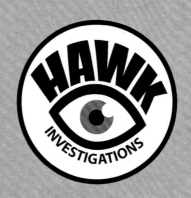

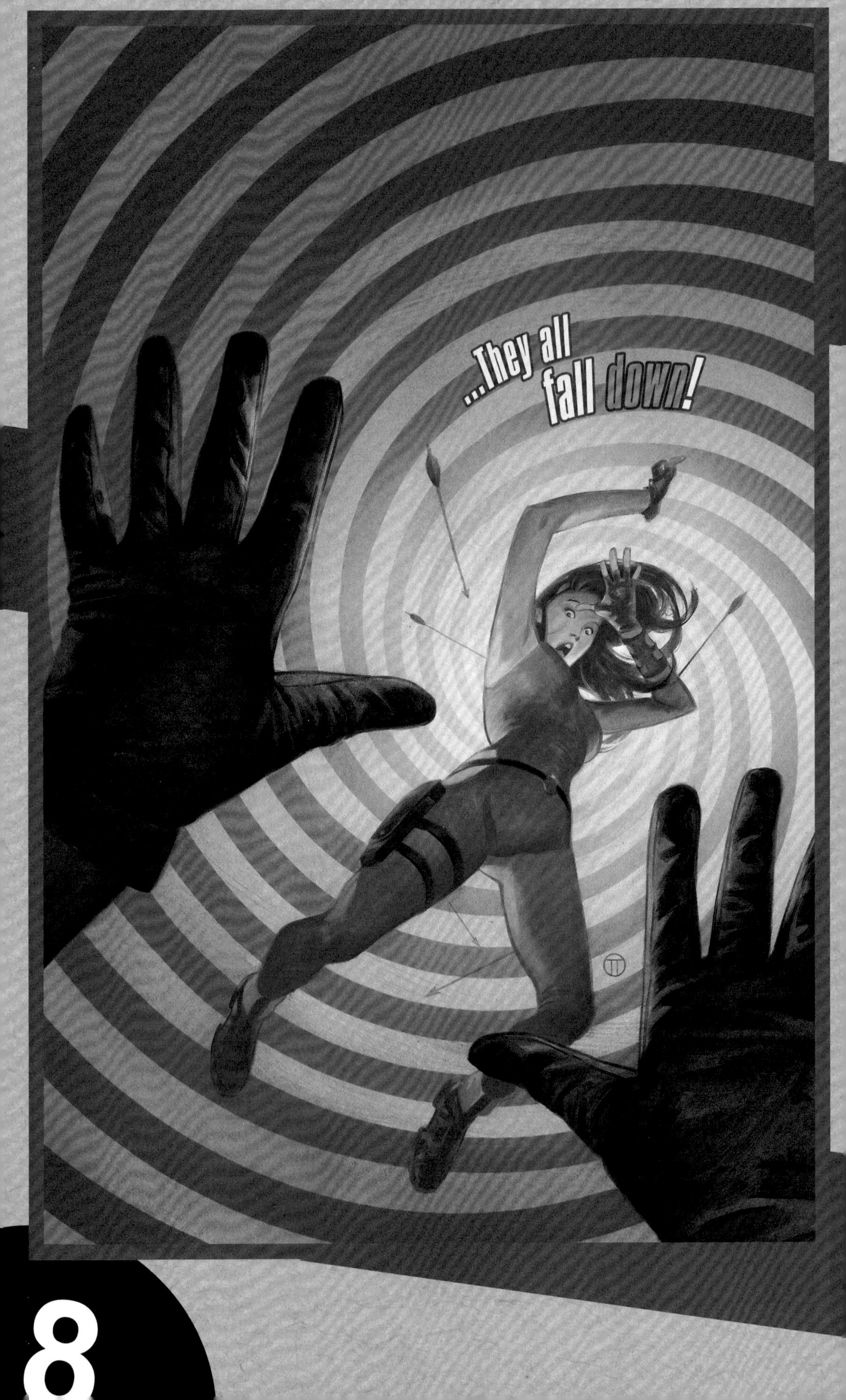

...They all fall down!
8

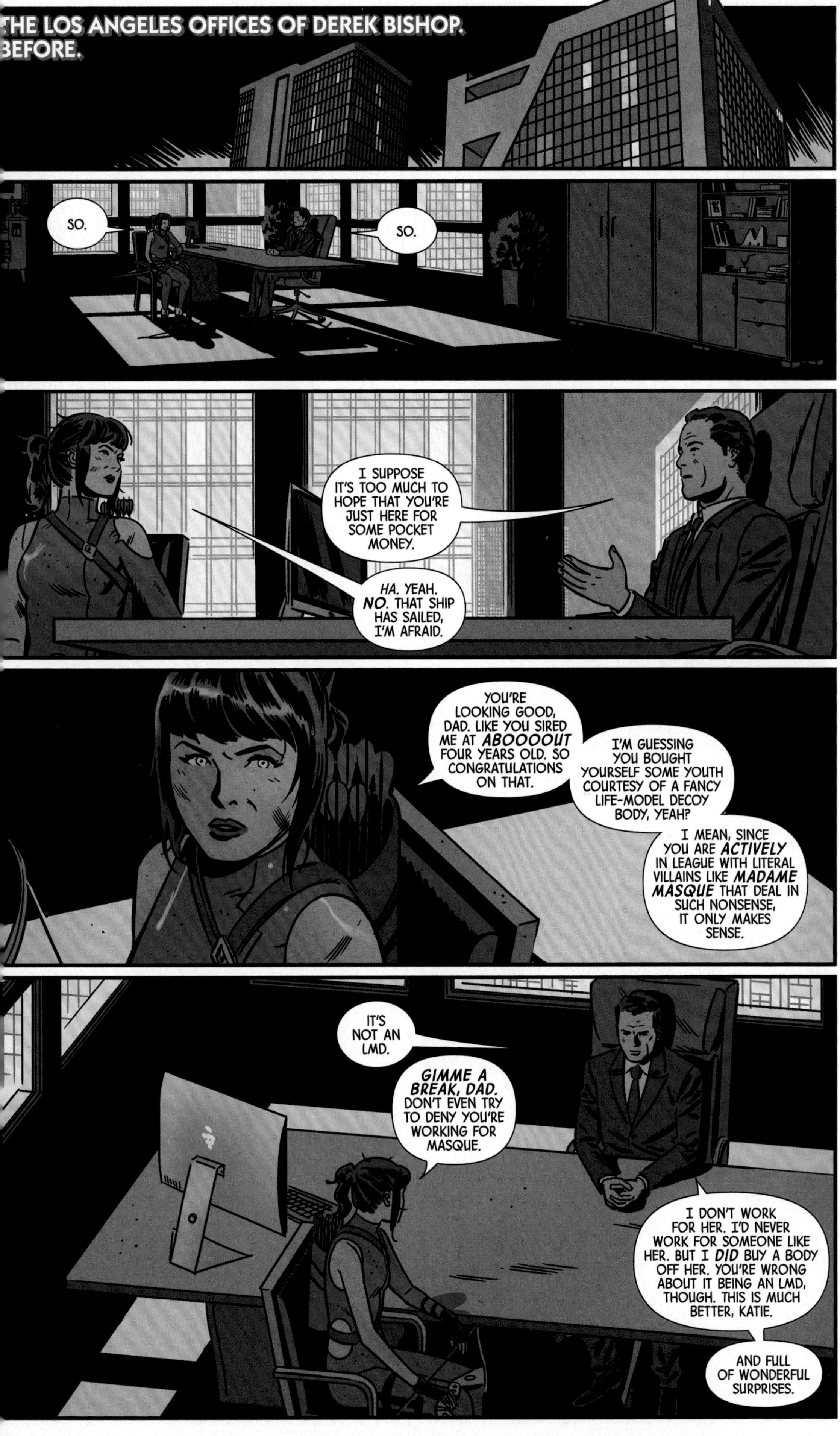
THE LOS ANGELES OFFICES OF DEREK BISHOP. BEFORE.
SO.
SO.
I SUPPOSE IT'S TOO MUCH TO HOPE THAT YOU'RE JUST HERE FOR SOME POCKET MONEY.
HA. YEAH. NO. THAT SHIP HAS SAILED, I'M AFRAID.
YOU'RE LOOKING GOOD, DAD. LIKE YOU SIRED ME AT ABOOOOUT FOUR YEARS OLD. SO CONGRATULATIONS ON THAT.
I'M GUESSING YOU BOUGHT YOURSELF SOME YOUTH COURTESY OF A FANCY LIFE-MODEL DECOY BODY, YEAH?
I MEAN, SINCE YOU ARE ACTIVELY IN LEAGUE WITH LITERAL VILLAINS LIKE MADAME MASQUE THAT DEAL IN SUCH NONSENSE, IT ONLY MAKES SENSE.
IT'S NOT AN LMD.
GIMME A BREAK, DAD. DON'T EVEN TRY TO DENY YOU'RE WORKING FOR MASQUE.
I DON'T WORK FOR HER. I'D NEVER WORK FOR SOMEONE LIKE HER. BUT I DID BUY A BODY OFF HER. YOU'RE WRONG ABOUT IT BEING AN LMD, THOUGH. THIS IS MUCH BETTER, KATIE.
AND FULL OF WONDERFUL SURPRISES.

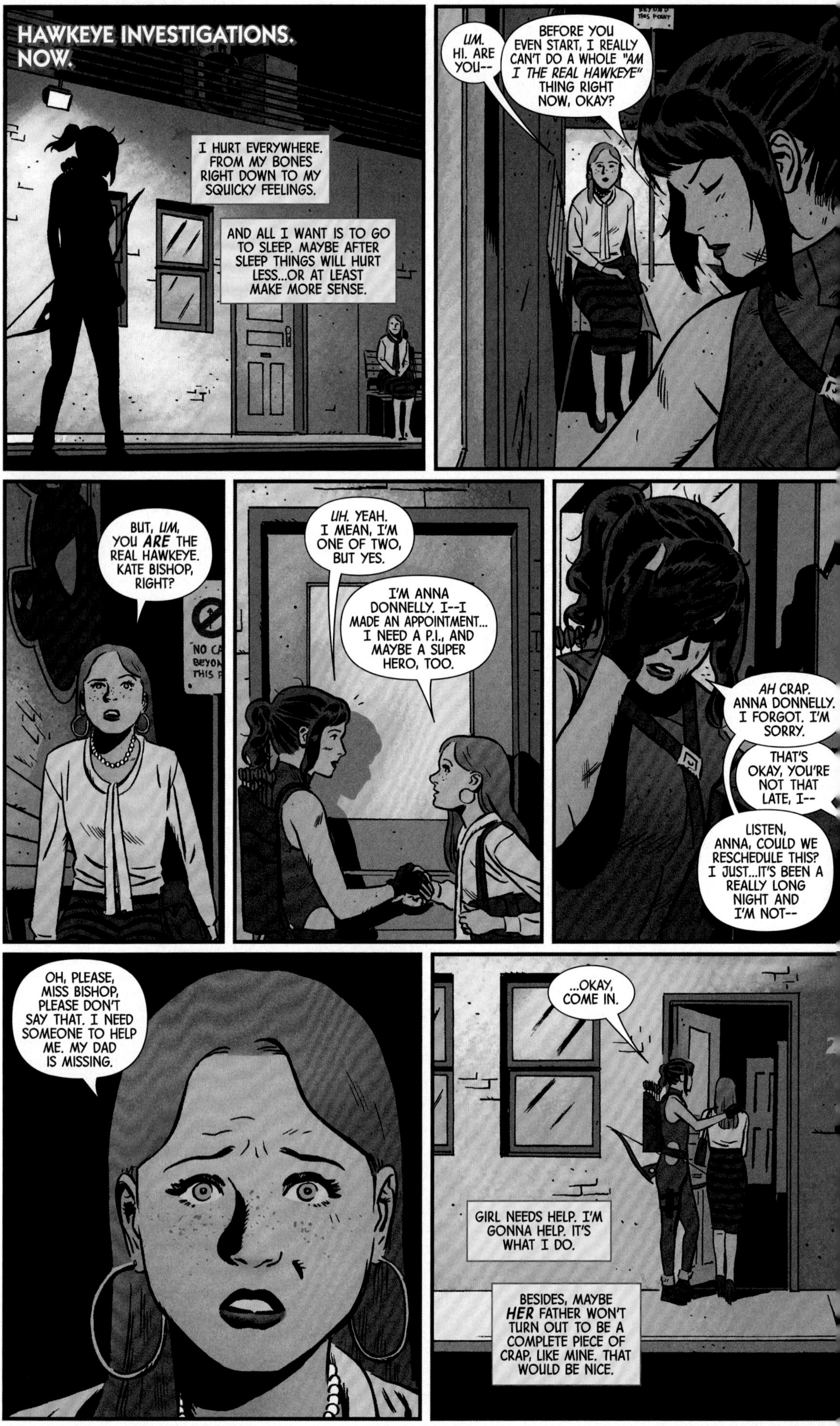
HAWKEYE INVESTIGATIONS. NOW.
I HURT EVERYWHERE. FROM MY BONES RIGHT DOWN TO MY SQUICKY FEELINGS.
AND ALL I WANT IS TO GO TO SLEEP. MAYBE AFTER SLEEP THINGS WILL HURT LESS...OR AT LEAST MAKE MORE SENSE.
UM. HI. ARE YOU--
BEFORE YOU EVEN START, I REALLY CAN'T DO A WHOLE "AM I THE REAL HAWKEYE" THING RIGHT NOW, OKAY?
BUT, UM, YOU ARE THE REAL HAWKEYE. KATE BISHOP, RIGHT?
UH. YEAH. I MEAN, I'M ONE OF TWO, BUT YES.
I'M ANNA DONNELLY. I--I MADE AN APPOINTMENT... I NEED A P.I., AND MAYBE A SUPER HERO, TOO.
AH CRAP. ANNA DONNELLY. I FORGOT. I'M SORRY.
THAT'S OKAY, YOU'RE NOT THAT LATE, I--
LISTEN, ANNA, COULD WE RESCHEDULE THIS? I JUST...IT'S BEEN A REALLY LONG NIGHT AND I'M NOT--
OH, PLEASE, MISS BISHOP, PLEASE DON'T SAY THAT. I NEED SOMEONE TO HELP ME. MY DAD IS MISSING.
...OKAY, COME IN.
GIRL NEEDS HELP. I'M GONNA HELP. IT'S WHAT I DO.
BESIDES, MAYBE HER FATHER WON'T TURN OUT TO BE A COMPLETE PIECE OF CRAP, LIKE MINE. THAT WOULD BE NICE.

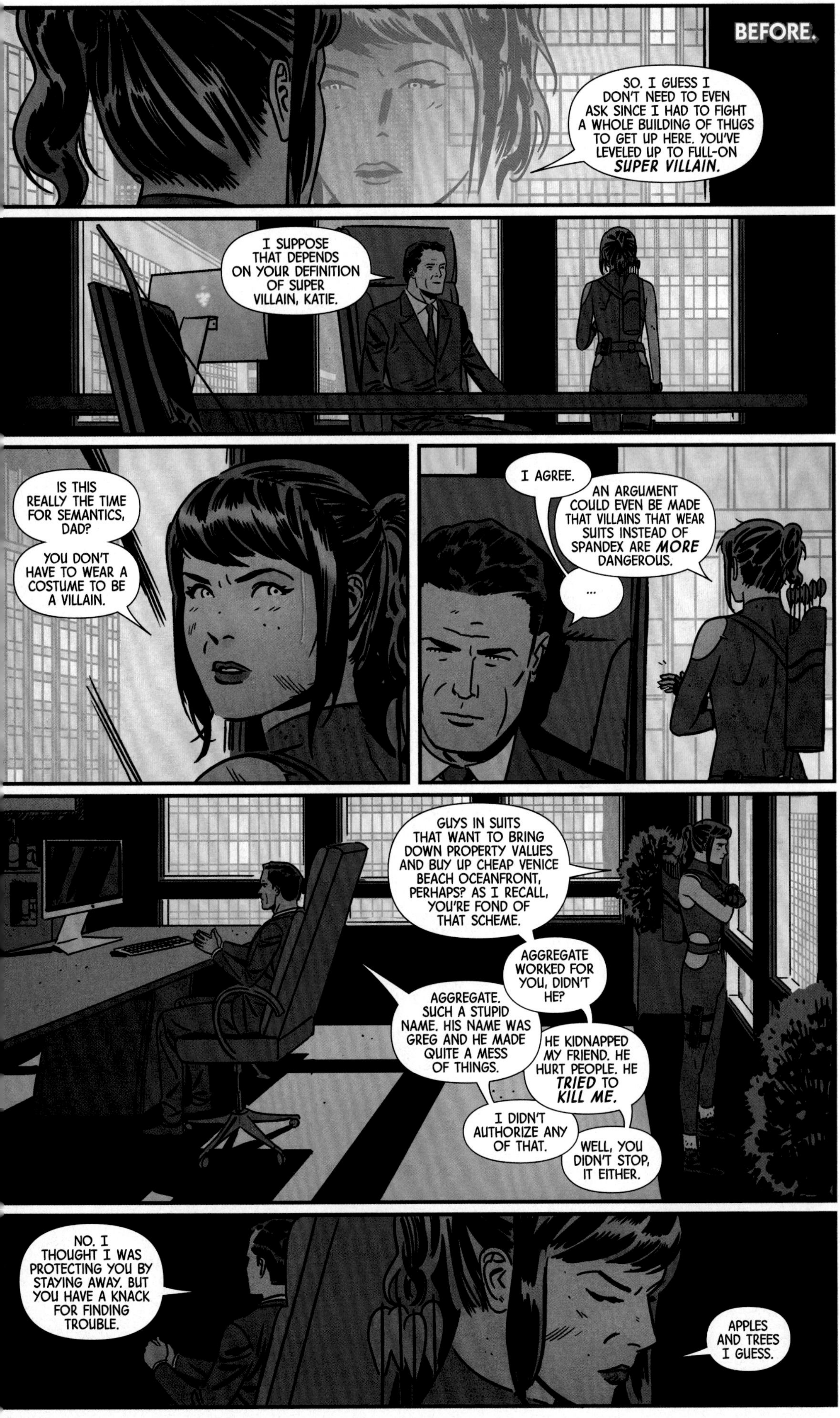
BEFORE.
SO. I GUESS I DON'T NEED TO EVEN ASK SINCE I HAD TO FIGHT A WHOLE BUILDING OF THUGS TO GET UP HERE. YOU'VE LEVELED UP TO FULL-ON SUPER VILLAIN.
I SUPPOSE THAT DEPENDS ON YOUR DEFINITION OF SUPER VILLAIN, KATIE.
IS THIS REALLY THE TIME FOR SEMANTICS, DAD?
YOU DON'T HAVE TO WEAR A COSTUME TO BE A VILLAIN.
I AGREE.
AN ARGUMENT COULD EVEN BE MADE THAT VILLAINS THAT WEAR SUITS INSTEAD OF SPANDEX ARE MORE DANGEROUS.
...
GUYS IN SUITS THAT WANT TO BRING DOWN PROPERTY VALUES AND BUY UP CHEAP VENICE BEACH OCEANFRONT, PERHAPS? AS I RECALL, YOU'RE FOND OF THAT SCHEME.
AGGREGATE WORKED FOR YOU, DIDN'T HE?
AGGREGATE. SUCH A STUPID NAME. HIS NAME WAS GREG AND HE MADE QUITE A MESS OF THINGS.
HE KIDNAPPED MY FRIEND. HE HURT PEOPLE. HE TRIED TO KILL ME.
I DIDN'T AUTHORIZE ANY OF THAT.
WELL, YOU DIDN'T STOP, IT EITHER.
NO. I THOUGHT I WAS PROTECTING YOU BY STAYING AWAY. BUT YOU HAVE A KNACK FOR FINDING TROUBLE.
APPLES AND TREES I GUESS.

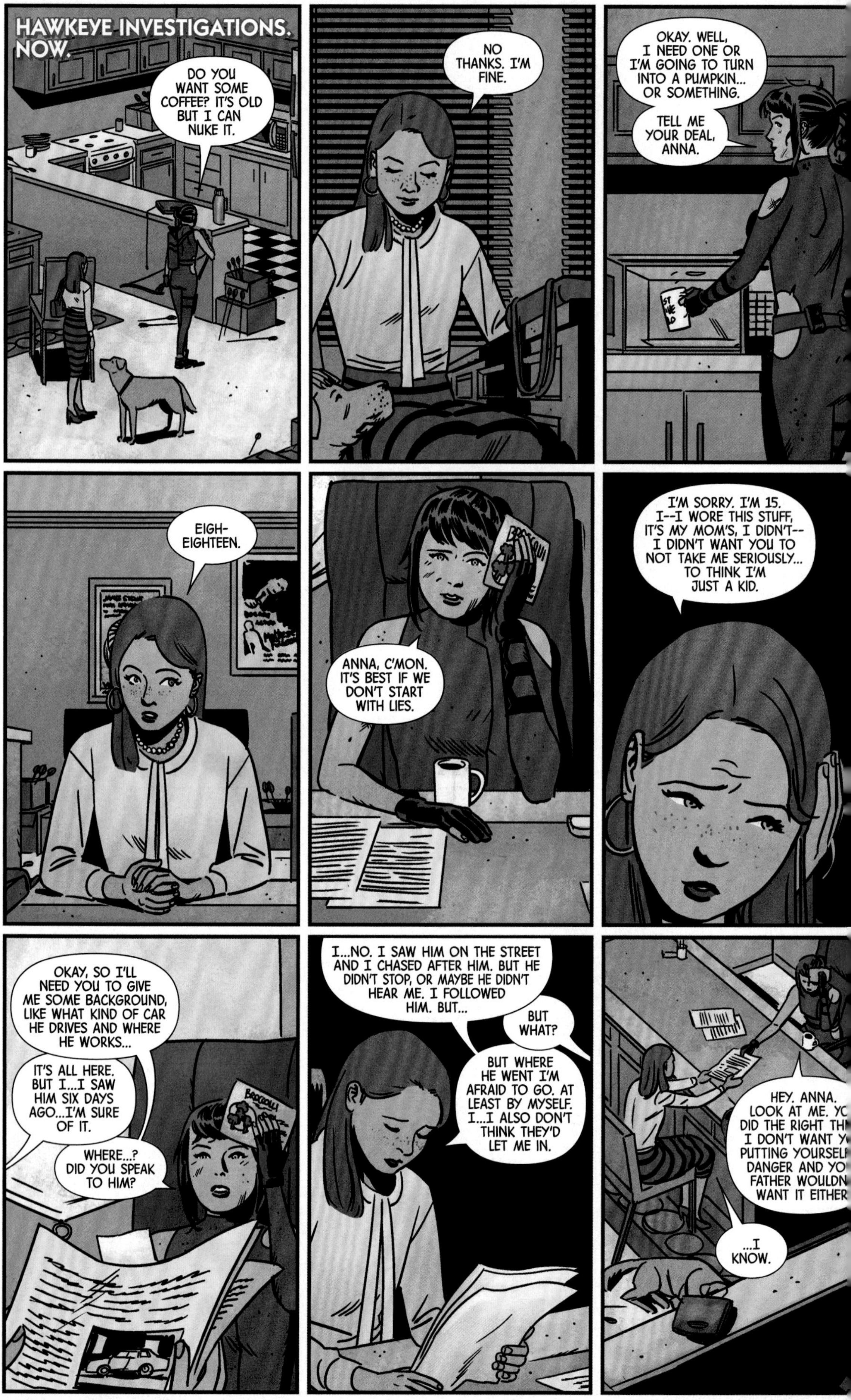
HAWKEYE INVESTIGATIONS. NOW.
DO YOU WANT SOME COFFEE? IT'S OLD BUT I CAN NUKE IT.
NO THANKS. I'M FINE.
OKAY. WELL, I NEED ONE OR I'M GOING TO TURN INTO A PUMPKIN... OR SOMETHING.
TELL ME YOUR DEAL, ANNA.
EIGH- EIGHTEEN.
ANNA, C'MON. IT'S BEST IF WE DON'T START WITH LIES.
I'M SORRY. I'M 15. I--I WORE THIS STUFF, IT'S MY MOM'S, I DIDN'T-- I DIDN'T WANT YOU TO NOT TAKE ME SERIOUSLY... TO THINK I'M JUST A KID.
OKAY, SO I'LL NEED YOU TO GIVE ME SOME BACKGROUND, LIKE WHAT KIND OF CAR HE DRIVES AND WHERE HE WORKS...
IT'S ALL HERE. BUT I...I SAW HIM SIX DAYS AGO...I'M SURE OF IT.
WHERE...? DID YOU SPEAK TO HIM?
I...NO. I SAW HIM ON THE STREET AND I CHASED AFTER HIM. BUT HE DIDN'T STOP, OR MAYBE HE DIDN'T HEAR ME. I FOLLOWED HIM. BUT...
BUT WHAT?
BUT WHERE HE WENT I'M AFRAID TO GO. AT LEAST BY MYSELF. I...I ALSO DON'T THINK THEY'D LET ME IN.
HEY. ANNA. LOOK AT ME. YO DID THE RIGHT TH I DON'T WANT Y PUTTING YOURSEL DANGER AND YO FATHER WOULDN WANT IT EITHER
...I KNOW.

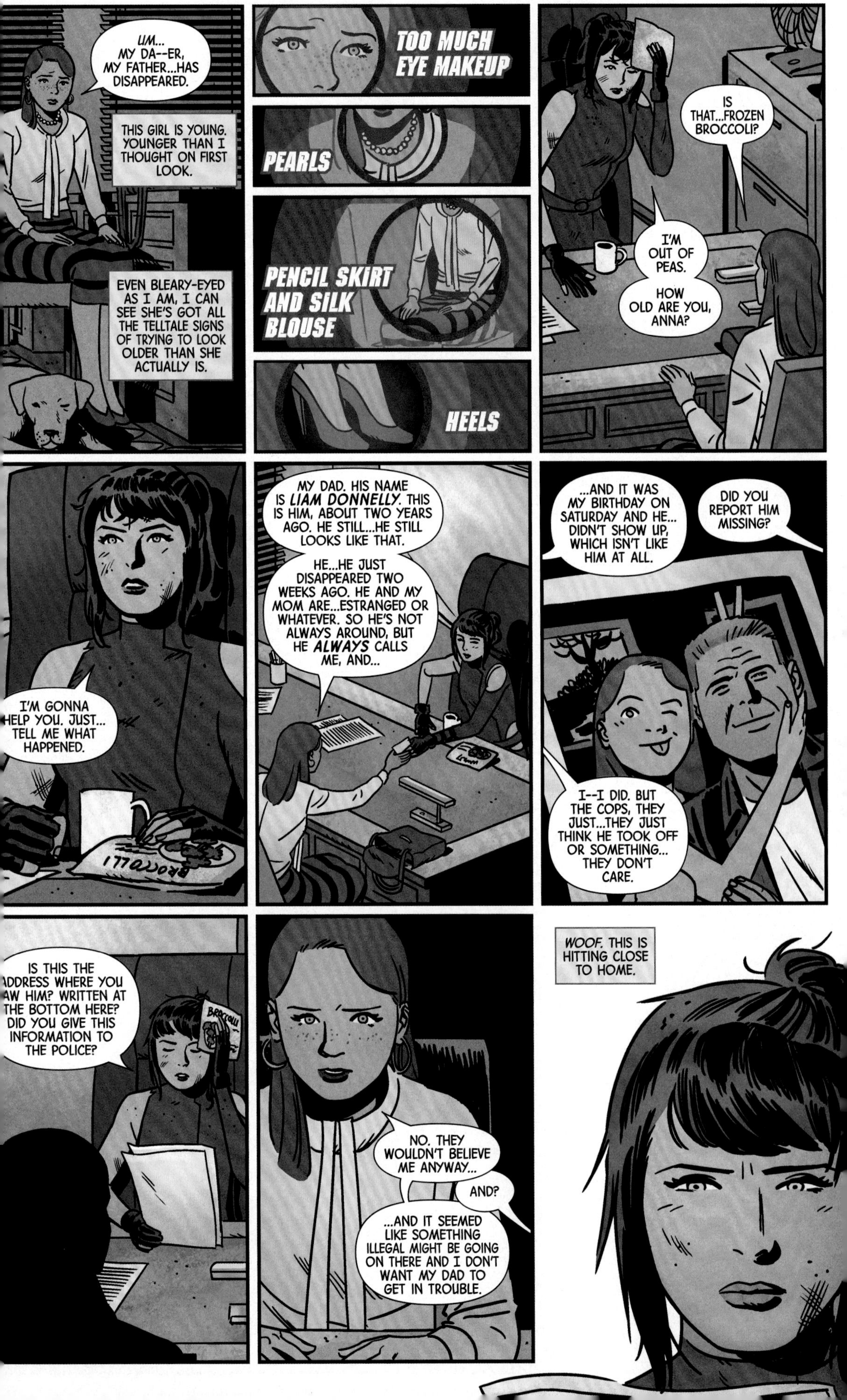

UM... MY DA--ER, MY FATHER...HAS DISAPPEARED.
THIS GIRL IS YOUNG. YOUNGER THAN I THOUGHT ON FIRST LOOK.
EVEN BLEARY-EYED AS I AM, I CAN SEE SHE'S GOT ALL THE TELLTALE SIGNS OF TRYING TO LOOK OLDER THAN SHE ACTUALLY IS.
TOO MUCH EYE MAKEUP
PEARLS
PENCIL SKIRT AND SILK BLOUSE
HEELS
IS THAT...FROZEN BROCCOLI?
I'M OUT OF PEAS.
HOW OLD ARE YOU, ANNA?
I'M GONNA HELP YOU. JUST... TELL ME WHAT HAPPENED.
BROCCOLI
MY DAD. HIS NAME IS LIAM DONNELLY. THIS IS HIM, ABOUT TWO YEARS AGO. HE STILL...HE STILL LOOKS LIKE THAT.
HE...HE JUST DISAPPEARED TWO WEEKS AGO. HE AND MY MOM ARE...ESTRANGED OR WHATEVER. SO HE'S NOT ALWAYS AROUND, BUT HE ALWAYS CALLS ME, AND...
...AND IT WAS MY BIRTHDAY ON SATURDAY AND HE... DIDN'T SHOW UP, WHICH ISN'T LIKE HIM AT ALL.
DID YOU REPORT HIM MISSING?
I--I DID. BUT THE COPS, THEY JUST...THEY JUST THINK HE TOOK OFF OR SOMETHING... THEY DON'T CARE.
IS THIS THE ADDRESS WHERE YOU SAW HIM? WRITTEN AT THE BOTTOM HERE? DID YOU GIVE THIS INFORMATION TO THE POLICE?
BROCCOLI
NO. THEY WOULDN'T BELIEVE ME ANYWAY...
AND?
...AND IT SEEMED LIKE SOMETHING ILLEGAL MIGHT BE GOING ON THERE AND I DON'T WANT MY DAD TO GET IN TROUBLE.
WOOF. THIS IS HITTING CLOSE TO HOME.

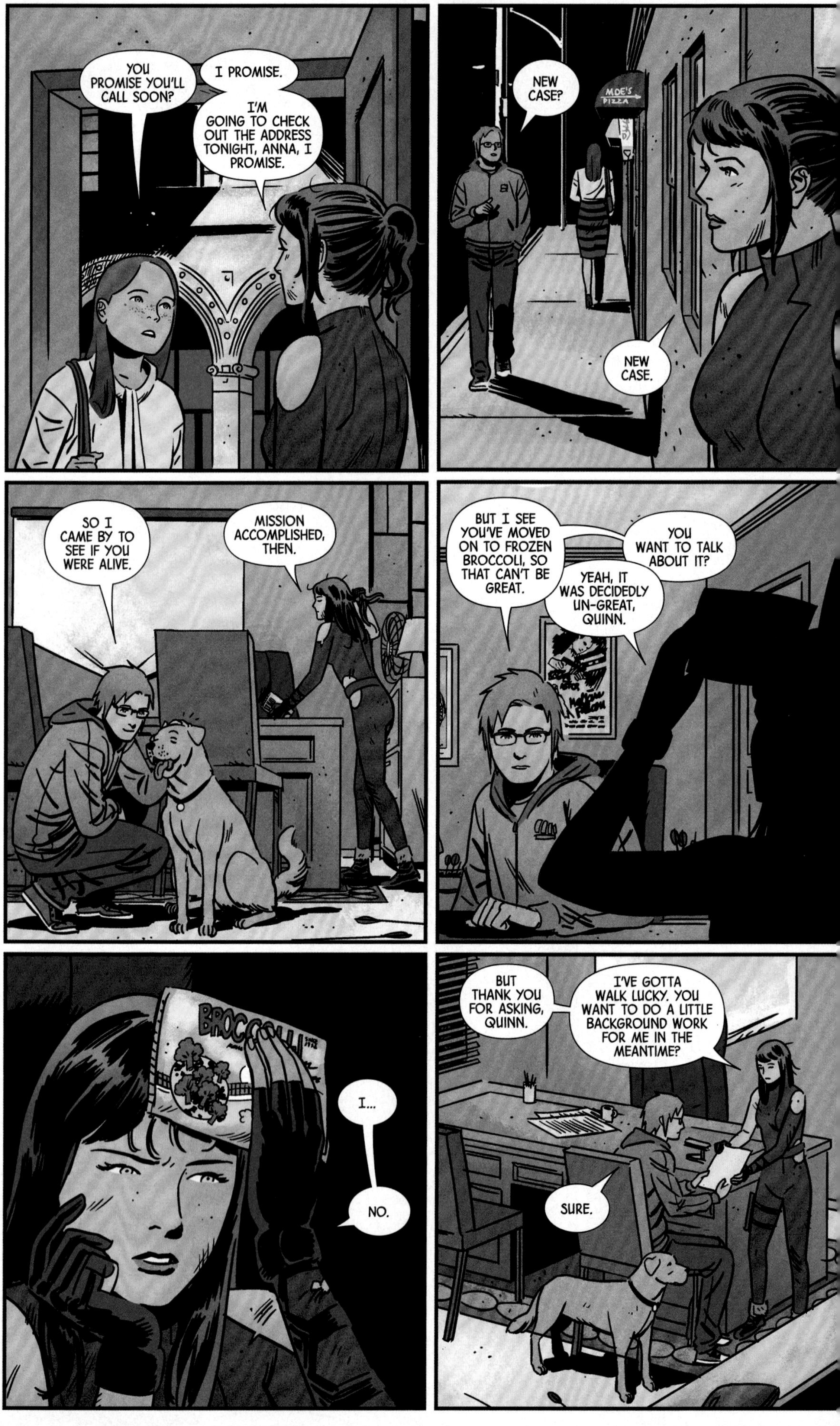

YOU PROMISE YOU'LL CALL SOON?
I PROMISE.
I'M GOING TO CHECK OUT THE ADDRESS TONIGHT, ANNA, I PROMISE.
NEW CASE?
MOE'S PIZZA
NEW CASE.
SO I CAME BY TO SEE IF YOU WERE ALIVE.
MISSION ACCOMPLISHED, THEN.
BUT I SEE YOU'VE MOVED ON TO FROZEN BROCCOLI, SO THAT CAN'T BE GREAT.
YOU WANT TO TALK ABOUT IT?
YEAH, IT WAS DECIDEDLY UN-GREAT, QUINN.
BROCCOLI
I...
NO.
BUT THANK YOU FOR ASKING, QUINN.
I'VE GOTTA WALK LUCKY. YOU WANT TO DO A LITTLE BACKGROUND WORK FOR ME IN THE MEANTIME?
SURE.

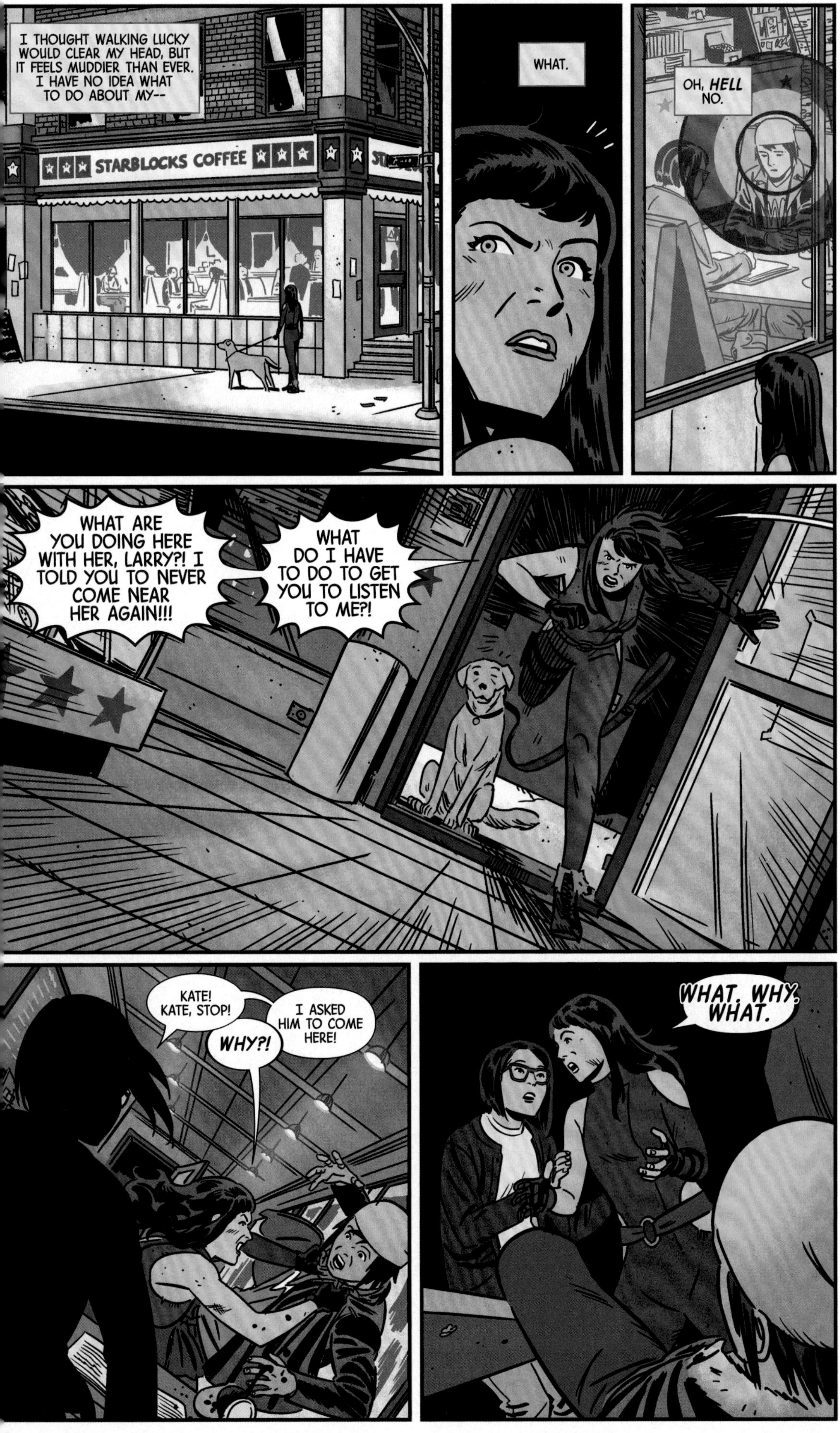
I THOUGHT WALKING LUCKY WOULD CLEAR MY HEAD, BUT IT FEELS MUDDIER THAN EVER. I HAVE NO IDEA WHAT TO DO ABOUT MY--
STARBLOCKS COFFEE
WHAT.
OH, HELL NO.
WHAT ARE YOU DOING HERE WITH HER, LARRY?! I TOLD YOU TO NEVER COME NEAR HER AGAIN!!!
WHAT DO I HAVE TO DO TO GET YOU TO LISTEN TO ME?!
KATE! KATE, STOP!
WHY?!
I ASKED HIM TO COME HERE!
WHAT. WHY. WHAT.

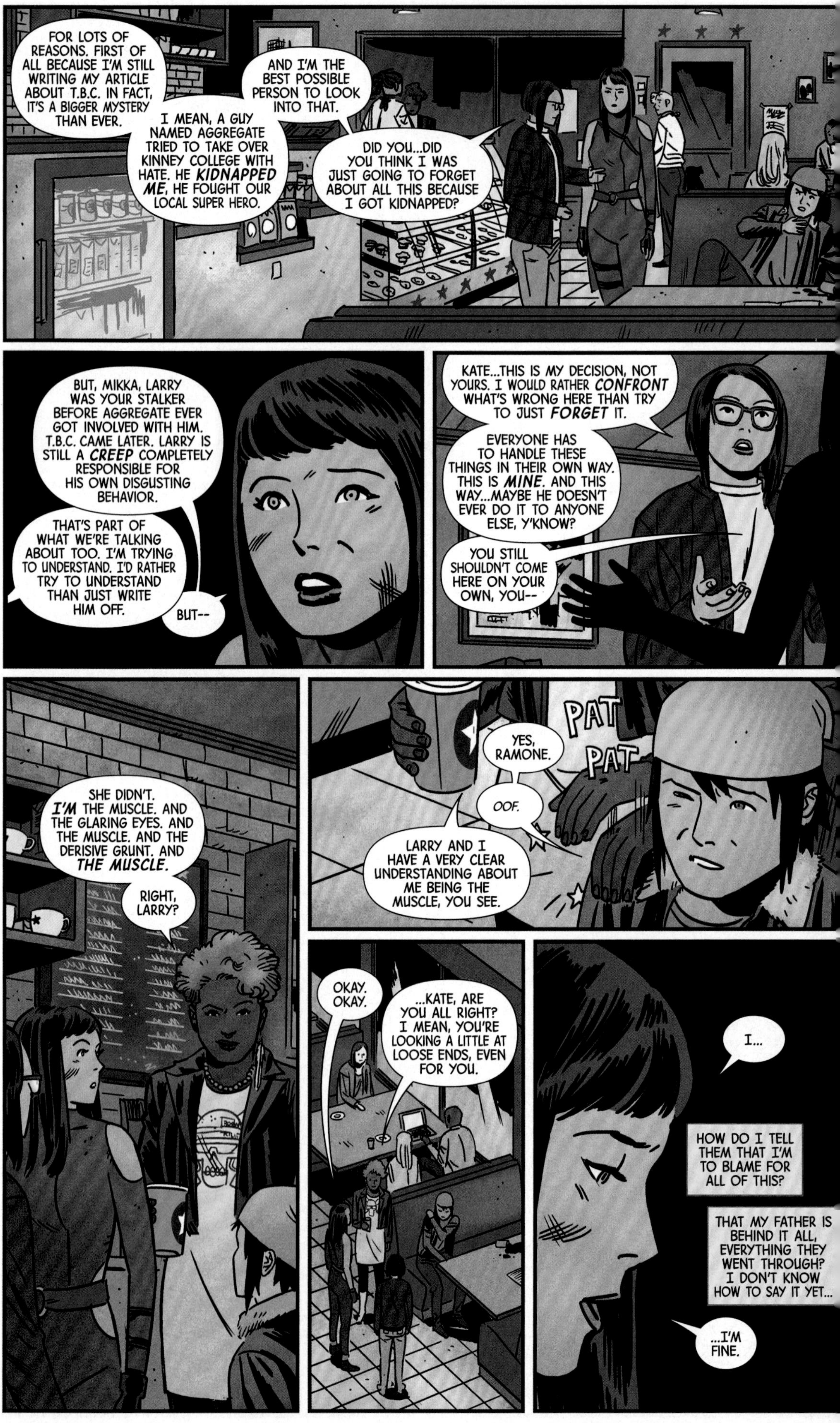
FOR LOTS OF REASONS. FIRST OF ALL BECAUSE I'M STILL WRITING MY ARTICLE ABOUT T.B.C. IN FACT, IT'S A BIGGER MYSTERY THAN EVER.
I MEAN, A GUY NAMED AGGREGATE TRIED TO TAKE OVER KINNEY COLLEGE WITH HATE. HE KIDNAPPED ME, HE FOUGHT OUR LOCAL SUPER HERO.
AND I'M THE BEST POSSIBLE PERSON TO LOOK INTO THAT.
DID YOU...DID YOU THINK I WAS JUST GOING TO FORGET ABOUT ALL THIS BECAUSE I GOT KIDNAPPED?
BUT, MIKKA, LARRY WAS YOUR STALKER BEFORE AGGREGATE EVER GOT INVOLVED WITH HIM. T.B.C. CAME LATER. LARRY IS STILL A CREEP COMPLETELY RESPONSIBLE FOR HIS OWN DISGUSTING BEHAVIOR.
THAT'S PART OF WHAT WE'RE TALKING ABOUT TOO. I'M TRYING TO UNDERSTAND. I'D RATHER TRY TO UNDERSTAND THAN JUST WRITE HIM OFF.
BUT--
KATE...THIS IS MY DECISION, NOT YOURS. I WOULD RATHER CONFRONT WHAT'S WRONG HERE THAN TRY TO JUST FORGET IT.
EVERYONE HAS TO HANDLE THESE THINGS IN THEIR OWN WAY. THIS IS MINE. AND THIS WAY...MAYBE HE DOESN'T EVER DO IT TO ANYONE ELSE, Y'KNOW?
YOU STILL SHOULDN'T COME HERE ON YOUR OWN, YOU--
SHE DIDN'T. I'M THE MUSCLE. AND THE GLARING EYES. AND THE MUSCLE. AND THE DERISIVE GRUNT. AND THE MUSCLE.
RIGHT, LARRY?
PAT PAT
YES, RAMONE.
OOF.
LARRY AND I HAVE A VERY CLEAR UNDERSTANDING ABOUT ME BEING THE MUSCLE, YOU SEE.
OKAY. OKAY.
...KATE, ARE YOU ALL RIGHT? I MEAN, YOU'RE LOOKING A LITTLE AT LOOSE ENDS, EVEN FOR YOU.
I...
HOW DO I TELL THEM THAT I'M TO BLAME FOR ALL OF THIS?
THAT MY FATHER IS BEHIND IT ALL, EVERYTHING THEY WENT THROUGH? I DON'T KNOW HOW TO SAY IT YET...
...I'M FINE.

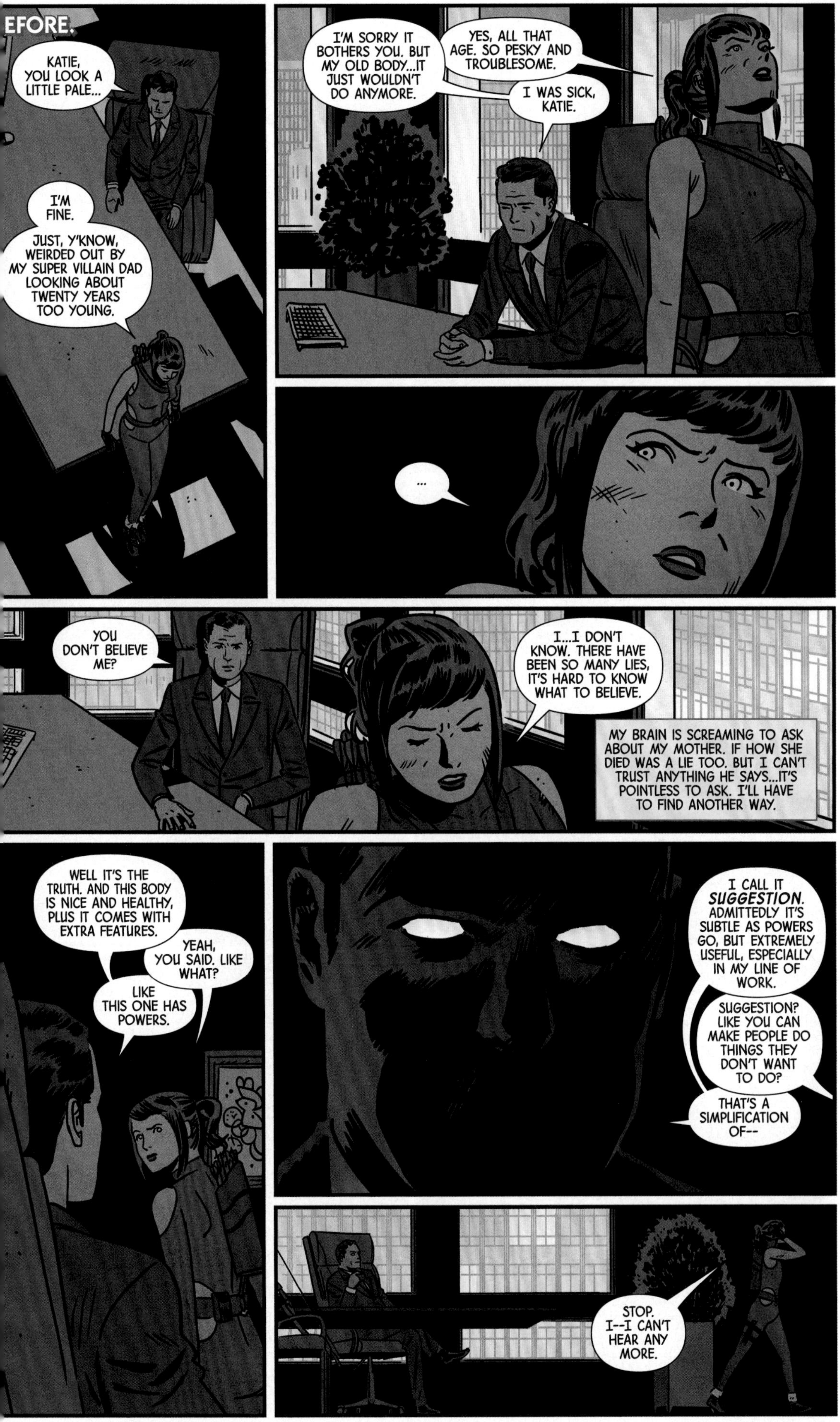
EFORE.
KATIE, YOU LOOK A LITTLE PALE...
I'M FINE.
JUST, Y'KNOW, WEIRDED OUT BY MY SUPER VILLAIN DAD LOOKING ABOUT TWENTY YEARS TOO YOUNG.
I'M SORRY IT BOTHERS YOU. BUT MY OLD BODY...IT JUST WOULDN'T DO ANYMORE.
YES, ALL THAT AGE. SO PESKY AND TROUBLESOME.
I WAS SICK, KATIE.
...
YOU DON'T BELIEVE ME?
I...I DON'T KNOW. THERE HAVE BEEN SO MANY LIES, IT'S HARD TO KNOW WHAT TO BELIEVE.
MY BRAIN IS SCREAMING TO ASK ABOUT MY MOTHER. IF HOW SHE DIED WAS A LIE TOO. BUT I CAN'T TRUST ANYTHING HE SAYS...IT'S POINTLESS TO ASK. I'LL HAVE TO FIND ANOTHER WAY.
WELL IT'S THE TRUTH. AND THIS BODY IS NICE AND HEALTHY, PLUS IT COMES WITH EXTRA FEATURES.
YEAH, YOU SAID. LIKE WHAT?
LIKE THIS ONE HAS POWERS.
I CALL IT SUGGESTION. ADMITTEDLY IT'S SUBTLE AS POWERS GO, BUT EXTREMELY USEFUL, ESPECIALLY IN MY LINE OF WORK.
SUGGESTION? LIKE YOU CAN MAKE PEOPLE DO THINGS THEY DON'T WANT TO DO?
THAT'S A SIMPLIFICATION OF--
STOP. I--I CAN'T HEAR ANY MORE.

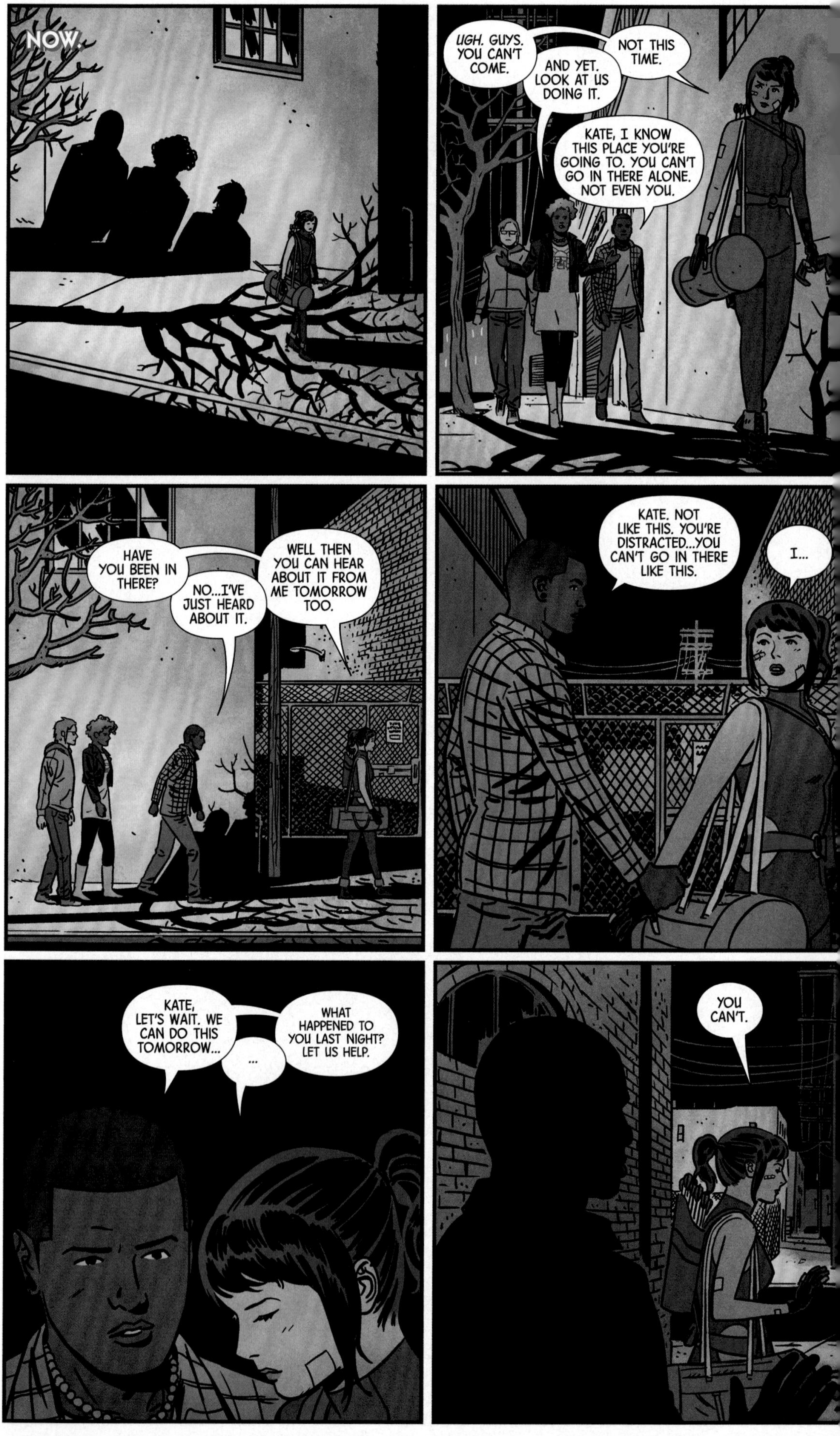
NOW.
UGH. GUYS. YOU CAN'T COME.
AND YET. LOOK AT US DOING IT.
NOT THIS TIME.
KATE, I KNOW THIS PLACE YOU'RE GOING TO. YOU CAN'T GO IN THERE ALONE. NOT EVEN YOU.
HAVE YOU BEEN IN THERE?
NO...I'VE JUST HEARD ABOUT IT.
WELL THEN YOU CAN HEAR ABOUT IT FROM ME TOMORROW TOO.
KATE. NOT LIKE THIS. YOU'RE DISTRACTED...YOU CAN'T GO IN THERE LIKE THIS.
I...
KATE, LET'S WAIT. WE CAN DO THIS TOMORROW...
...
WHAT HAPPENED TO YOU LAST NIGHT? LET US HELP.
YOU CAN'T.

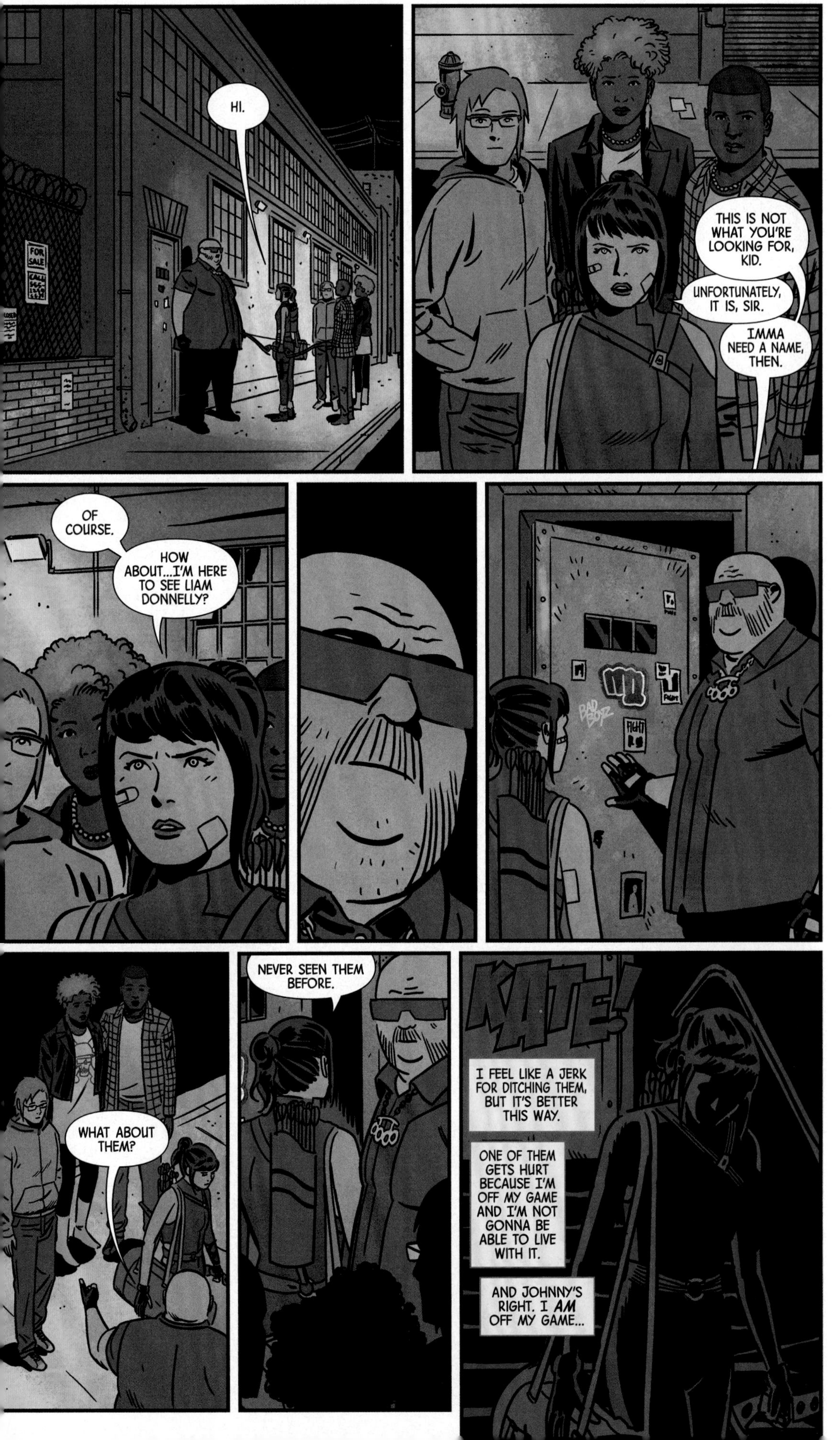

HI.
THIS IS NOT WHAT YOU'RE LOOKING FOR, KID.
UNFORTUNATELY, IT IS, SIR.
IMMA NEED A NAME, THEN.
OF COURSE.
HOW ABOUT...I'M HERE TO SEE LIAM DONNELLY?
WHAT ABOUT THEM?
NEVER SEEN THEM BEFORE.
KATE!
I FEEL LIKE A JERK FOR DITCHING THEM, BUT IT'S BETTER THIS WAY.
ONE OF THEM GETS HURT BECAUSE I'M OFF MY GAME AND I'M NOT GONNA BE ABLE TO LIVE WITH IT.
AND JOHNNY'S RIGHT. I *AM* OFF MY GAME...

...AND IT'S A BAAAAD TIME FOR THAT TO BE TRUE.

HOO BOY.

TROUBLE TROUBLE TROUBLE TROUBLE TROUBLE

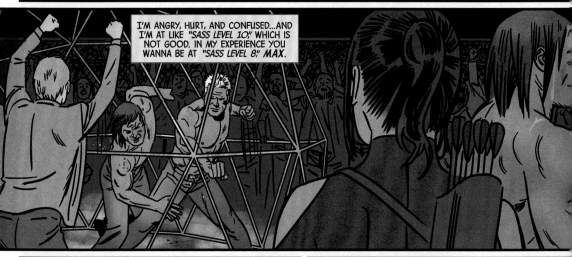

I'M ANGRY, HURT, AND CONFUSED...AND I'M AT LIKE *"SASS LEVEL 10,"* WHICH IS NOT GOOD. IN MY EXPERIENCE YOU WANNA BE AT *"SASS LEVEL 8,"* MAX.

ANYTHING ELSE GETS YOU PUMMELED. CASE IN POINT... THIS GUY. THIS GUY'S ABOUT TO PUMMEL ME.

YOU DON'T BELONG HERE.

OH YEAH? WHAT TIPPED YOU OFF? I'M NOT COVERED IN A METRIC TON OF SWEAT?

THUNK

YOU'RE MOUTHY.

MUST BE YOUR FIRST NIGHT... IF IT'S YOUR FIRST NIGHT, THEN YOU FIGHT, GIRLIE.

AH, CRAP.

IT'S ONE OF THOSE FIGHT CLUB THINGAMAJIGS.

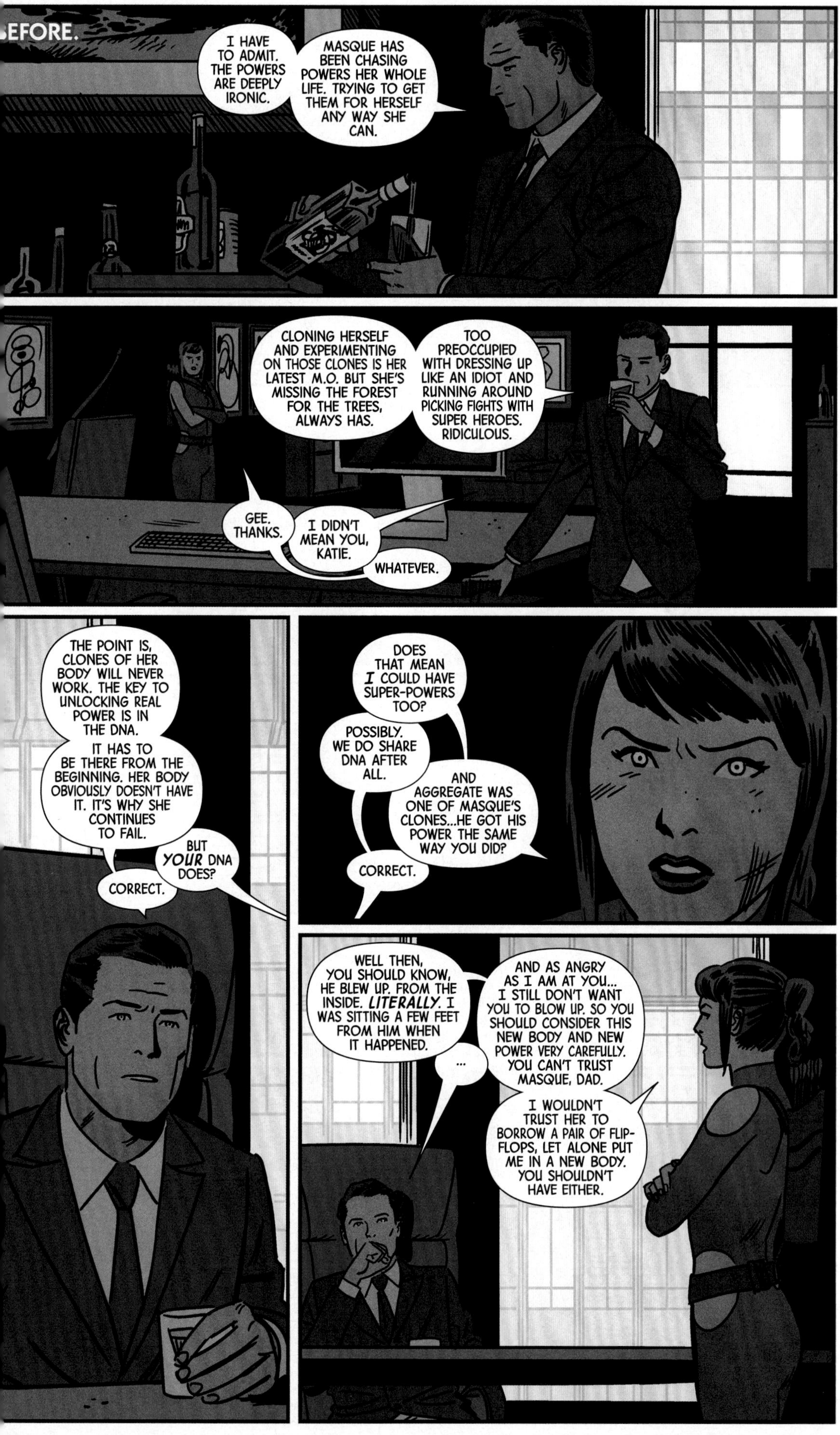

EFORE.
I HAVE TO ADMIT. THE POWERS ARE DEEPLY IRONIC.
MASQUE HAS BEEN CHASING POWERS HER WHOLE LIFE. TRYING TO GET THEM FOR HERSELF ANY WAY SHE CAN.
CLONING HERSELF AND EXPERIMENTING ON THOSE CLONES IS HER LATEST M.O. BUT SHE'S MISSING THE FOREST FOR THE TREES, ALWAYS HAS.
TOO PREOCCUPIED WITH DRESSING UP LIKE AN IDIOT AND RUNNING AROUND PICKING FIGHTS WITH SUPER HEROES. RIDICULOUS.
GEE. THANKS.
I DIDN'T MEAN YOU, KATIE.
WHATEVER.
THE POINT IS, CLONES OF HER BODY WILL NEVER WORK. THE KEY TO UNLOCKING REAL POWER IS IN THE DNA.
IT HAS TO BE THERE FROM THE BEGINNING. HER BODY OBVIOUSLY DOESN'T HAVE IT. IT'S WHY SHE CONTINUES TO FAIL.
BUT *YOUR* DNA DOES?
CORRECT.
DOES THAT MEAN *I* COULD HAVE SUPER-POWERS TOO?
POSSIBLY. WE DO SHARE DNA AFTER ALL.
AND AGGREGATE WAS ONE OF MASQUE'S CLONES...HE GOT HIS POWER THE SAME WAY YOU DID?
CORRECT.
WELL THEN, YOU SHOULD KNOW, HE BLEW UP. FROM THE INSIDE. *LITERALLY.* I WAS SITTING A FEW FEET FROM HIM WHEN IT HAPPENED.
...
AND AS ANGRY AS I AM AT YOU... I STILL DON'T WANT YOU TO BLOW UP. SO YOU SHOULD CONSIDER THIS NEW BODY AND NEW POWER VERY CAREFULLY. YOU CAN'T TRUST MASQUE, DAD.
I WOULDN'T TRUST HER TO BORROW A PAIR OF FLIP-FLOPS, LET ALONE PUT ME IN A NEW BODY. YOU SHOULDN'T HAVE EITHER.

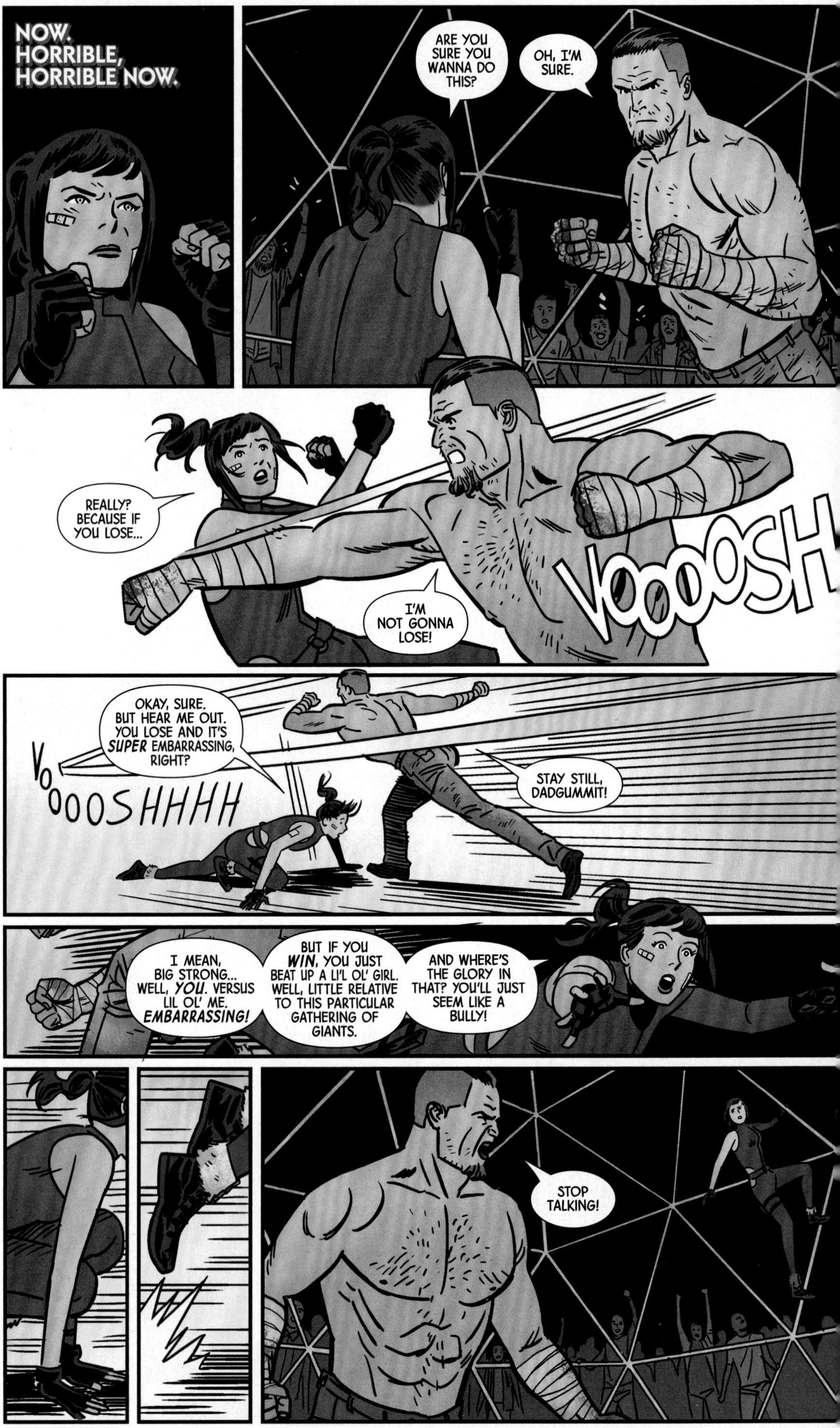
NOW. HORRIBLE, HORRIBLE NOW.
ARE YOU SURE YOU WANNA DO THIS?
OH, I'M SURE.
REALLY? BECAUSE IF YOU LOSE...
I'M NOT GONNA LOSE!
VOOOOSH
OKAY, SURE. BUT HEAR ME OUT. YOU LOSE AND IT'S SUPER EMBARRASSING, RIGHT?
VOOOOSHHHH
STAY STILL, DADGUMMIT!
I MEAN, BIG STRONG... WELL, YOU. VERSUS LIL OL' ME. EMBARRASSING!
BUT IF YOU WIN, YOU JUST BEAT UP A LI'L OL' GIRL. WELL, LITTLE RELATIVE TO THIS PARTICULAR GATHERING OF GIANTS.
AND WHERE'S THE GLORY IN THAT? YOU'LL JUST SEEM LIKE A BULLY!
STOP TALKING!

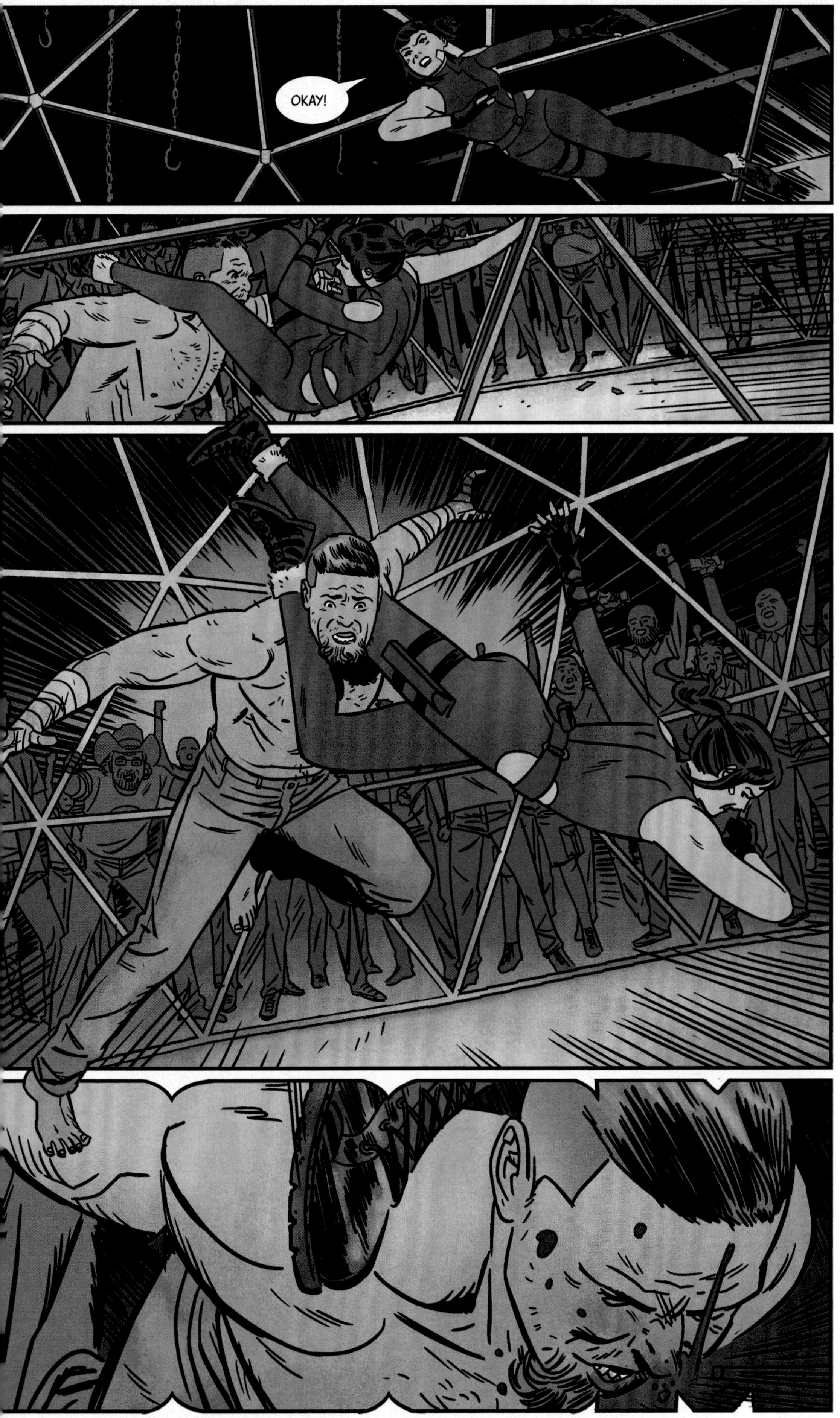
OKAY!

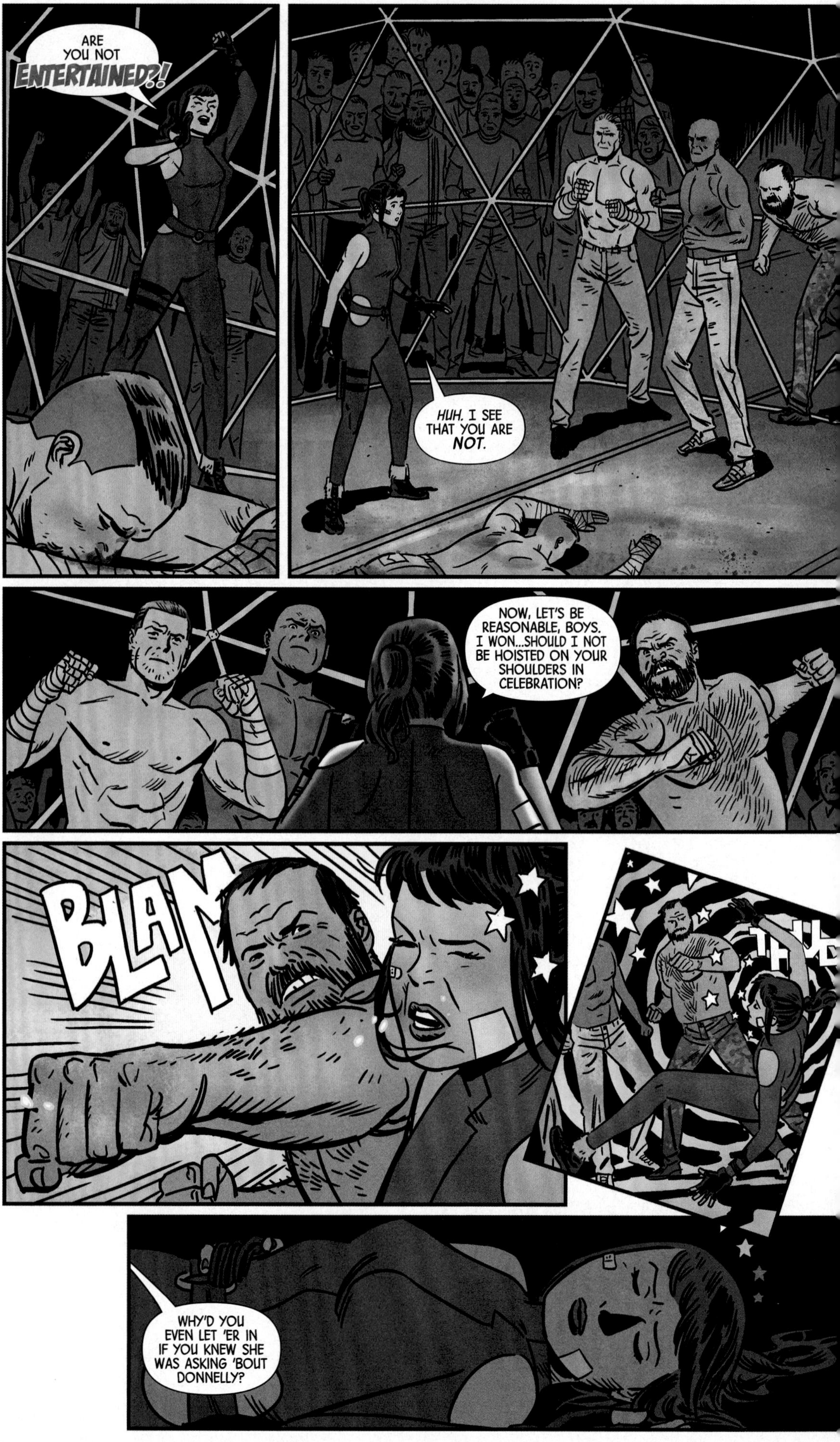

ARE YOU NOT ENTERTAINED?!
HUH. I SEE THAT YOU ARE NOT.
NOW, LET'S BE REASONABLE, BOYS. I WON...SHOULD I NOT BE HOISTED ON YOUR SHOULDERS IN CELEBRATION?
BLAM
WHY'D YOU EVEN LET 'ER IN IF YOU KNEW SHE WAS ASKING 'BOUT DONNELLY?

WELL, IT'S BEEN REAL, DAD. BUT I NEED TO GO.

I'M AFRAID THAT'S NOT POSSIBLE, KATIE. I HAD HOPED YOU WOULD COME AROUND...SEE THINGS MY WAY, BUT YOU'RE JUST AS STUBBORN AS EVER.

YOU'RE GONNA STOP ME? YOU AND WHAT ARMY? OH YEAH, THE ARMY I ALREADY FOUGHT ONCE TODAY.

WELL, I DEFEATED THEM ONCE, I'LL JUST DO IT AGAIN. IT'LL BE ANNOYING, BUT IT'S TOTALLY DOABLE.

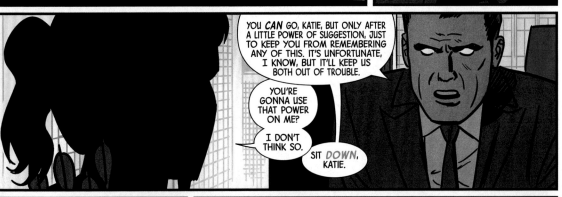

YOU *CAN* GO, KATIE, BUT ONLY AFTER A LITTLE POWER OF SUGGESTION, JUST TO KEEP YOU FROM REMEMBERING ANY OF THIS. IT'S UNFORTUNATE, I KNOW, BUT IT'LL KEEP US BOTH OUT OF TROUBLE.

YOU'RE GONNA USE THAT POWER ON ME?

I DON'T THINK SO.

SIT *DOWN*, KATIE.

OOF. DAD. STOP IT.

OUR RELATIONSHIP IS IN A BAD ENOUGH STATE. IF YOU USE THAT POWER TO ERASE MY MEMORIES WE'RE GOING TO HAVE EXTRA SERIOUS PROBLEMS.

I'M AFRAID YOU'VE LEFT ME NO CHOICE, KATIE. YOU NEVER SHOULD HAVE COME HERE.

FWUMP

POSSIBLY TRUE. BUT I'M HAWKEYE, DAD, AND I'VE *ALWAYS* GOT MY EYE ON AN EXIT.

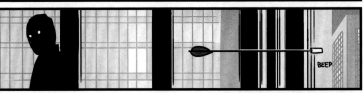

BEEP

BOOM

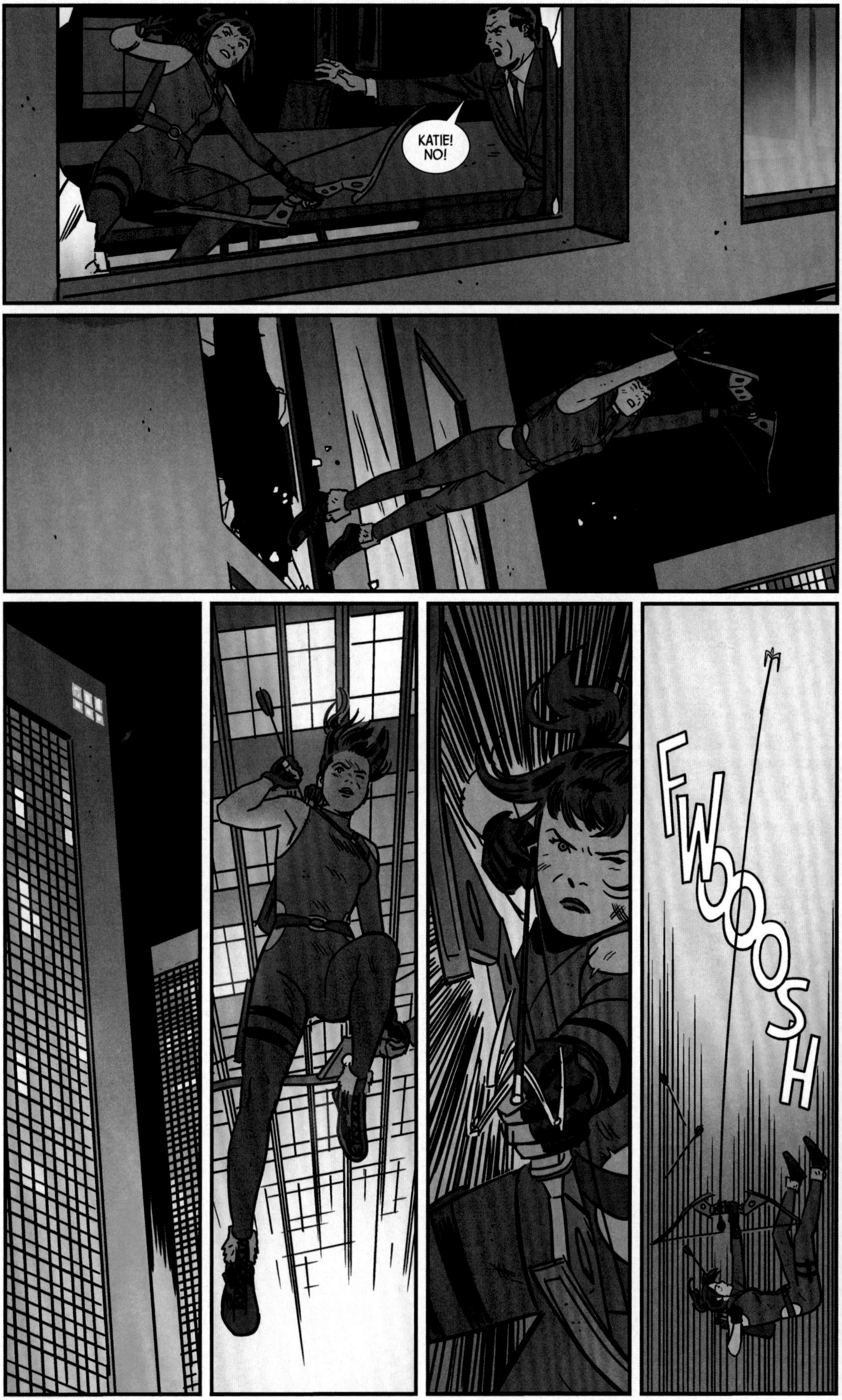
KATIE! NO!
FWOOOSH

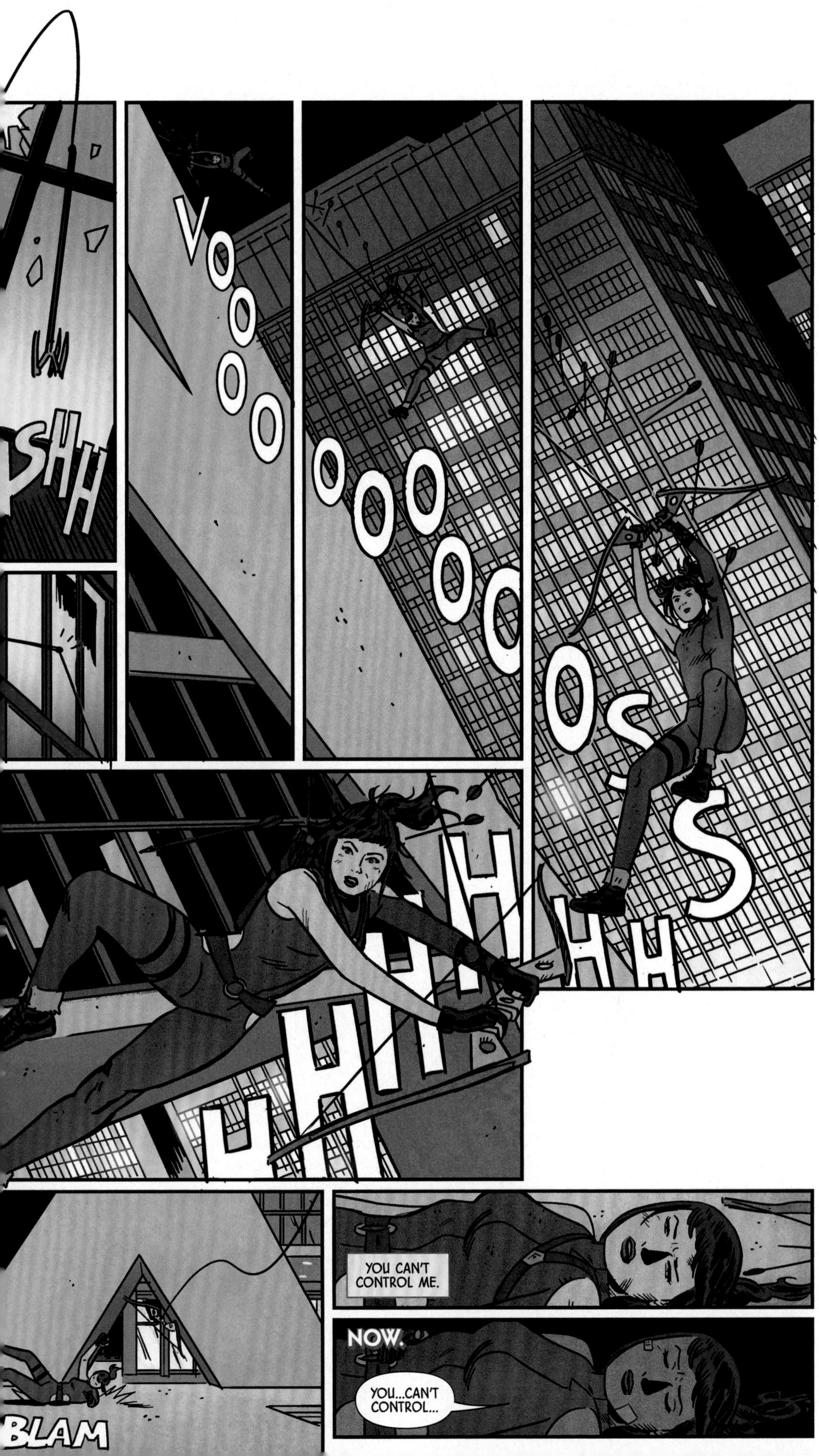
SHH
VOOOOOOOOOOOSSHHHHHHH
YOU CAN'T CONTROL ME.
BLAM
NOW.
YOU...CAN'T CONTROL...

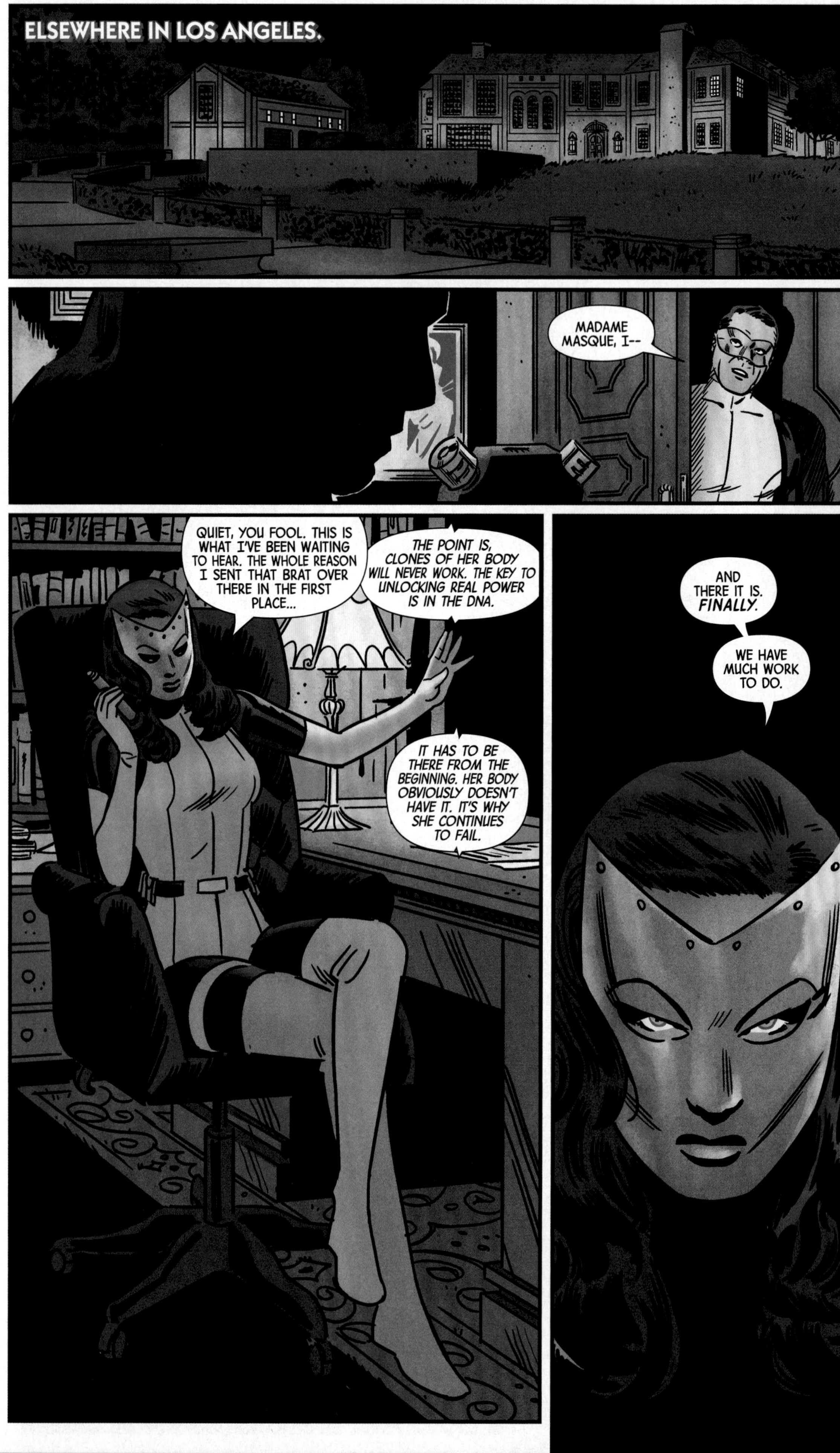
ELSEWHERE IN LOS ANGELES.
MADAME MASQUE, I--
QUIET, YOU FOOL. THIS IS WHAT I'VE BEEN WAITING TO HEAR. THE WHOLE REASON I SENT THAT BRAT OVER THERE IN THE FIRST PLACE...
THE POINT IS, CLONES OF HER BODY WILL NEVER WORK. THE KEY TO UNLOCKING REAL POWER IS IN THE DNA.
IT HAS TO BE THERE FROM THE BEGINNING. HER BODY OBVIOUSLY DOESN'T HAVE IT. IT'S WHY SHE CONTINUES TO FAIL.
AND THERE IT IS. FINALLY.
WE HAVE MUCH WORK TO DO.

HAWK
INVESTIGATIONS

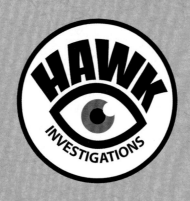

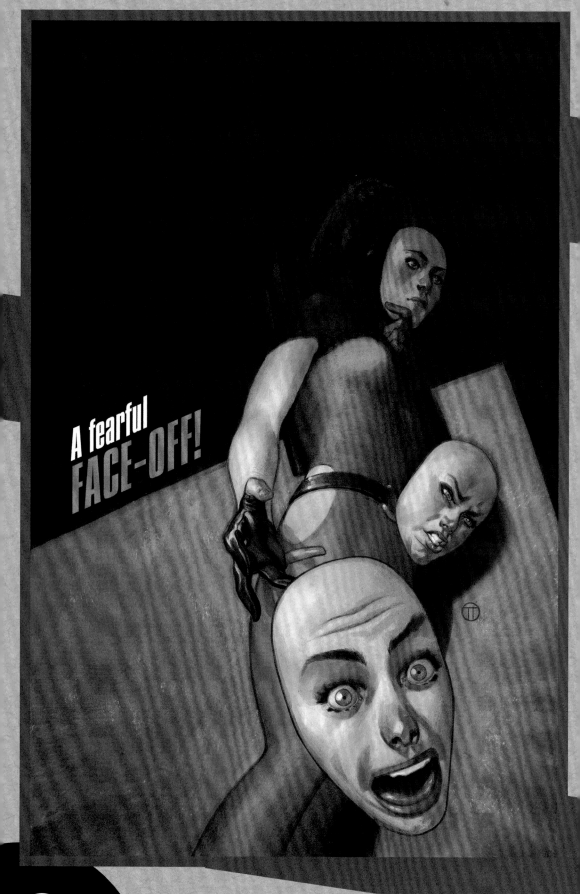

A fearful
FACE-OFF!

9

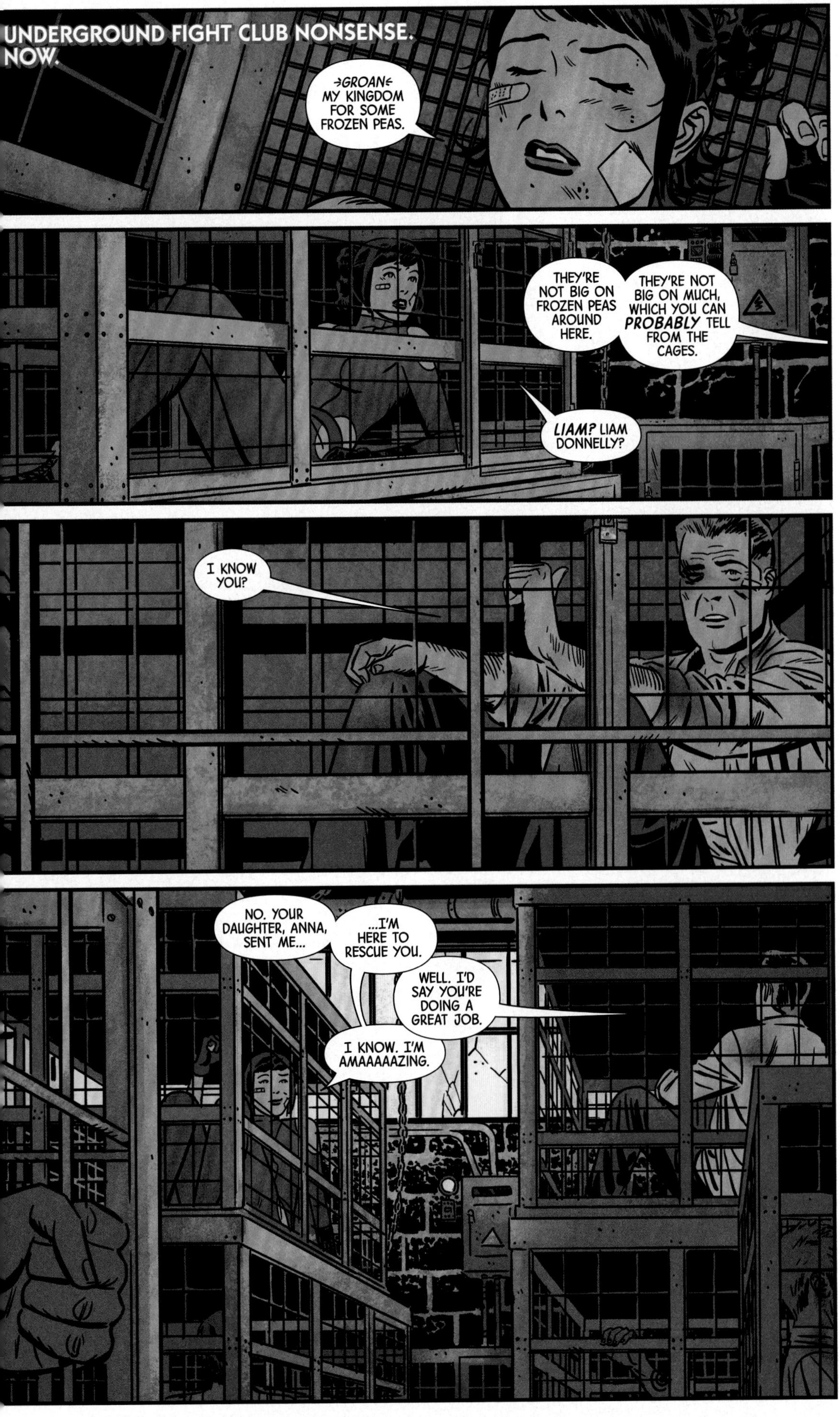
UNDERGROUND FIGHT CLUB NONSENSE. NOW.
→GROAN← MY KINGDOM FOR SOME FROZEN PEAS.
THEY'RE NOT BIG ON FROZEN PEAS AROUND HERE.
THEY'RE NOT BIG ON MUCH, WHICH YOU CAN *PROBABLY* TELL FROM THE CAGES.
LIAM? LIAM DONNELLY?
I KNOW YOU?
NO. YOUR DAUGHTER, ANNA, SENT ME...
...I'M HERE TO RESCUE YOU.
WELL. I'D SAY YOU'RE DOING A GREAT JOB.
I KNOW. I'M AMAAAAAAZING.

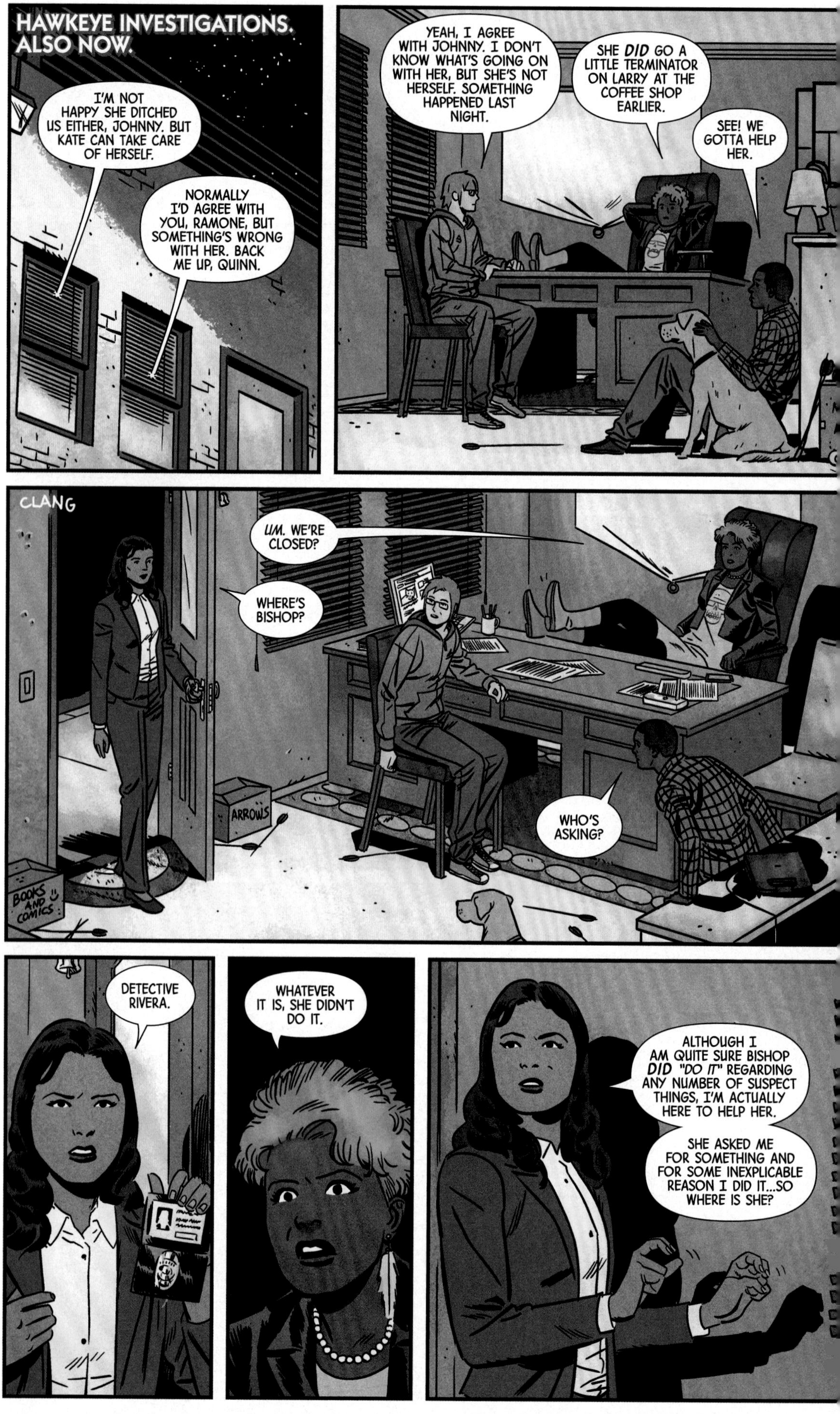
HAWKEYE INVESTIGATIONS. ALSO NOW.
I'M NOT HAPPY SHE DITCHED US EITHER, JOHNNY. BUT KATE CAN TAKE CARE OF HERSELF.
NORMALLY I'D AGREE WITH YOU, RAMONE, BUT SOMETHING'S WRONG WITH HER. BACK ME UP, QUINN.
YEAH, I AGREE WITH JOHNNY. I DON'T KNOW WHAT'S GOING ON WITH HER, BUT SHE'S NOT HERSELF. SOMETHING HAPPENED LAST NIGHT.
SHE DID GO A LITTLE TERMINATOR ON LARRY AT THE COFFEE SHOP EARLIER.
SEE! WE GOTTA HELP HER.
CLANG
UM. WE'RE CLOSED?
WHERE'S BISHOP?
ARROWS
BOOKS AND COMICS
WHO'S ASKING?
DETECTIVE RIVERA.
WHATEVER IT IS, SHE DIDN'T DO IT.
ALTHOUGH I AM QUITE SURE BISHOP DID "DO IT" REGARDING ANY NUMBER OF SUSPECT THINGS, I'M ACTUALLY HERE TO HELP HER.
SHE ASKED ME FOR SOMETHING AND FOR SOME INEXPLICABLE REASON I DID IT...SO WHERE IS SHE?

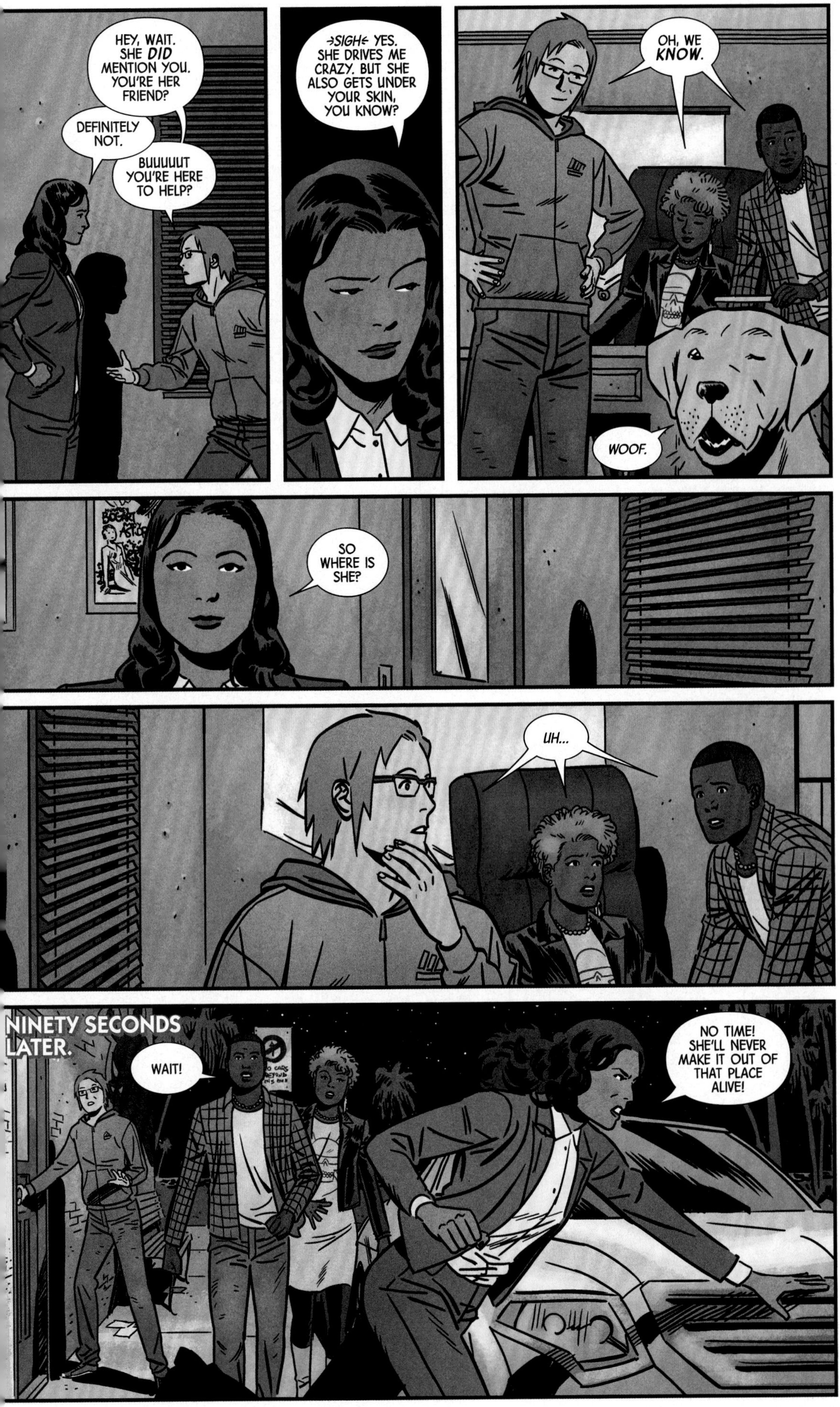
HEY, WAIT. SHE DID MENTION YOU. YOU'RE HER FRIEND?
DEFINITELY NOT.
BUUUUUT YOU'RE HERE TO HELP?
>SIGH< YES. SHE DRIVES ME CRAZY. BUT SHE ALSO GETS UNDER YOUR SKIN, YOU KNOW?
OH, WE KNOW.
WOOF.
SO WHERE IS SHE?
UH...
NINETY SECONDS LATER.
WAIT!
NO TIME! SHE'LL NEVER MAKE IT OUT OF THAT PLACE ALIVE!

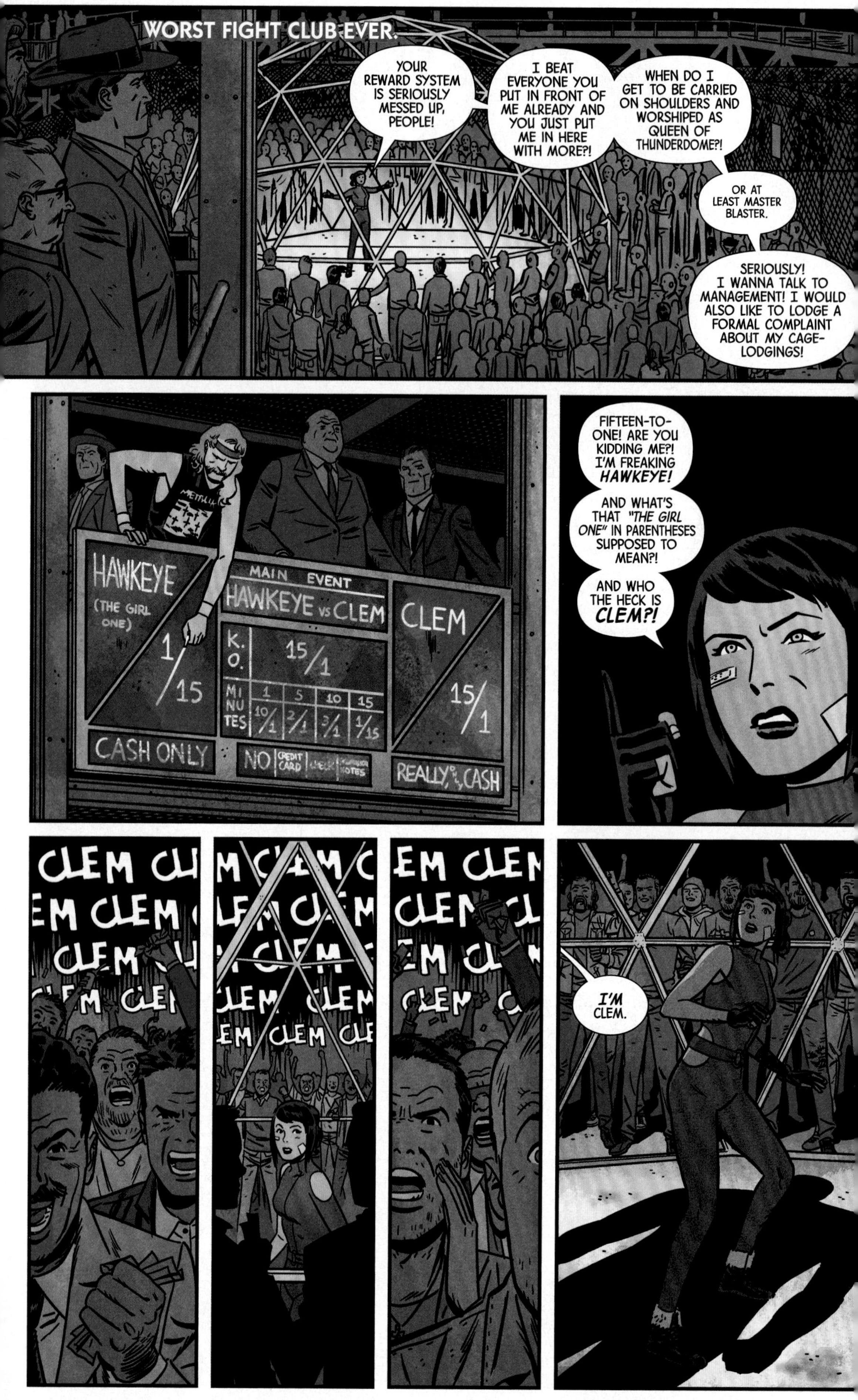
WORST FIGHT CLUB EVER.
YOUR REWARD SYSTEM IS SERIOUSLY MESSED UP, PEOPLE!
I BEAT EVERYONE YOU PUT IN FRONT OF ME ALREADY AND YOU JUST PUT ME IN HERE WITH MORE?!
WHEN DO I GET TO BE CARRIED ON SHOULDERS AND WORSHIPED AS QUEEN OF THUNDERDOME?!
OR AT LEAST MASTER BLASTER.
SERIOUSLY! I WANNA TALK TO MANAGEMENT! I WOULD ALSO LIKE TO LODGE A FORMAL COMPLAINT ABOUT MY CAGE-LODGINGS!
HAWKEYE (THE GIRL ONE) 1/15
MAIN EVENT
HAWKEYE vs CLEM
K.O. 15/1
MINUTES 1 5 10 15
10/1 2/1 3/1 1/15
CLEM 15/1
CASH ONLY
NO CREDIT CARD CHECK
REALLY, CASH
FIFTEEN-TO-ONE! ARE YOU KIDDING ME?! I'M FREAKING *HAWKEYE!*
AND WHAT'S THAT *"THE GIRL ONE"* IN PARENTHESES SUPPOSED TO MEAN?!
AND WHO THE HECK IS ***CLEM?!***
CLEM CLEM CLEM CLEM CLEM CLEM
I'M CLEM.

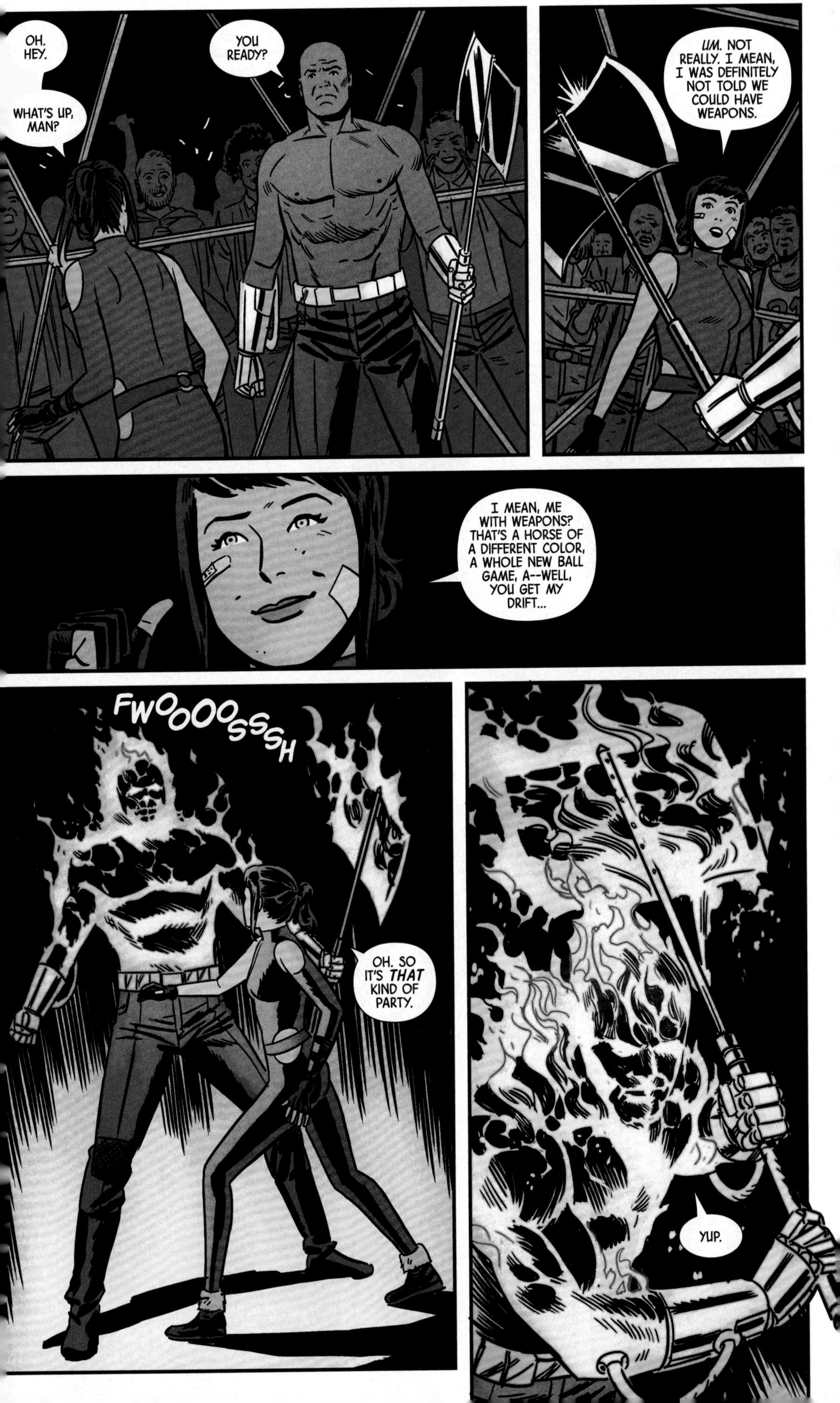
OH. HEY.
WHAT'S UP, MAN?
YOU READY?
UM. NOT REALLY. I MEAN, I WAS DEFINITELY NOT TOLD WE COULD HAVE WEAPONS.
I MEAN, ME WITH WEAPONS? THAT'S A HORSE OF A DIFFERENT COLOR, A WHOLE NEW BALL GAME, A--WELL, YOU GET MY DRIFT...
FWOOOOSSSH
OH. SO IT'S THAT KIND OF PARTY.
YUP.

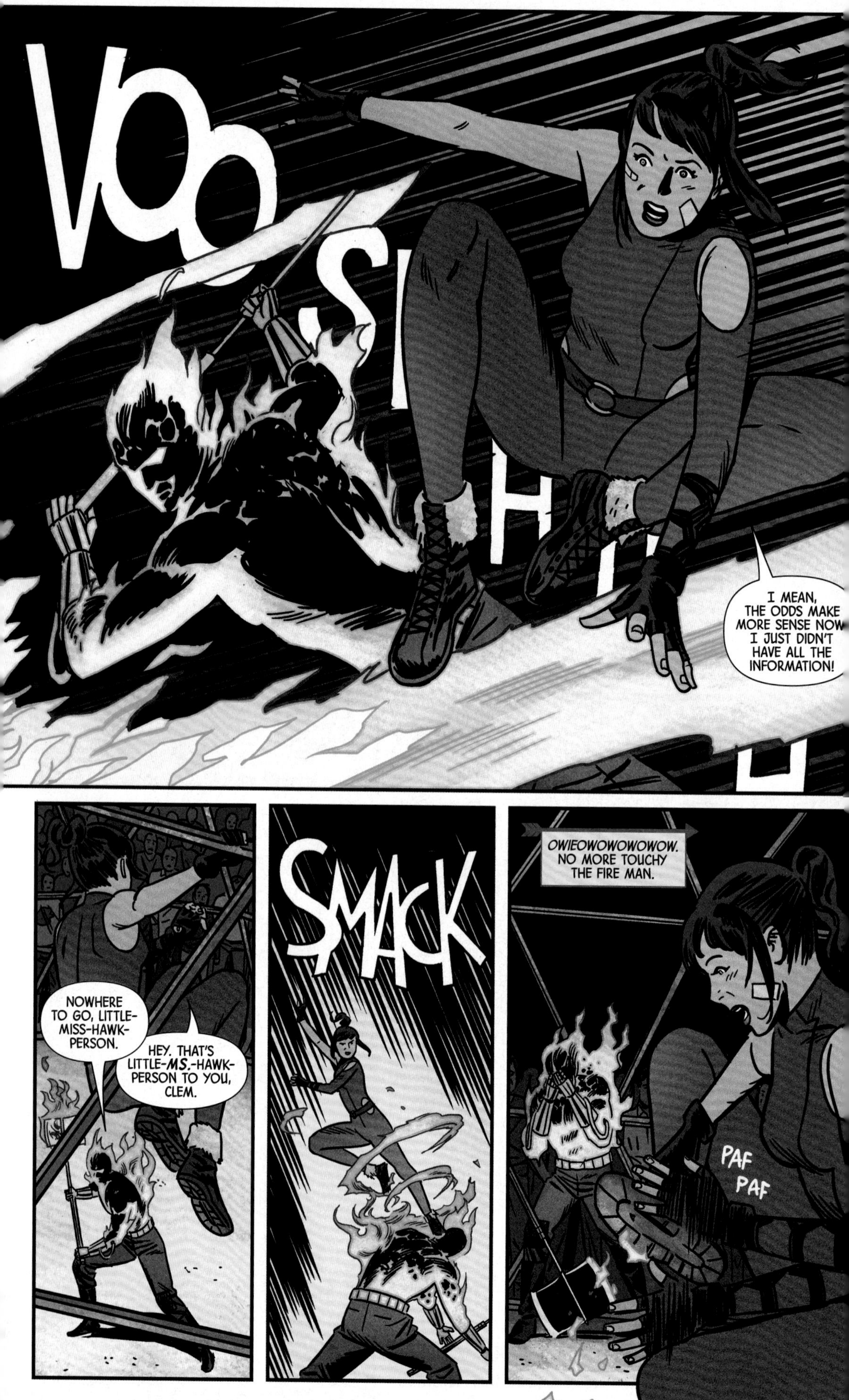
VOO
I MEAN, THE ODDS MAKE MORE SENSE NOW. I JUST DIDN'T HAVE ALL THE INFORMATION!
NOWHERE TO GO, LITTLE-MISS-HAWK-PERSON.
HEY. THAT'S LITTLE-*MS.*-HAWK-PERSON TO YOU, CLEM.
SMACK
OWIEOWOWOWOWOW. NO MORE TOUCHY THE FIRE MAN.
PAF
PAF

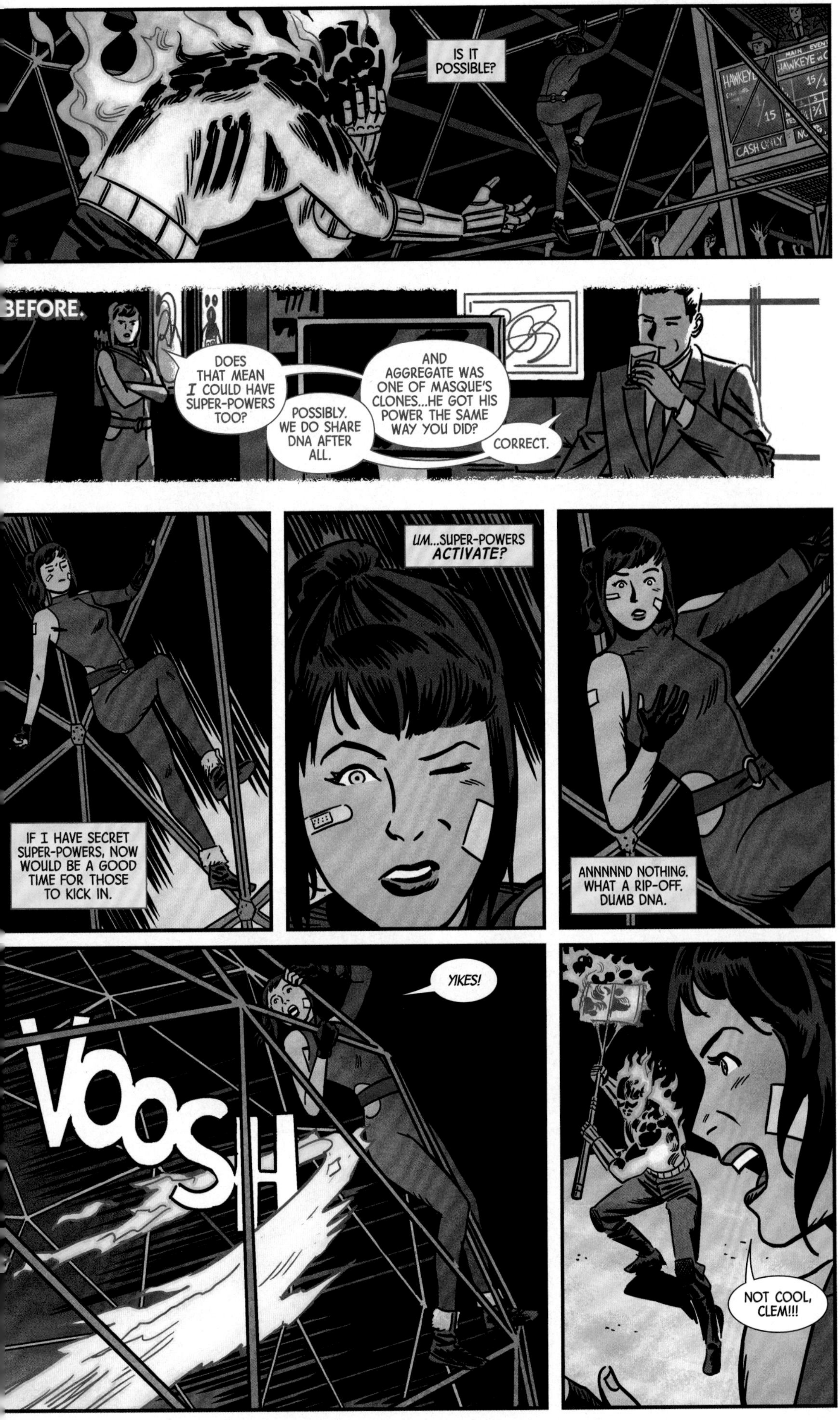
IS IT POSSIBLE?
HAWKEYE
MAIN EVENT
HAWKEYE vs C
15/1
1/15
CASH ONLY
BEFORE.
DOES THAT MEAN I COULD HAVE SUPER-POWERS TOO?
POSSIBLY. WE DO SHARE DNA AFTER ALL.
AND AGGREGATE WAS ONE OF MASQUE'S CLONES...HE GOT HIS POWER THE SAME WAY YOU DID?
CORRECT.
IF I HAVE SECRET SUPER-POWERS, NOW WOULD BE A GOOD TIME FOR THOSE TO KICK IN.
UM...SUPER-POWERS ACTIVATE?
ANNNNND NOTHING. WHAT A RIP-OFF. DUMB DNA.
YIKES!
VOOSH
NOT COOL, CLEM!!!

MAY NOT HAVE SHINY NEW SUPER-POWERS...
POPCORN?
BLOODTHIRSTY HORDES
BLOOD HORDE
INAPPROPRIATE COCKTAIL DRESS
REFRESHING BEVERAGE
BLOODTHIRS HORDES
GAH.

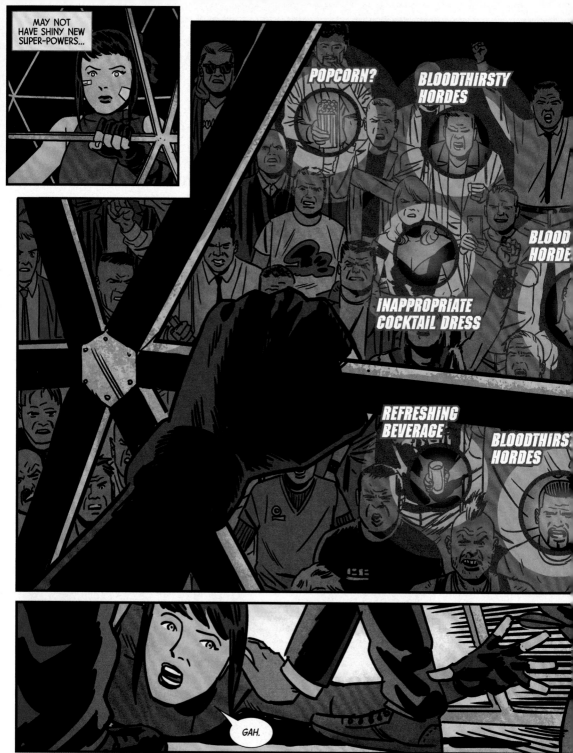

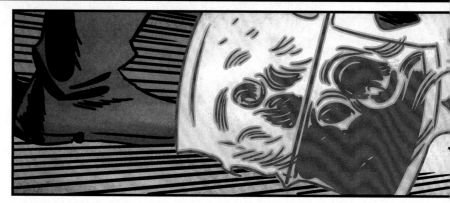

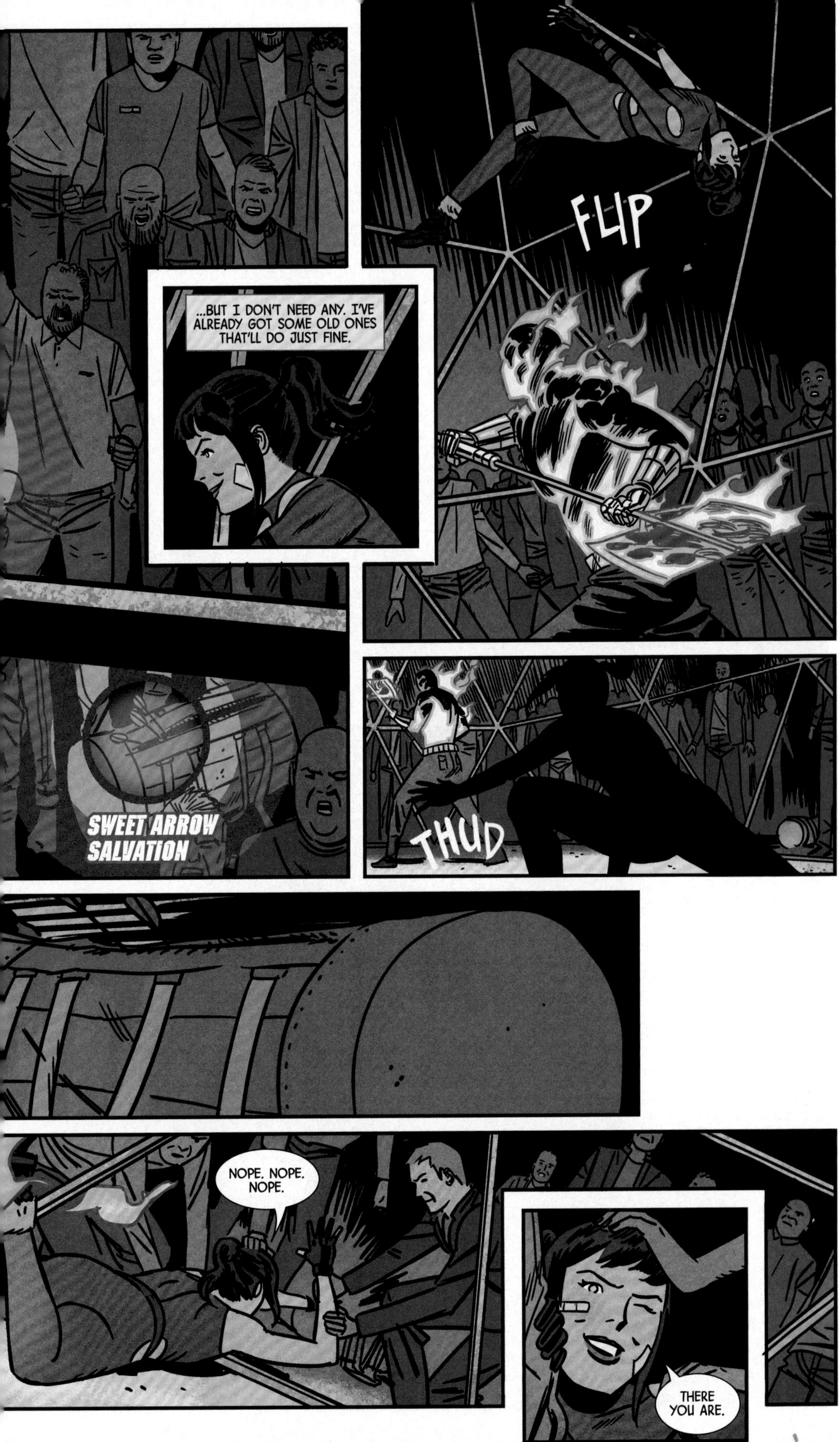
...BUT I DON'T NEED ANY. I'VE ALREADY GOT SOME OLD ONES THAT'LL DO JUST FINE.
FLIP
SWEET ARROW SALVATION
THUD
NOPE. NOPE. NOPE.
THERE YOU ARE.

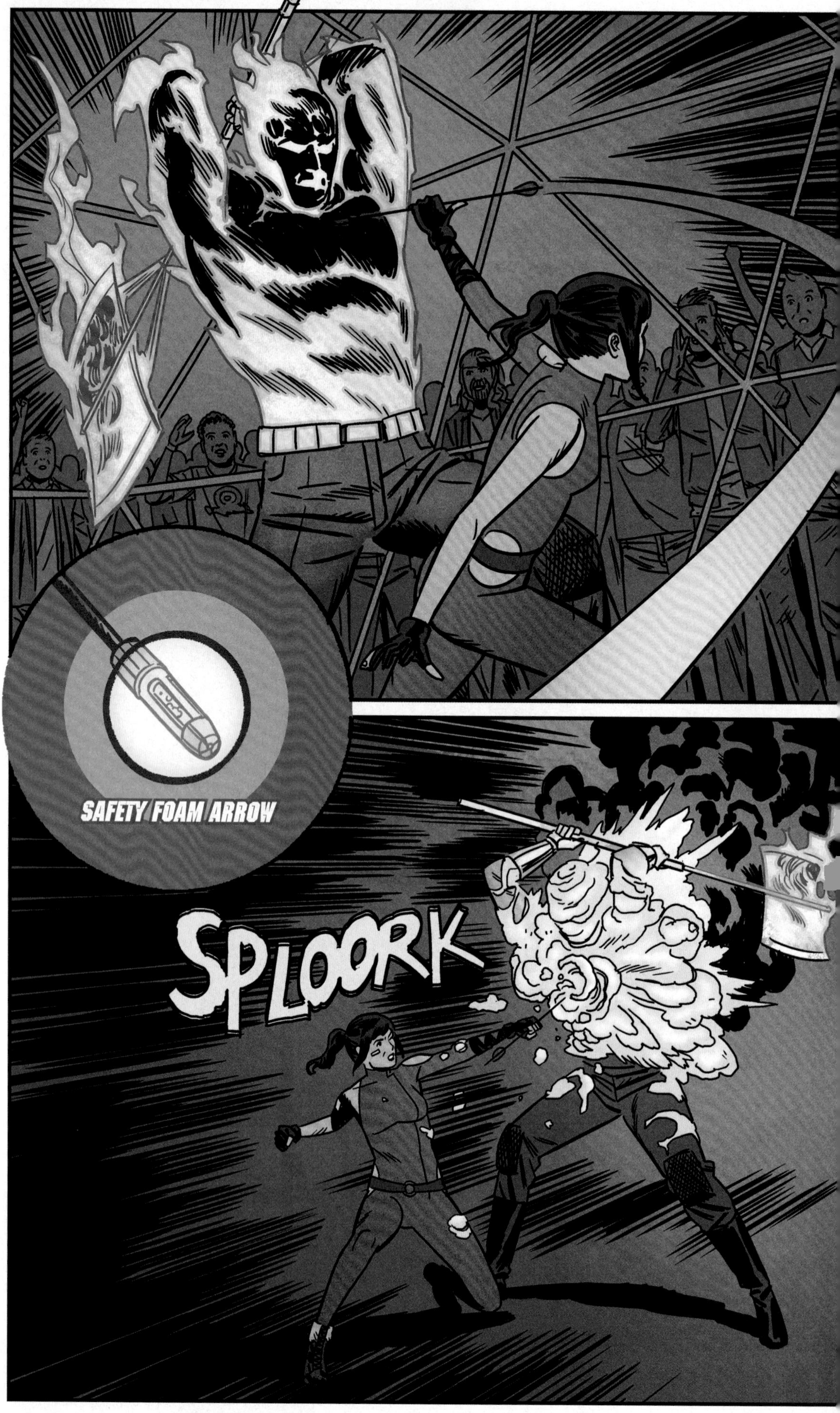
SAFETY FOAM ARROW
SPLOORK

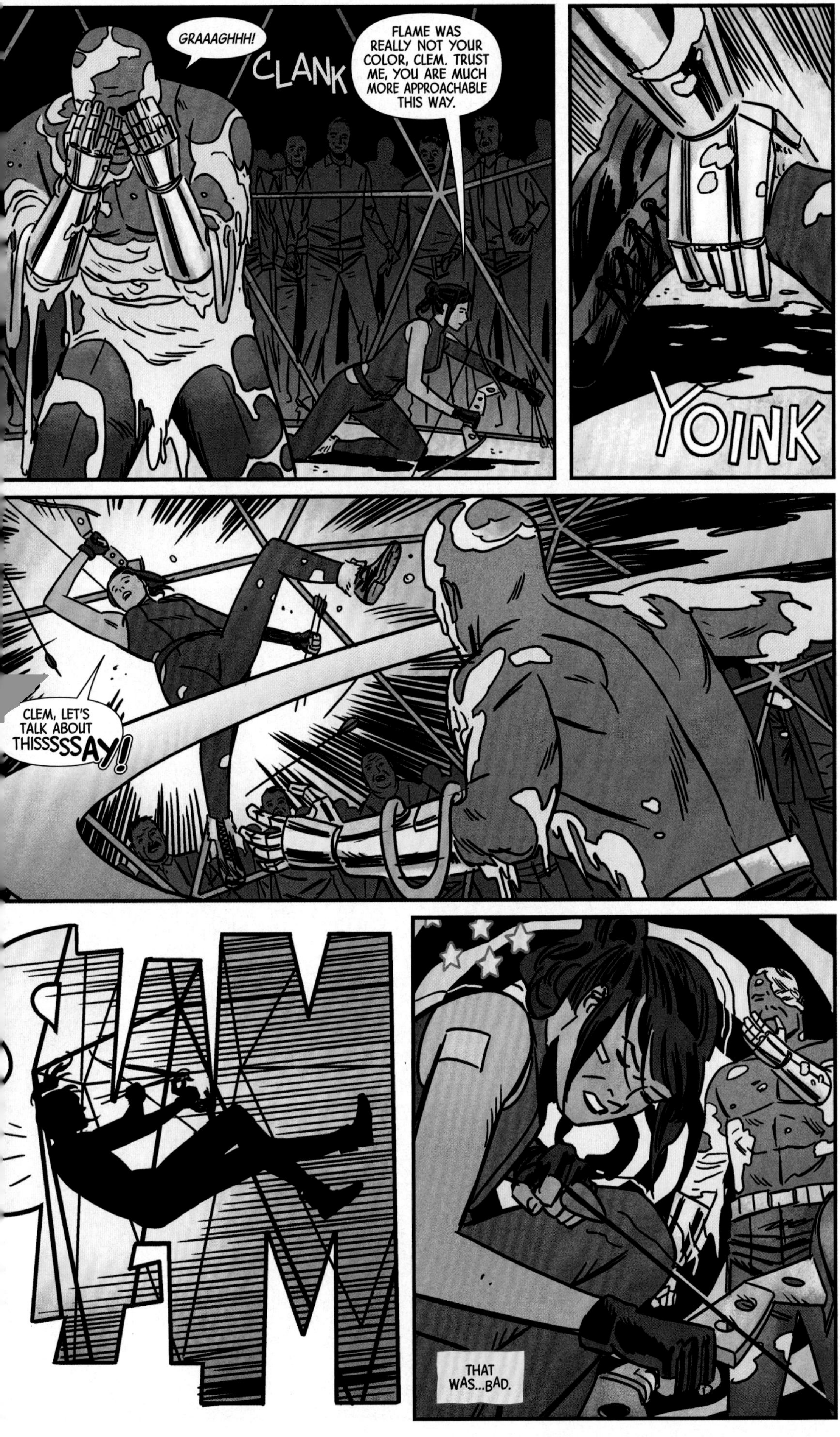
GRAAAGHHH!
CLANK
FLAME WAS REALLY NOT YOUR COLOR, CLEM. TRUST ME, YOU ARE MUCH MORE APPROACHABLE THIS WAY.
YOINK
CLEM, LET'S TALK ABOUT THISSSSSAY!
THAT WAS...BAD.

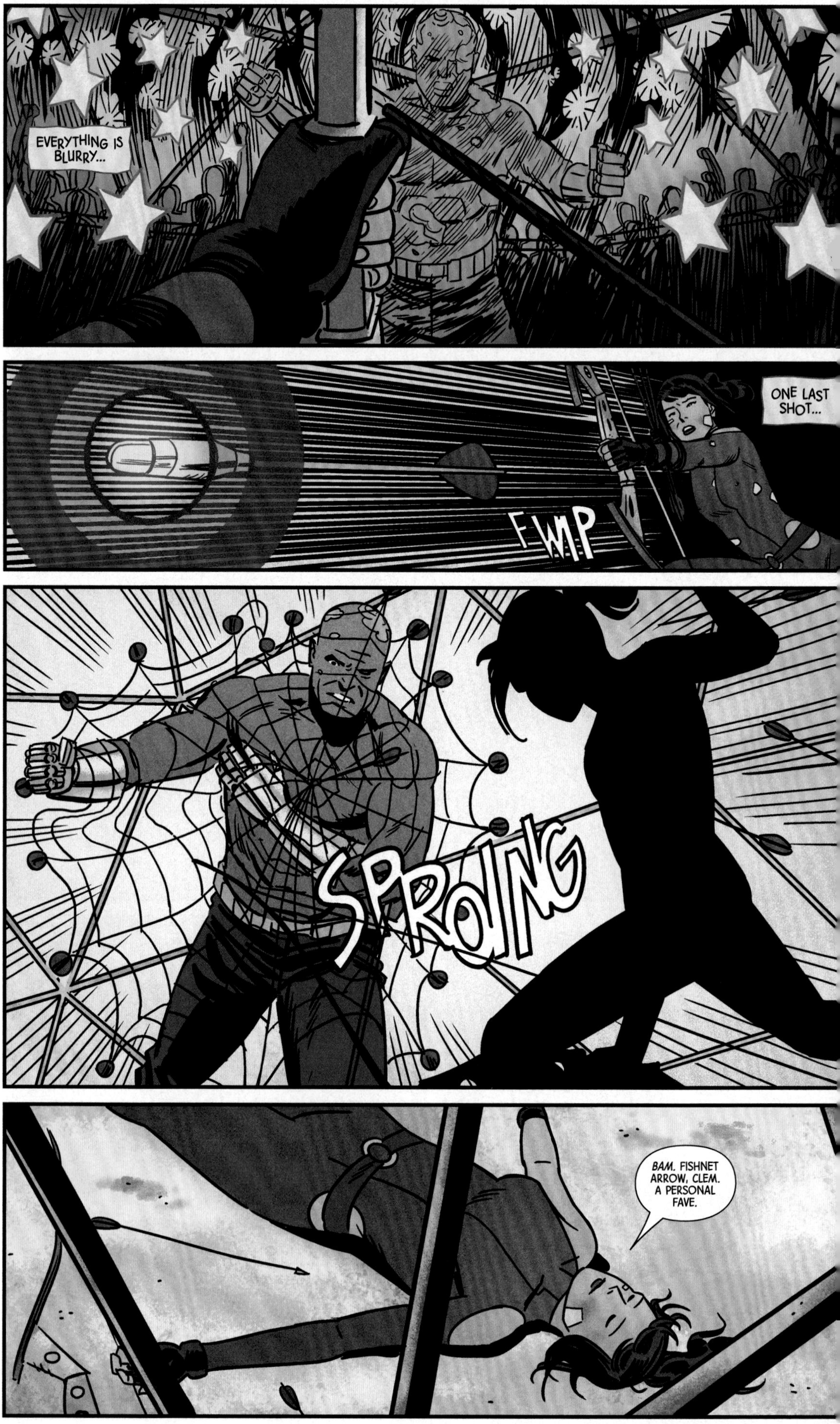
EVERYTHING IS BLURRY...
ONE LAST SHOT...
FWIP
SPROING
BAM. FISHNET ARROW, CLEM. A PERSONAL FAVE.

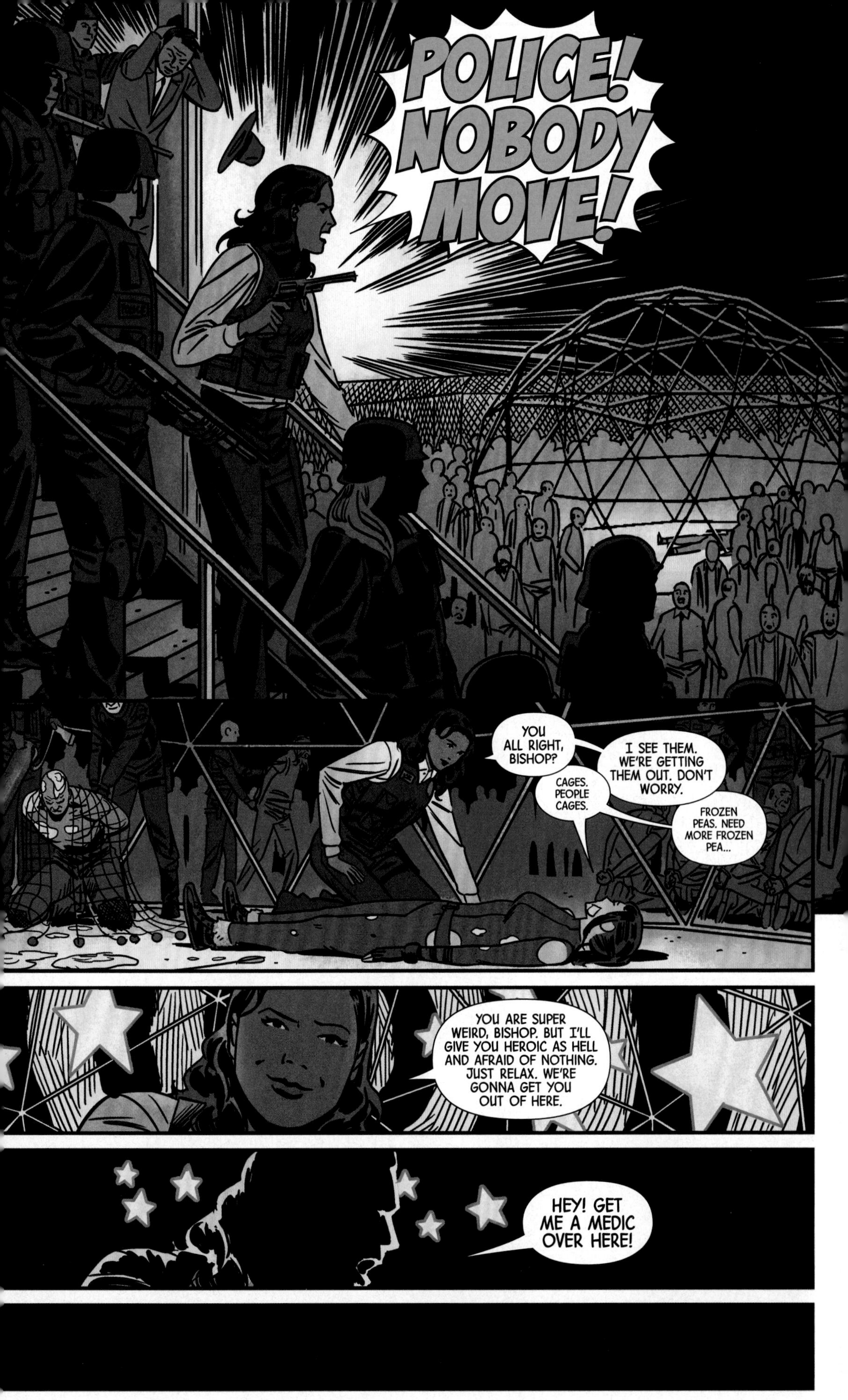
POLICE! NOBODY MOVE!
YOU ALL RIGHT, BISHOP?
I SEE THEM. WE'RE GETTING THEM OUT. DON'T WORRY.
CAGES. PEOPLE CAGES.
FROZEN PEAS. NEED MORE FROZEN PEA...
YOU ARE SUPER WEIRD, BISHOP. BUT I'LL GIVE YOU HEROIC AS HELL AND AFRAID OF NOTHING. JUST RELAX. WE'RE GONNA GET YOU OUT OF HERE.
HEY! GET ME A MEDIC OVER HERE!

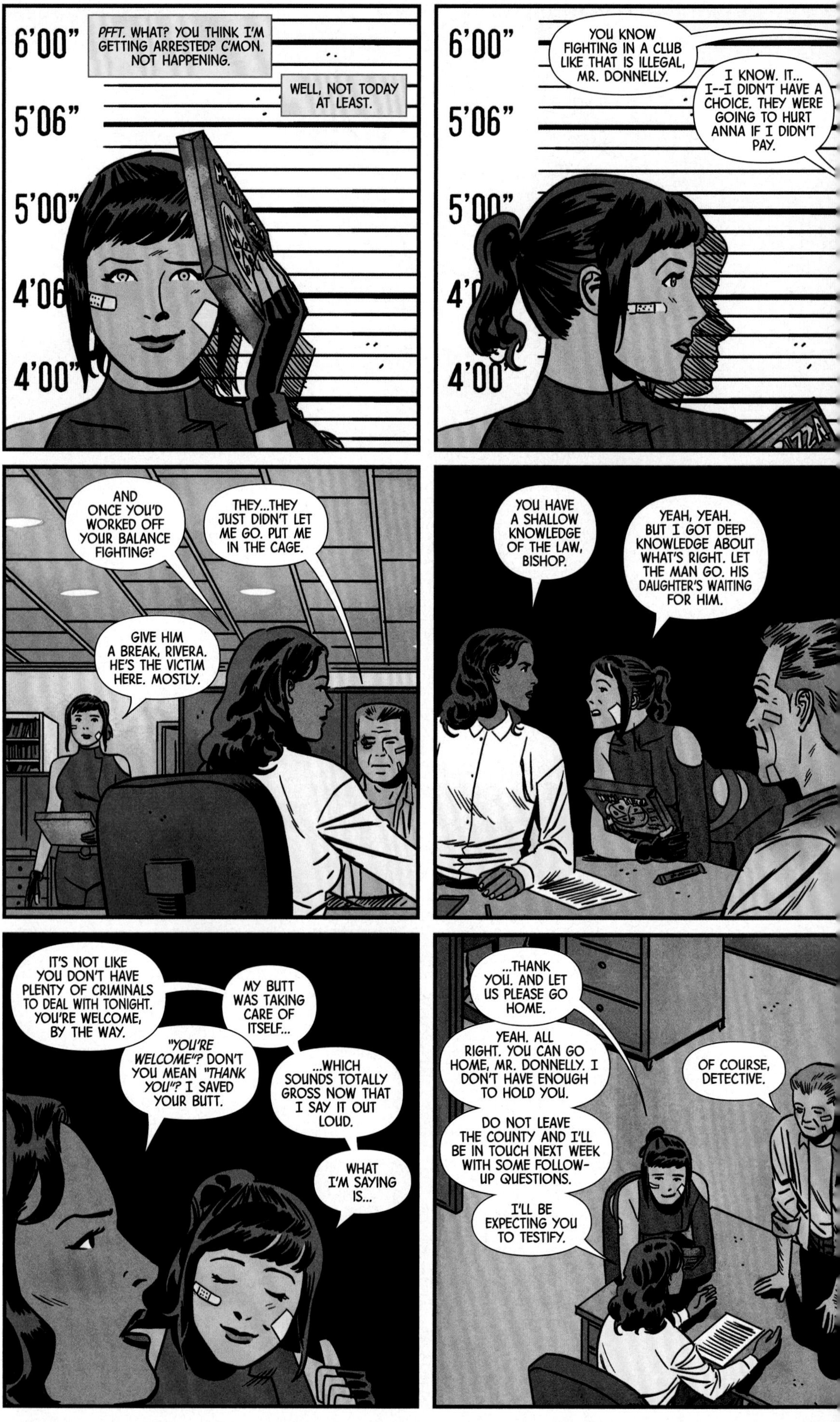
6'00"
5'06"
5'00"
4'06
4'00"
PFFT. WHAT? YOU THINK I'M GETTING ARRESTED? C'MON. NOT HAPPENING.
WELL, NOT TODAY AT LEAST.
6'00"
5'06"
5'00"
4'00
YOU KNOW FIGHTING IN A CLUB LIKE THAT IS ILLEGAL, MR. DONNELLY.
I KNOW. IT... I--I DIDN'T HAVE A CHOICE. THEY WERE GOING TO HURT ANNA IF I DIDN'T PAY.
AND ONCE YOU'D WORKED OFF YOUR BALANCE FIGHTING?
THEY...THEY JUST DIDN'T LET ME GO. PUT ME IN THE CAGE.
GIVE HIM A BREAK, RIVERA. HE'S THE VICTIM HERE. MOSTLY.
YOU HAVE A SHALLOW KNOWLEDGE OF THE LAW, BISHOP.
YEAH, YEAH. BUT I GOT DEEP KNOWLEDGE ABOUT WHAT'S RIGHT. LET THE MAN GO. HIS DAUGHTER'S WAITING FOR HIM.
IT'S NOT LIKE YOU DON'T HAVE PLENTY OF CRIMINALS TO DEAL WITH TONIGHT. YOU'RE WELCOME, BY THE WAY.
"YOU'RE WELCOME"? DON'T YOU MEAN "THANK YOU"? I SAVED YOUR BUTT.
MY BUTT WAS TAKING CARE OF ITSELF...
...WHICH SOUNDS TOTALLY GROSS NOW THAT I SAY IT OUT LOUD.
WHAT I'M SAYING IS...
...THANK YOU. AND LET US PLEASE GO HOME.
YEAH. ALL RIGHT. YOU CAN GO HOME, MR. DONNELLY. I DON'T HAVE ENOUGH TO HOLD YOU.
DO NOT LEAVE THE COUNTY AND I'LL BE IN TOUCH NEXT WEEK WITH SOME FOLLOW-UP QUESTIONS.
I'LL BE EXPECTING YOU TO TESTIFY.
OF COURSE, DETECTIVE.

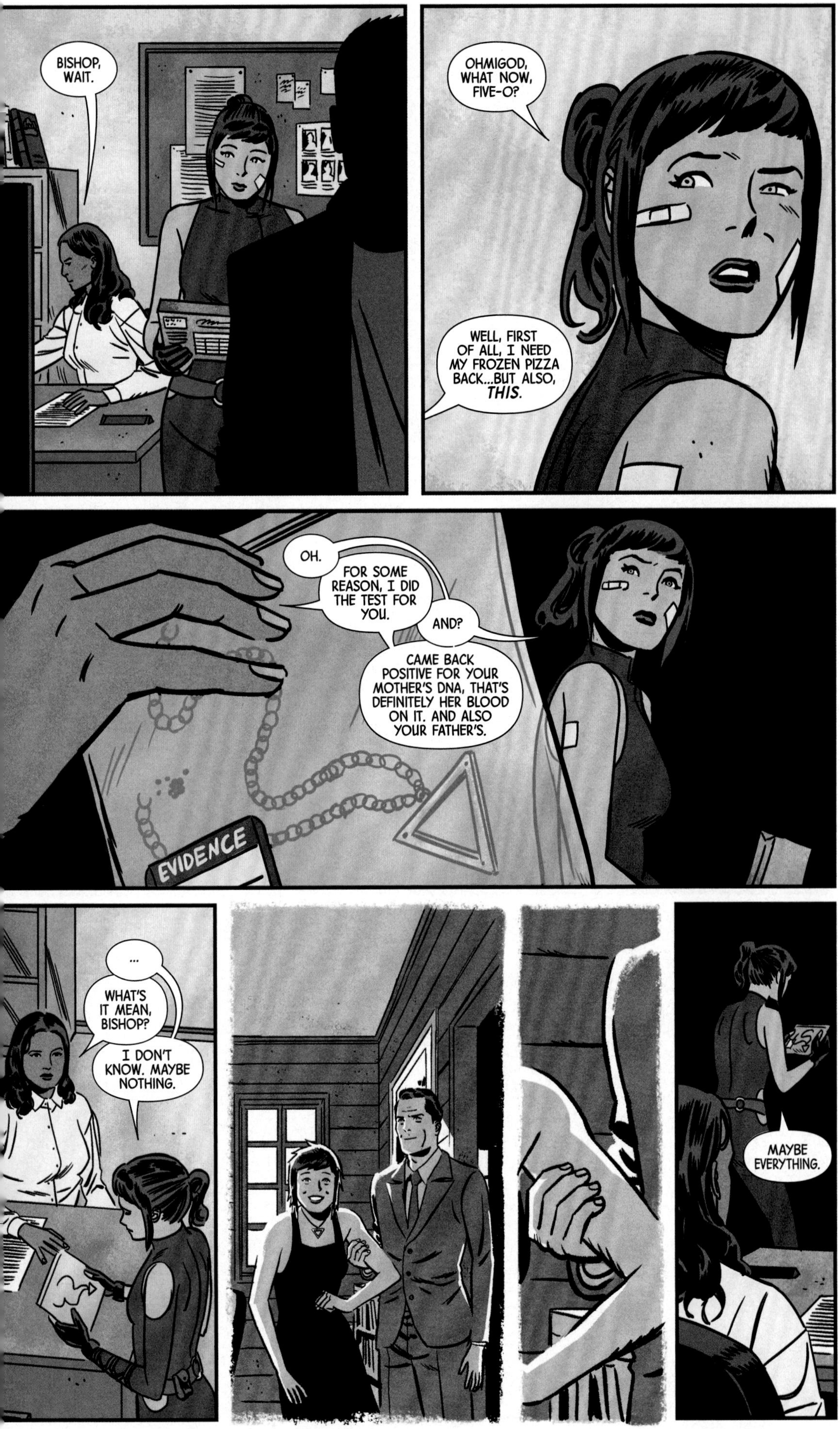

BISHOP, WAIT.
OHMIGOD, WHAT NOW, FIVE-O?
WELL, FIRST OF ALL, I NEED MY FROZEN PIZZA BACK...BUT ALSO, *THIS.*
OH.
FOR SOME REASON, I DID THE TEST FOR YOU.
AND?
CAME BACK POSITIVE FOR YOUR MOTHER'S DNA, THAT'S DEFINITELY HER BLOOD ON IT. AND ALSO YOUR FATHER'S.
EVIDENCE
...
WHAT'S IT MEAN, BISHOP?
I DON'T KNOW. MAYBE NOTHING.
MAYBE EVERYTHING.

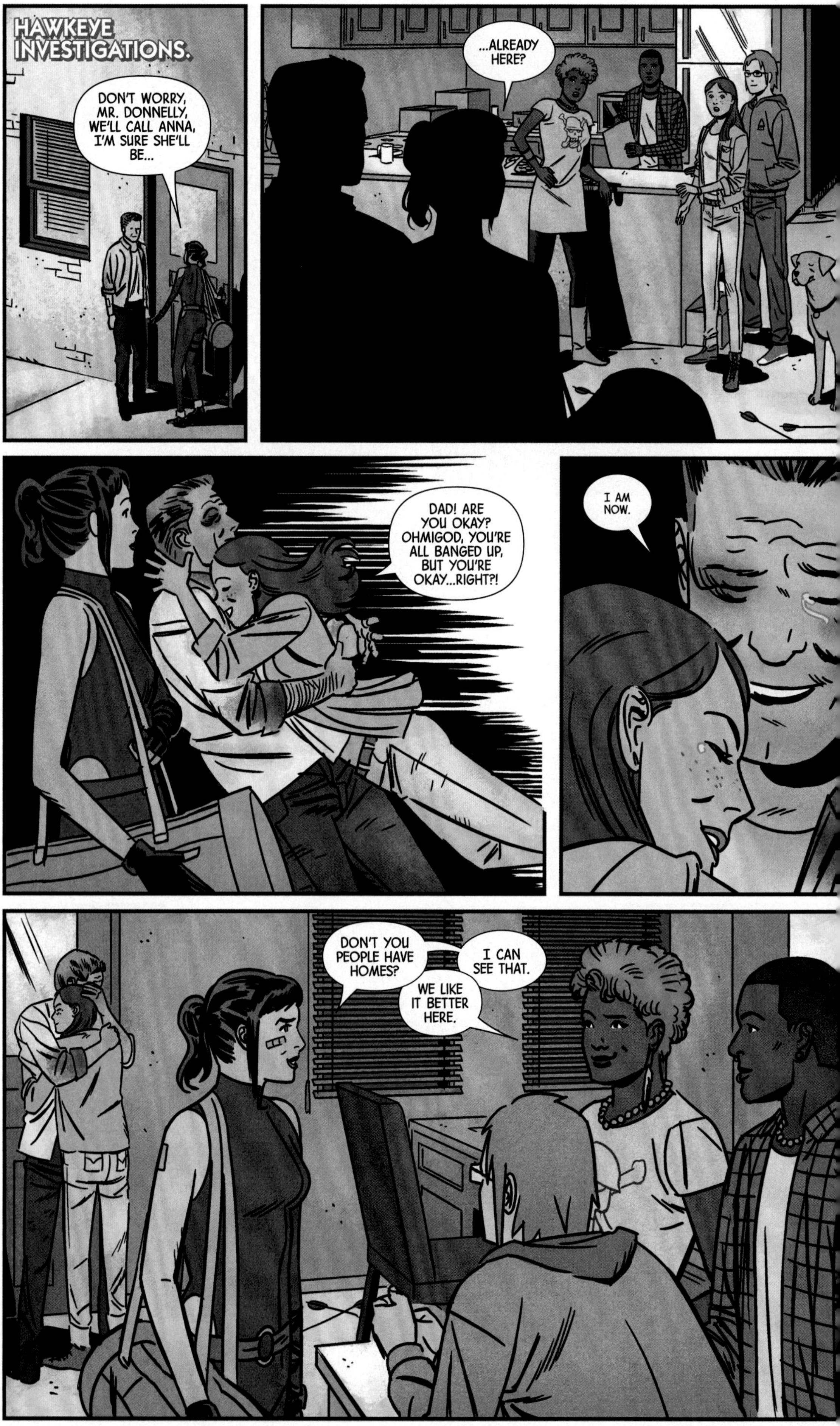
HAWKEYE INVESTIGATIONS.
DON'T WORRY, MR. DONNELLY, WE'LL CALL ANNA, I'M SURE SHE'LL BE...
...ALREADY HERE?
DAD! ARE YOU OKAY? OHMIGOD, YOU'RE ALL BANGED UP, BUT YOU'RE OKAY...RIGHT?!
I AM NOW.
DON'T YOU PEOPLE HAVE HOMES?
WE LIKE IT BETTER HERE.
I CAN SEE THAT.

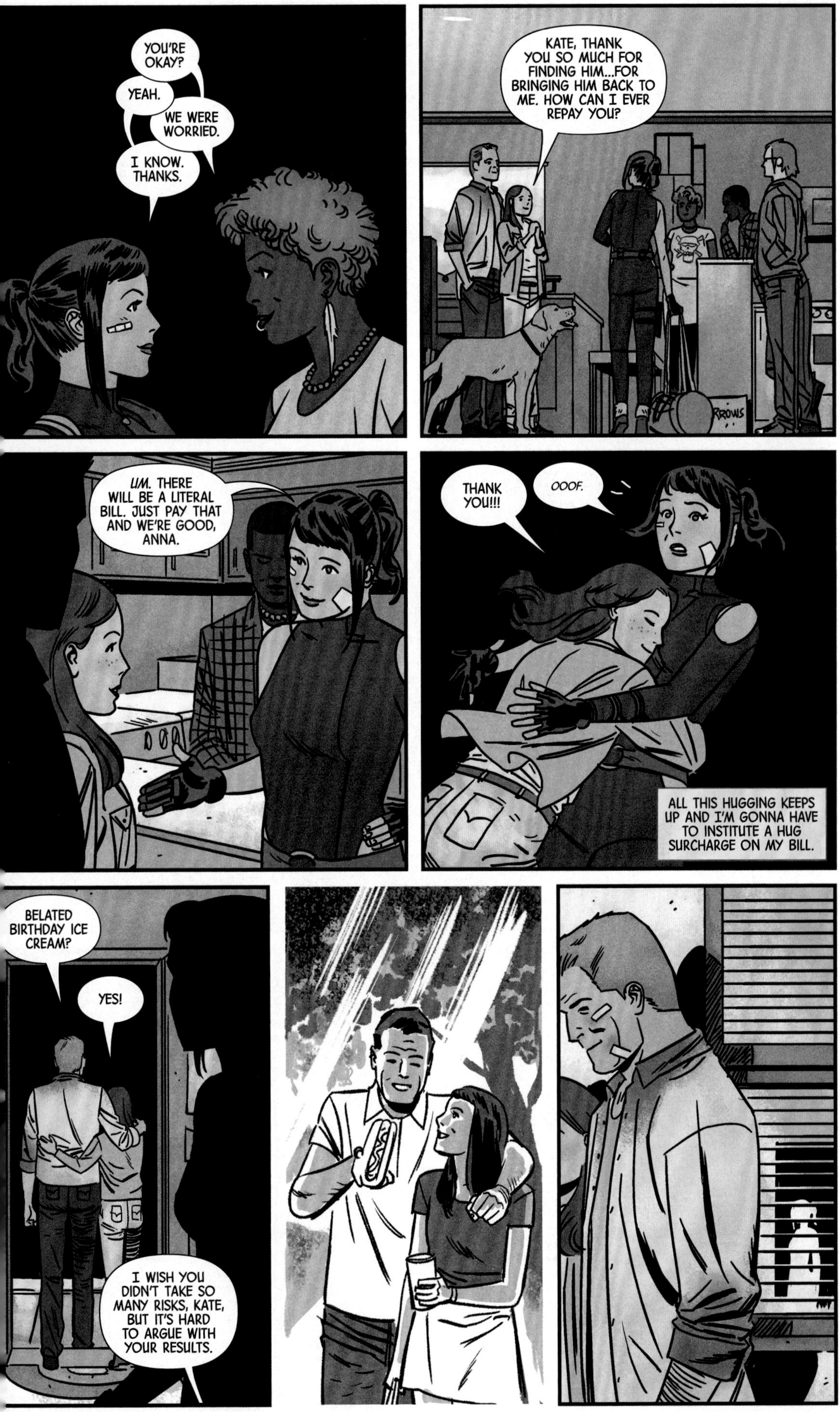

YOU'RE OKAY?
YEAH.
WE WERE WORRIED.
I KNOW. THANKS.
KATE, THANK YOU SO MUCH FOR FINDING HIM...FOR BRINGING HIM BACK TO ME. HOW CAN I EVER REPAY YOU?
ARROWS
UM. THERE WILL BE A LITERAL BILL. JUST PAY THAT AND WE'RE GOOD, ANNA.
THANK YOU!!!
OOOF.
ALL THIS HUGGING KEEPS UP AND I'M GONNA HAVE TO INSTITUTE A HUG SURCHARGE ON MY BILL.
BELATED BIRTHDAY ICE CREAM?
YES!
I WISH YOU DIDN'T TAKE SO MANY RISKS, KATE, BUT IT'S HARD TO ARGUE WITH YOUR RESULTS.

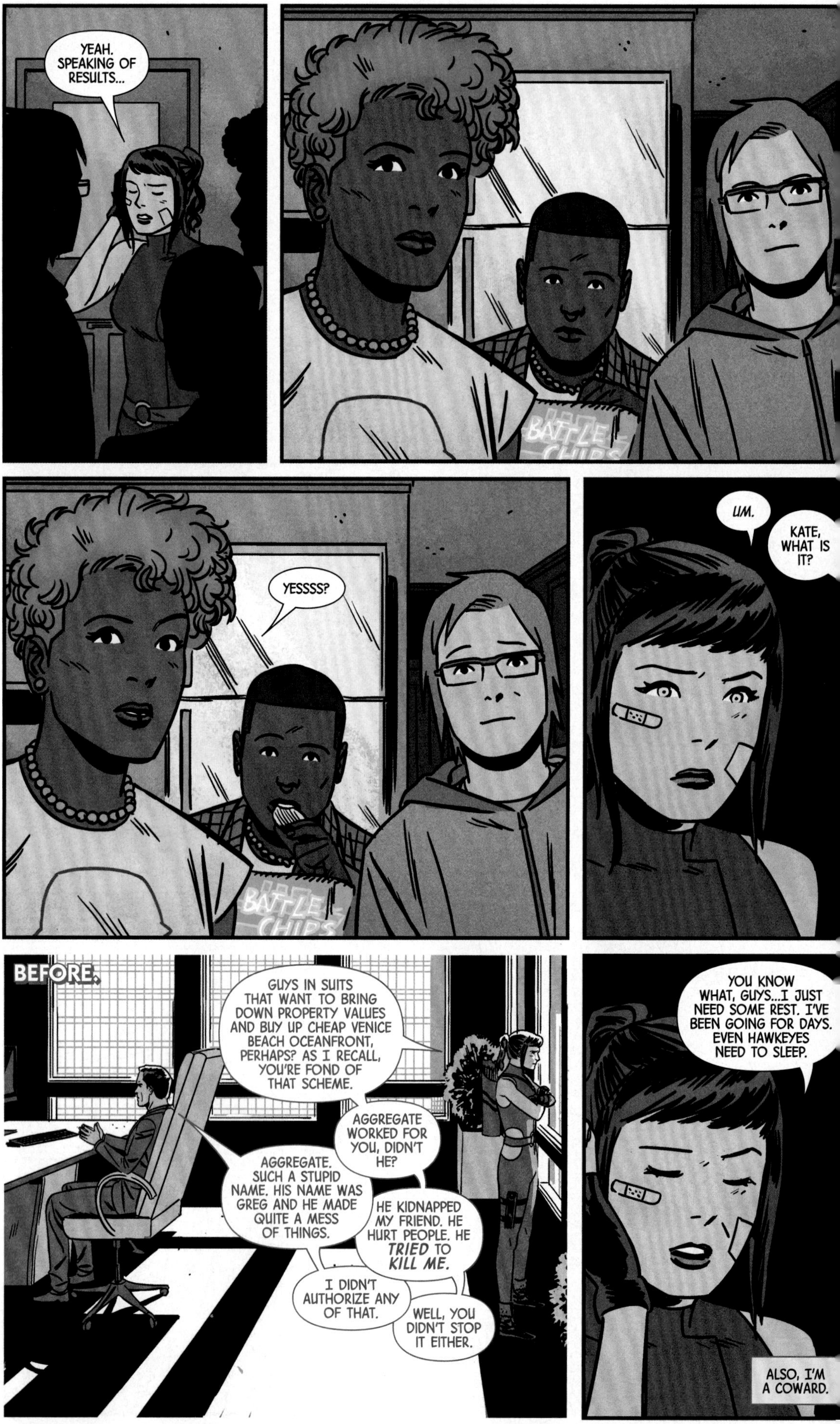
YEAH. SPEAKING OF RESULTS...
YESSSS?
UM.
KATE, WHAT IS IT?
BATTLE CHIPS
BEFORE.
GUYS IN SUITS THAT WANT TO BRING DOWN PROPERTY VALUES AND BUY UP CHEAP VENICE BEACH OCEANFRONT, PERHAPS? AS I RECALL, YOU'RE FOND OF THAT SCHEME.
AGGREGATE WORKED FOR YOU, DIDN'T HE?
AGGREGATE. SUCH A STUPID NAME. HIS NAME WAS GREG AND HE MADE QUITE A MESS OF THINGS.
HE KIDNAPPED MY FRIEND. HE HURT PEOPLE. HE *TRIED* TO *KILL ME.*
I DIDN'T AUTHORIZE ANY OF THAT.
WELL, YOU DIDN'T STOP IT EITHER.
YOU KNOW WHAT, GUYS...I JUST NEED SOME REST. I'VE BEEN GOING FOR DAYS. EVEN HAWKEYES NEED TO SLEEP.
ALSO, I'M A COWARD.

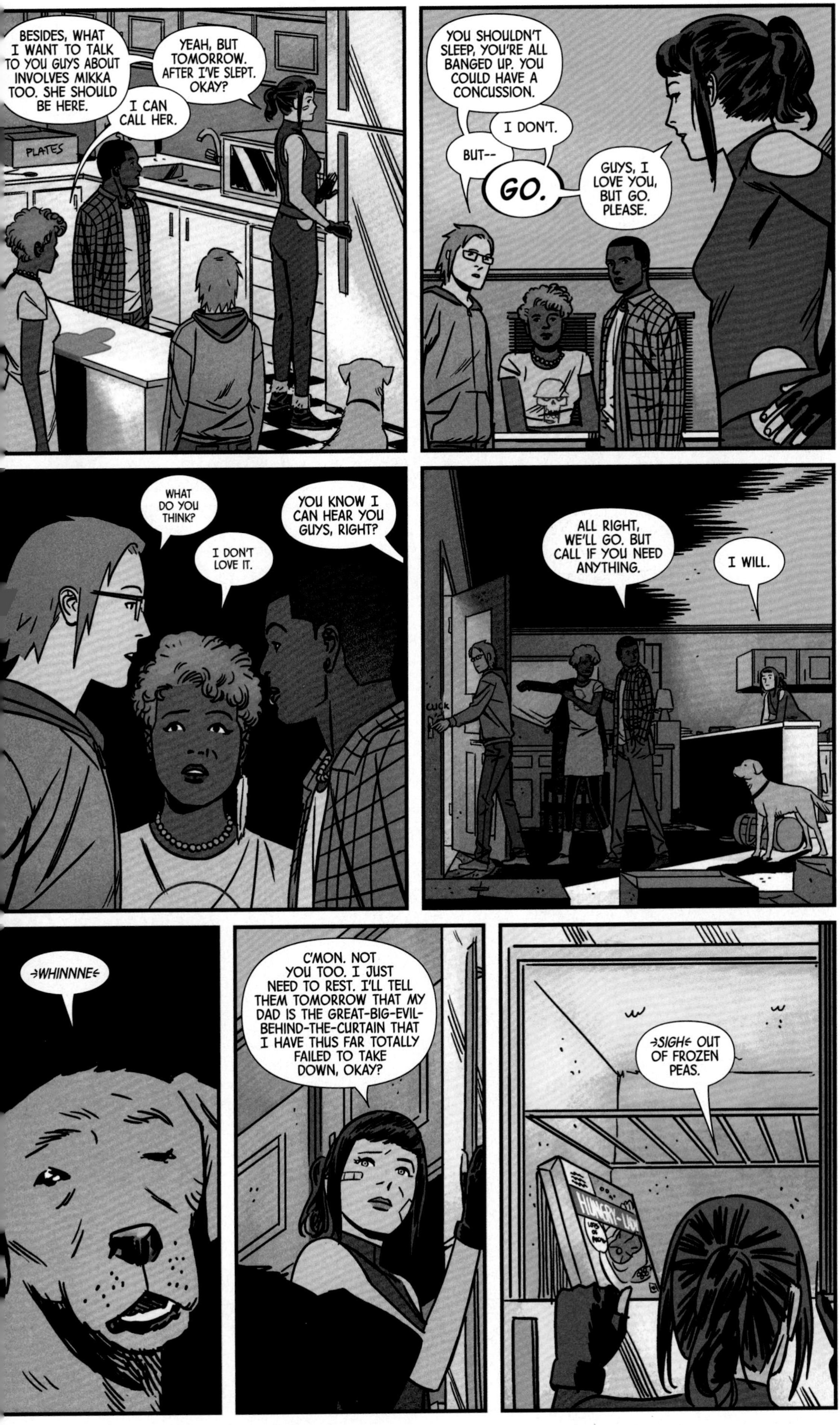
BESIDES, WHAT I WANT TO TALK TO YOU GUYS ABOUT INVOLVES MIKKA TOO. SHE SHOULD BE HERE.
I CAN CALL HER.
YEAH, BUT TOMORROW. AFTER I'VE SLEPT. OKAY?
PLATES
YOU SHOULDN'T SLEEP, YOU'RE ALL BANGED UP. YOU COULD HAVE A CONCUSSION.
I DON'T.
BUT--
GO.
GUYS, I LOVE YOU, BUT GO. PLEASE.
WHAT DO YOU THINK?
I DON'T LOVE IT.
YOU KNOW I CAN HEAR YOU GUYS, RIGHT?
ALL RIGHT, WE'LL GO. BUT CALL IF YOU NEED ANYTHING.
I WILL.
CLICK
WHINNNE
C'MON. NOT YOU TOO. I JUST NEED TO REST. I'LL TELL THEM TOMORROW THAT MY DAD IS THE GREAT-BIG-EVIL-BEHIND-THE-CURTAIN THAT I HAVE THUS FAR TOTALLY FAILED TO TAKE DOWN, OKAY?
SIGH OUT OF FROZEN PEAS.
HUNGRY-LADY

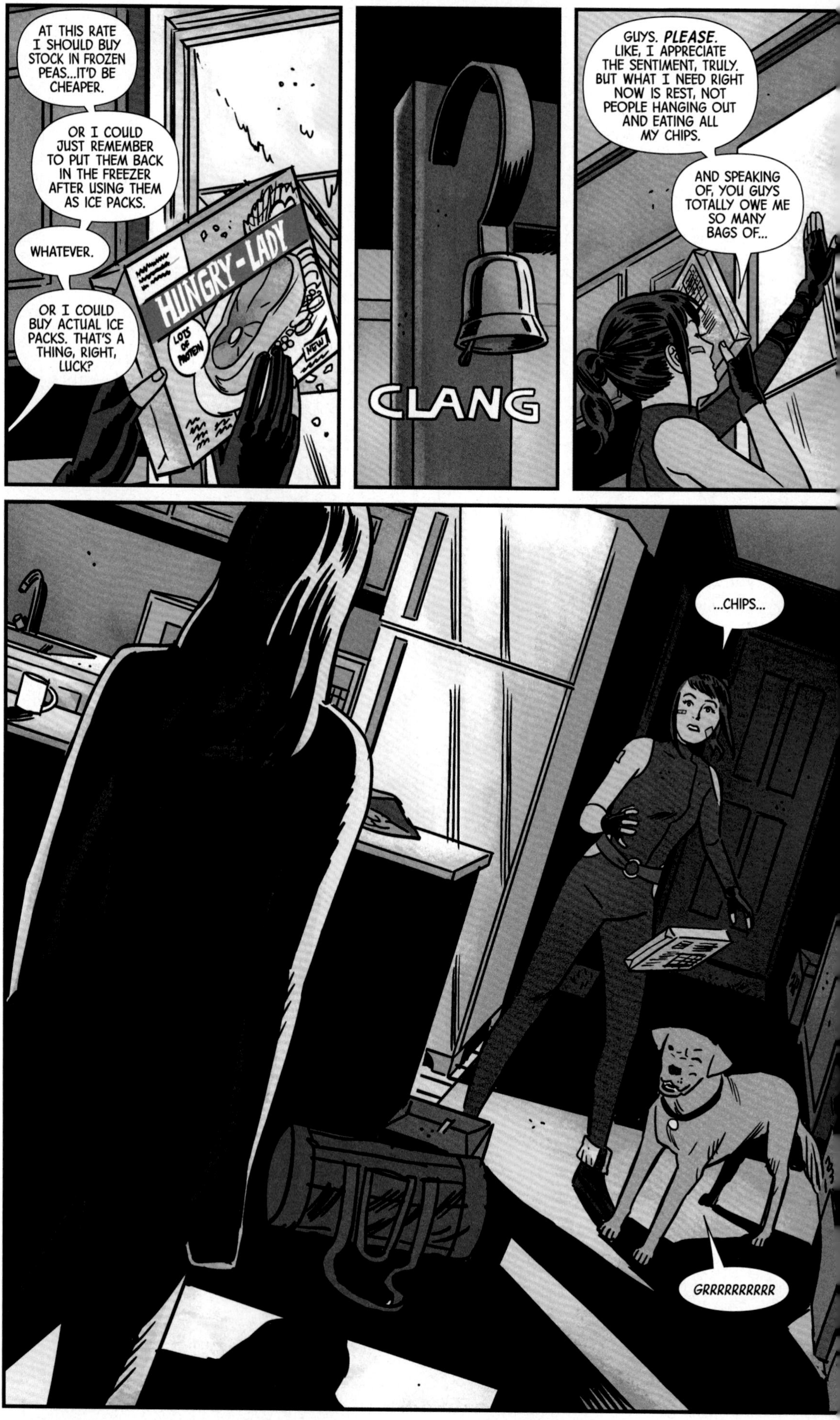
AT THIS RATE I SHOULD BUY STOCK IN FROZEN PEAS...IT'D BE CHEAPER.
OR I COULD JUST REMEMBER TO PUT THEM BACK IN THE FREEZER AFTER USING THEM AS ICE PACKS.
WHATEVER.
OR I COULD BUY ACTUAL ICE PACKS. THAT'S A THING, RIGHT, LUCK?
HUNGRY-LADY
LOTS OF PROTEIN
NEW
CLANG
GUYS. PLEASE. LIKE, I APPRECIATE THE SENTIMENT, TRULY. BUT WHAT I NEED RIGHT NOW IS REST, NOT PEOPLE HANGING OUT AND EATING ALL MY CHIPS.
AND SPEAKING OF, YOU GUYS TOTALLY OWE ME SO MANY BAGS OF...
...CHIPS...
GRRRRRRRRRR

HAWK
INVESTIGATIONS

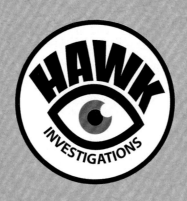

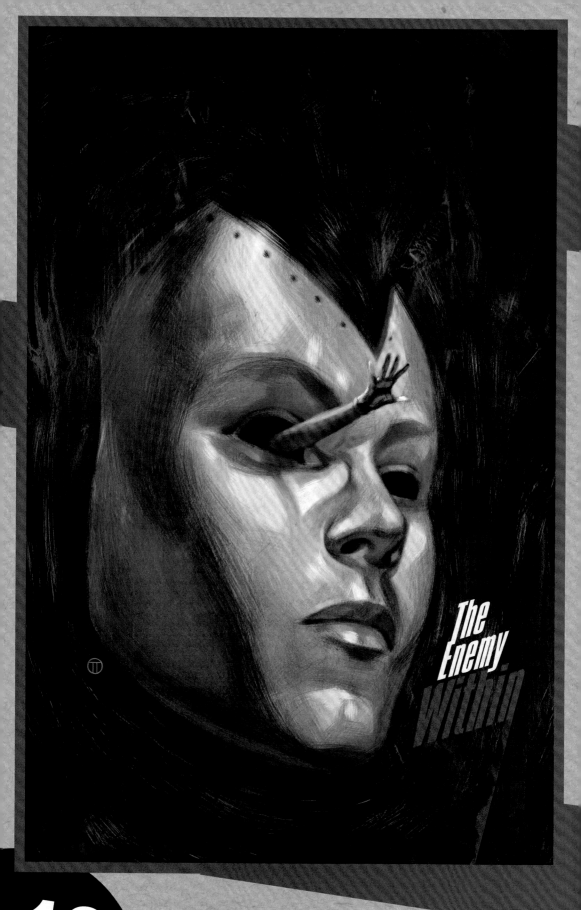

The Enemy
Within

10

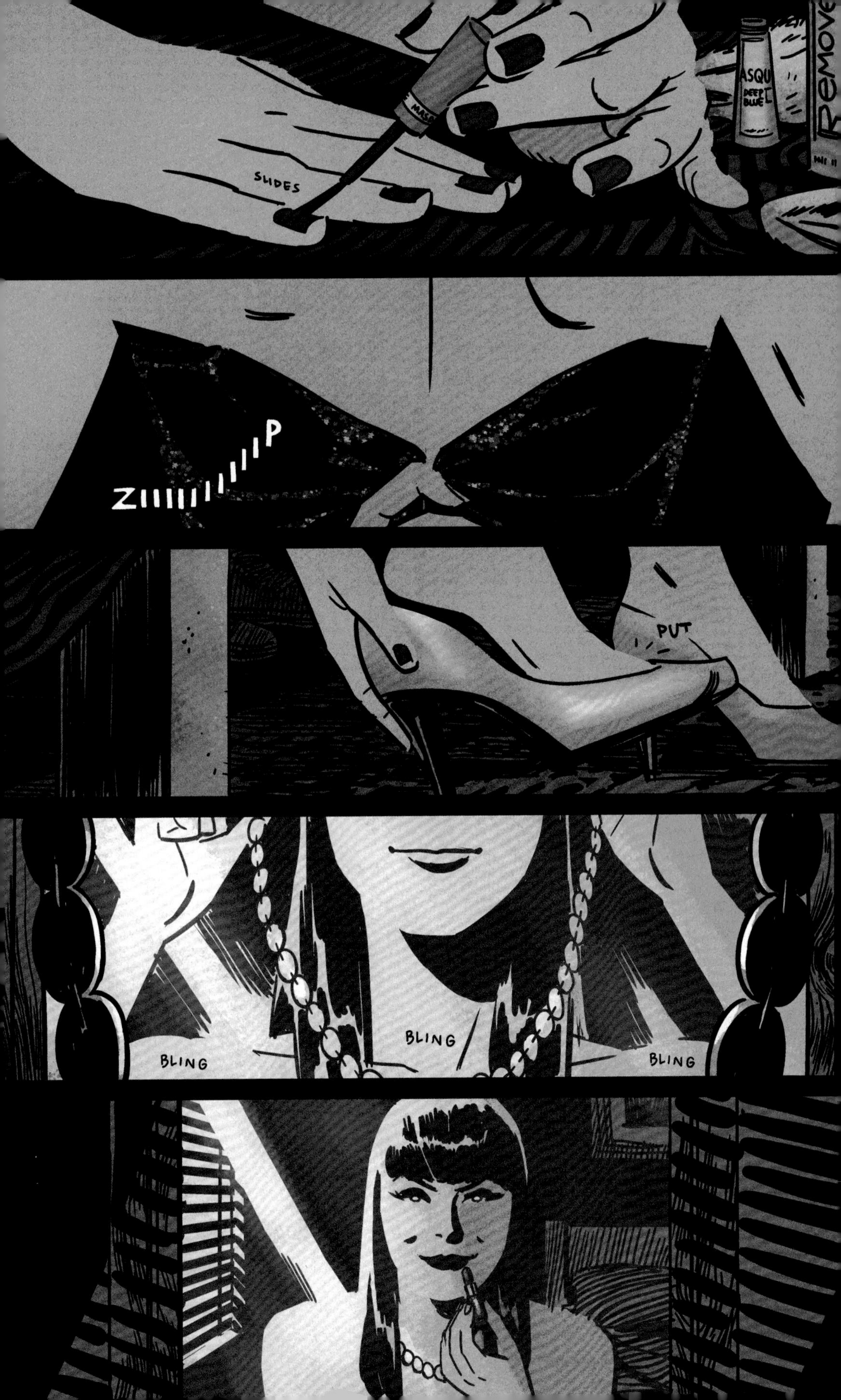

SLIDES
DEEP BLUE
Remove
ZIIIIIIIIIIP
PUT
BLING
BLING
BLING

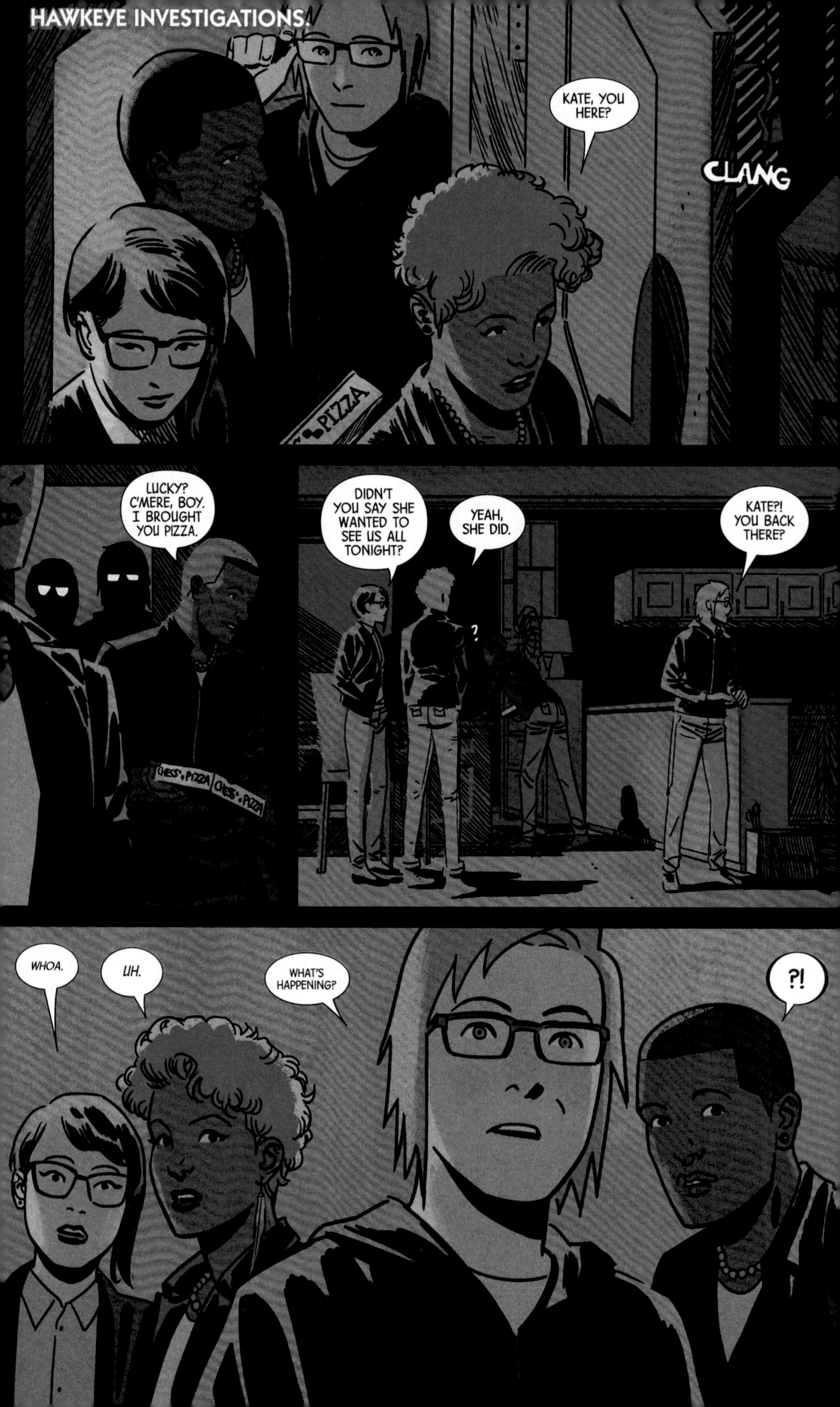
HAWKEYE INVESTIGATIONS.
KATE, YOU HERE?
CLANG
PIZZA
LUCKY? C'MERE, BOY. I BROUGHT YOU PIZZA.
CHESS • PIZZA
CHESS • PIZZA
DIDN'T YOU SAY SHE WANTED TO SEE US ALL TONIGHT?
YEAH, SHE DID.
?
KATE?! YOU BACK THERE?
WHOA.
UH.
WHAT'S HAPPENING?
?!

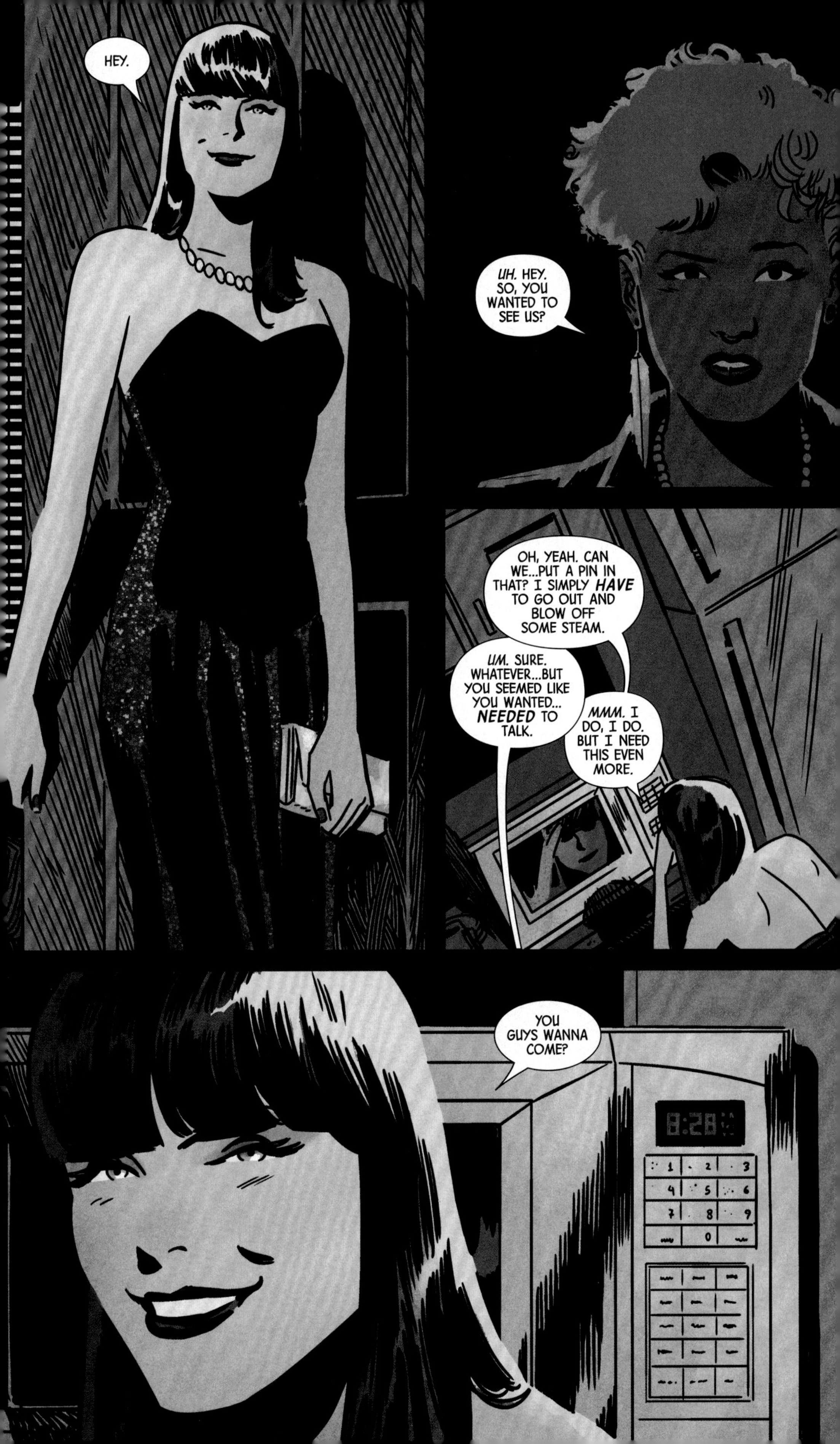
HEY.
UH. HEY. SO, YOU WANTED TO SEE US?
OH, YEAH. CAN WE...PUT A PIN IN THAT? I SIMPLY HAVE TO GO OUT AND BLOW OFF SOME STEAM.
UM. SURE. WHATEVER...BUT YOU SEEMED LIKE YOU WANTED... NEEDED TO TALK.
MMM. I DO, I DO. BUT I NEED THIS EVEN MORE.
YOU GUYS WANNA COME?

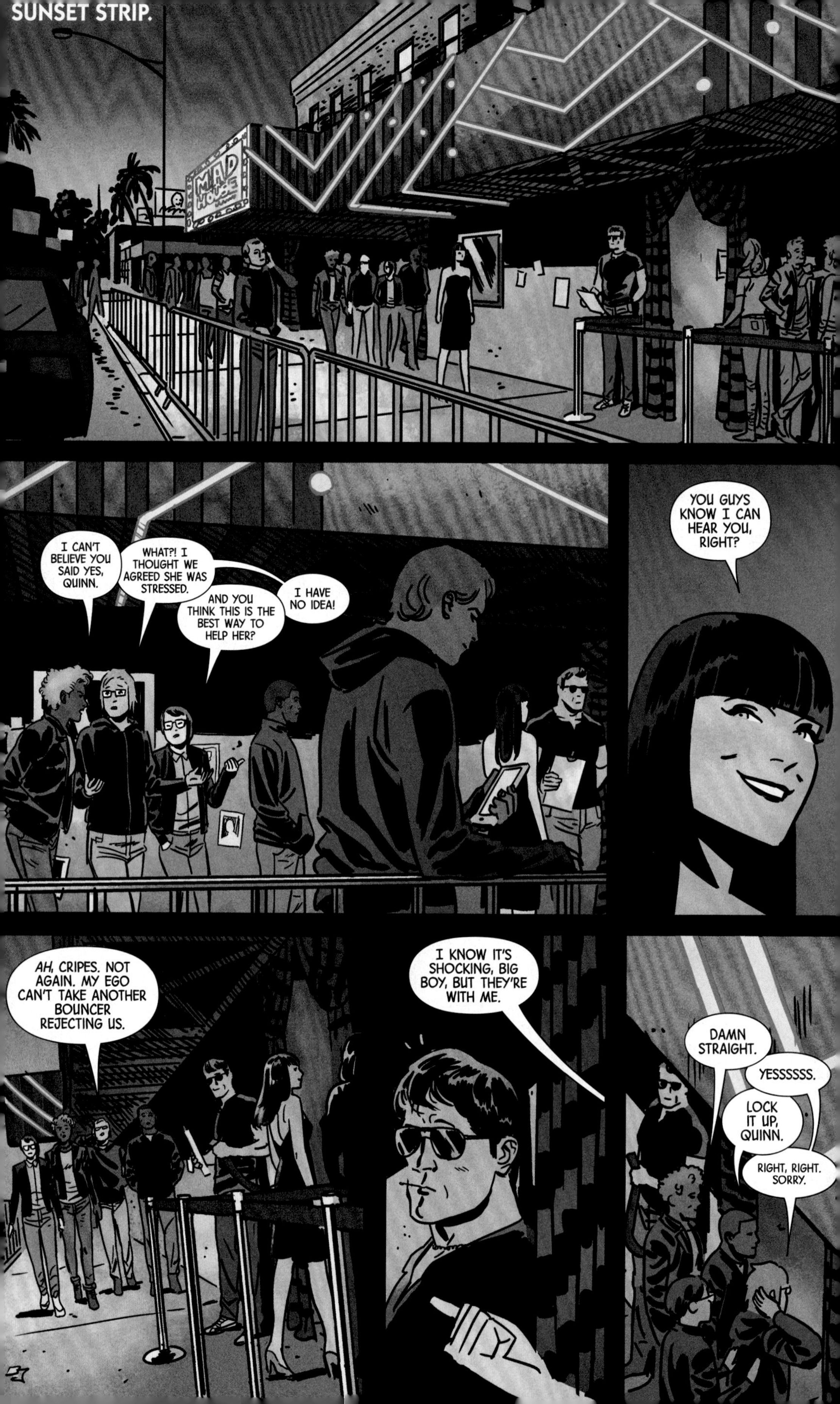
SUNSET STRIP.
MAD HOUSE
I CAN'T BELIEVE YOU SAID YES, QUINN.
WHAT?! I THOUGHT WE AGREED SHE WAS STRESSED.
AND YOU THINK THIS IS THE BEST WAY TO HELP HER?
I HAVE NO IDEA!
YOU GUYS KNOW I CAN HEAR YOU, RIGHT?
AH, CRIPES. NOT AGAIN. MY EGO CAN'T TAKE ANOTHER BOUNCER REJECTING US.
I KNOW IT'S SHOCKING, BIG BOY, BUT THEY'RE WITH ME.
DAMN STRAIGHT.
YESSSSSS.
LOCK IT UP, QUINN.
RIGHT, RIGHT. SORRY.

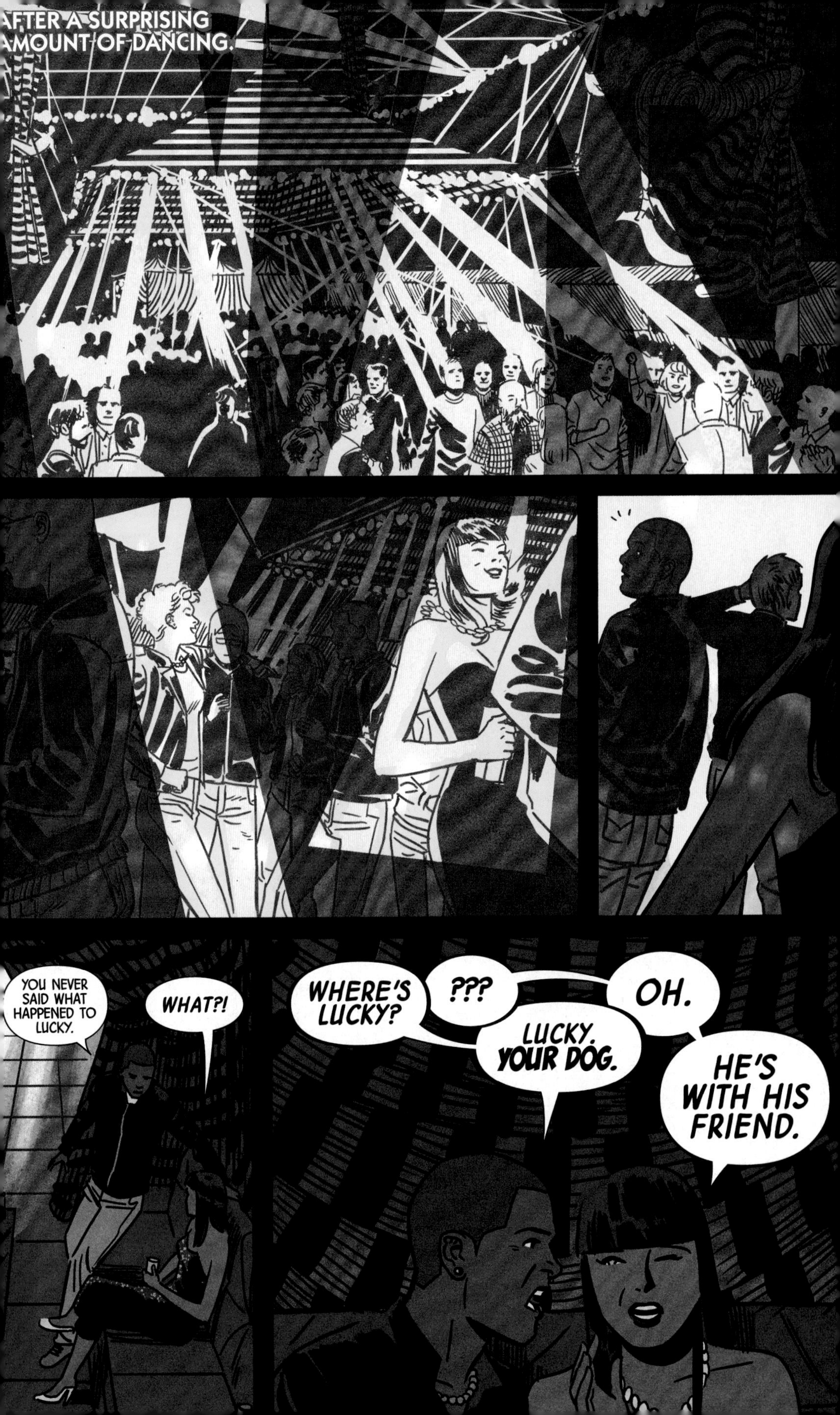
AFTER A SURPRISING AMOUNT OF DANCING.
YOU NEVER SAID WHAT HAPPENED TO LUCKY.
WHAT?!
WHERE'S LUCKY?
???
LUCKY. YOUR DOG.
OH.
HE'S WITH HIS FRIEND.

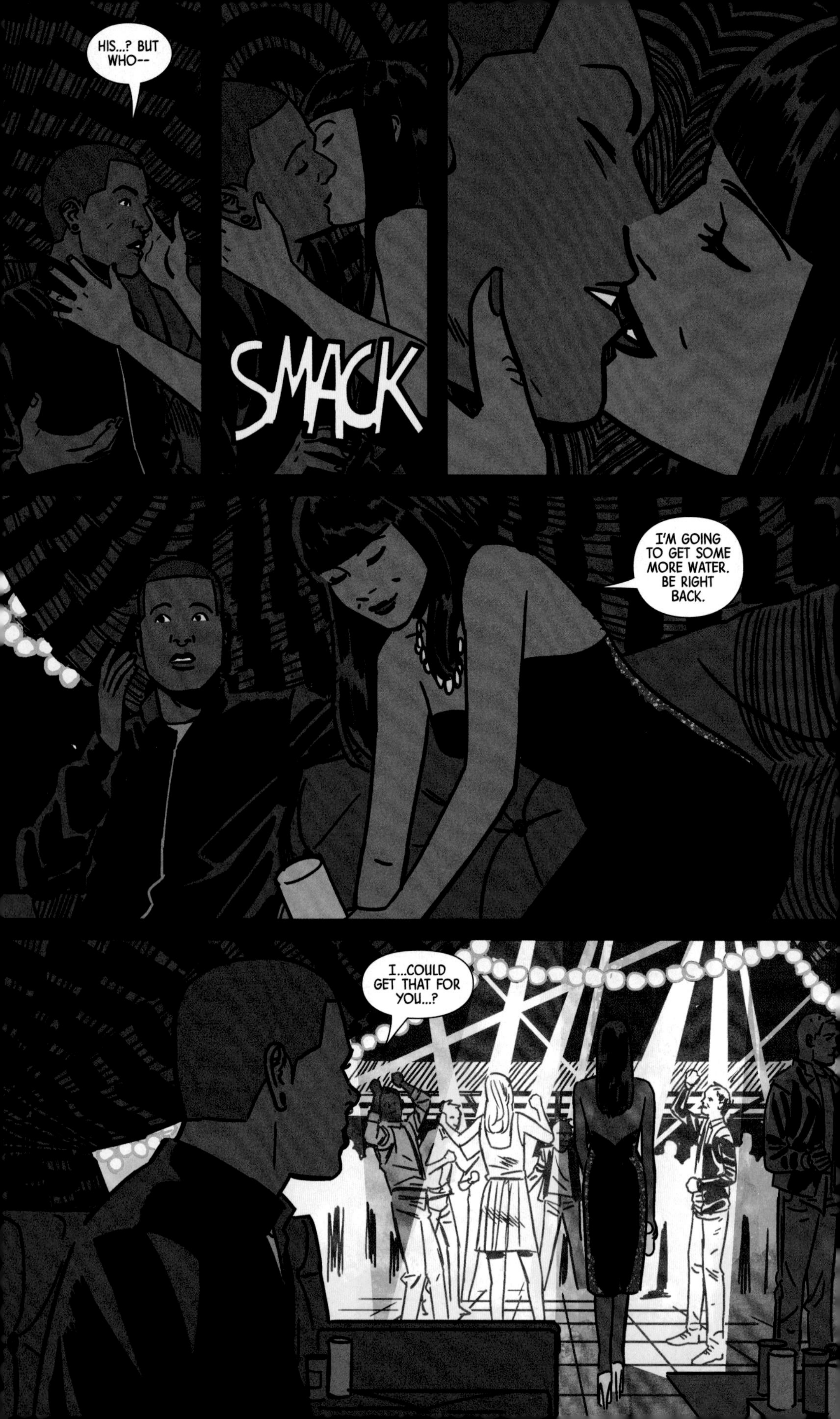
HIS...? BUT WHO--
SMACK
I'M GOING TO GET SOME MORE WATER. BE RIGHT BACK.
I...COULD GET THAT FOR YOU...?

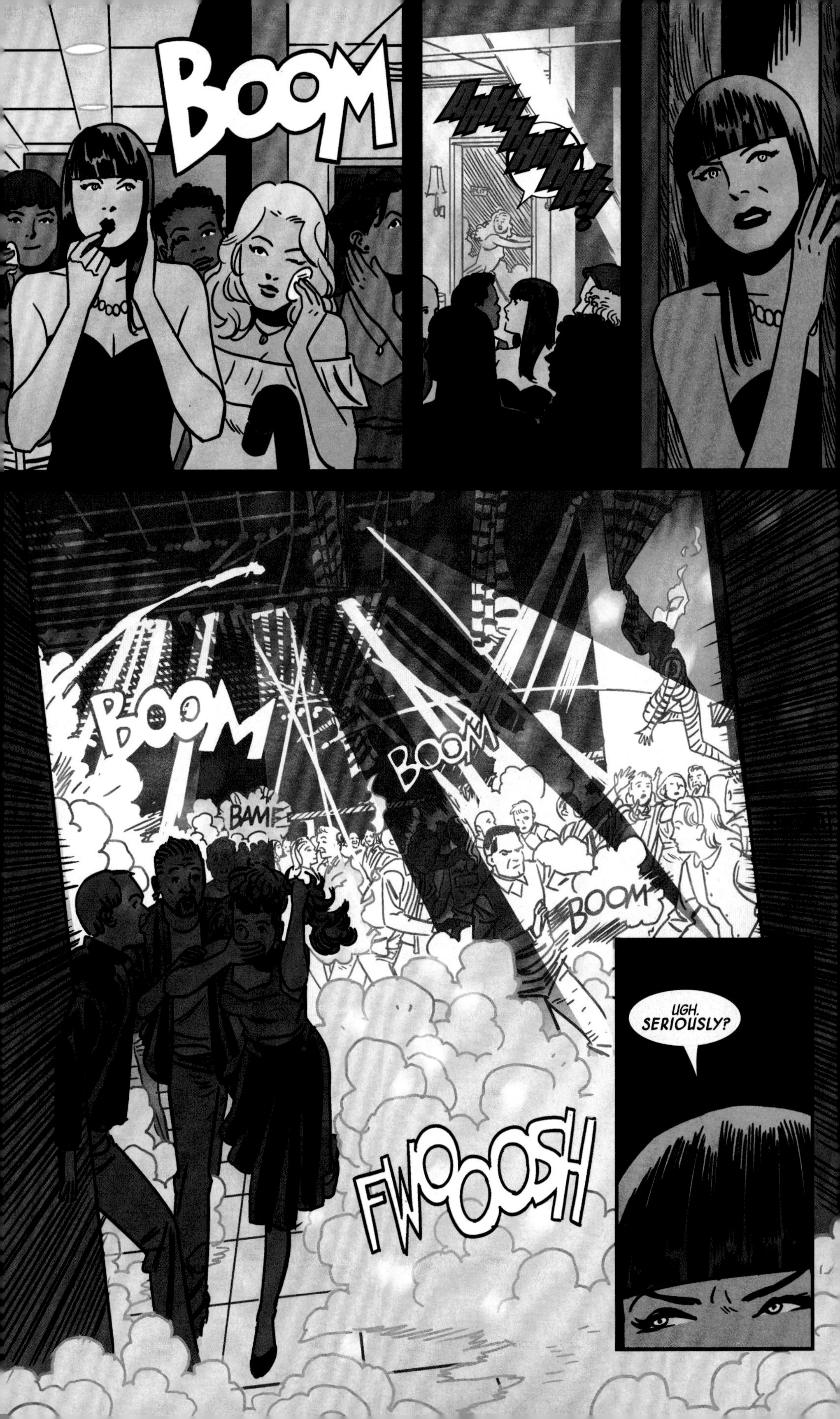
BOOM
AHHHHHHHH!!
BOOM
BOOM
BAM
BOOM
UGH. SERIOUSLY?
FWOOOSH

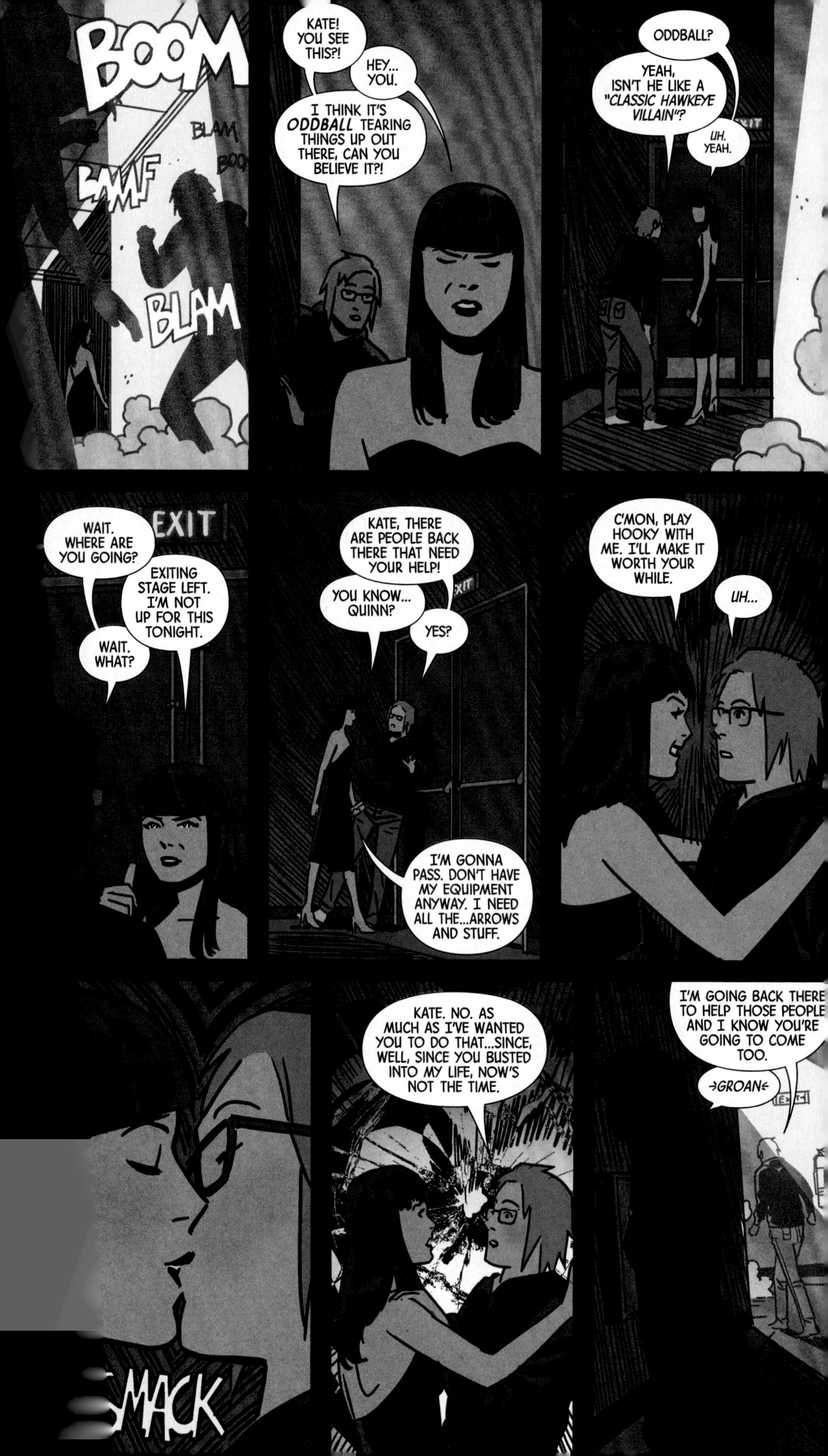
BOOM
BLAM
BAMF
BLAM
KATE! YOU SEE THIS?!
HEY... YOU.
I THINK IT'S ODDBALL TEARING THINGS UP OUT THERE, CAN YOU BELIEVE IT?!
ODDBALL?
YEAH, ISN'T HE LIKE A "CLASSIC HAWKEYE VILLAIN"?
UH. YEAH.
EXIT
WAIT. WHERE ARE YOU GOING?
EXITING STAGE LEFT. I'M NOT UP FOR THIS TONIGHT.
WAIT. WHAT?
KATE, THERE ARE PEOPLE BACK THERE THAT NEED YOUR HELP!
YOU KNOW... QUINN?
YES?
I'M GONNA PASS. DON'T HAVE MY EQUIPMENT ANYWAY. I NEED ALL THE...ARROWS AND STUFF.
C'MON, PLAY HOOKY WITH ME. I'LL MAKE IT WORTH YOUR WHILE.
UH...
MACK
KATE. NO. AS MUCH AS I'VE WANTED YOU TO DO THAT...SINCE, WELL, SINCE YOU BUSTED INTO MY LIFE, NOW'S NOT THE TIME.
I'M GOING BACK THERE TO HELP THOSE PEOPLE AND I KNOW YOU'RE GOING TO COME TOO.
GROAN

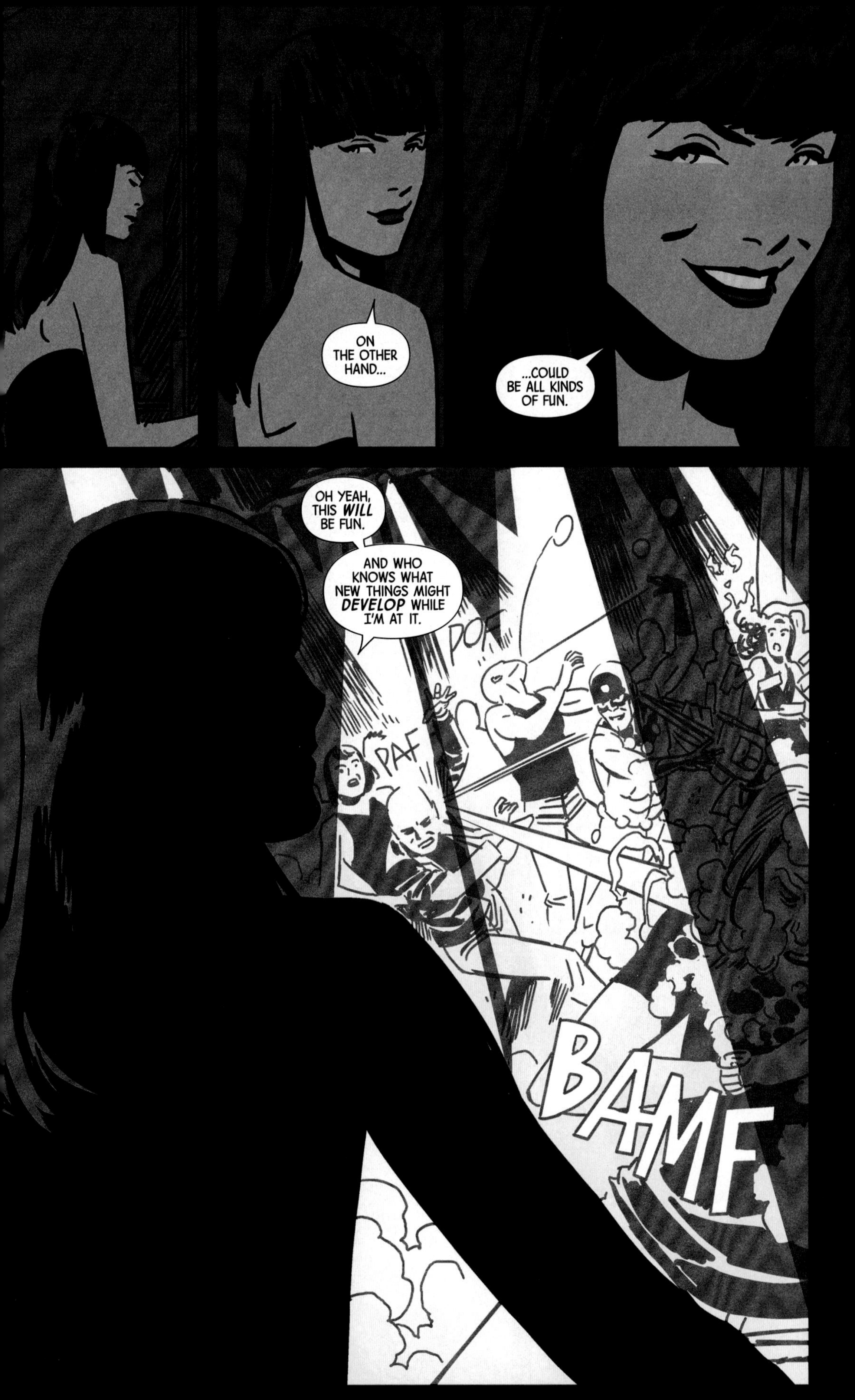
ON THE OTHER HAND...
...COULD BE ALL KINDS OF FUN.
OH YEAH, THIS WILL BE FUN.
AND WHO KNOWS WHAT NEW THINGS MIGHT DEVELOP WHILE I'M AT IT.
POF
PAF
BAMF

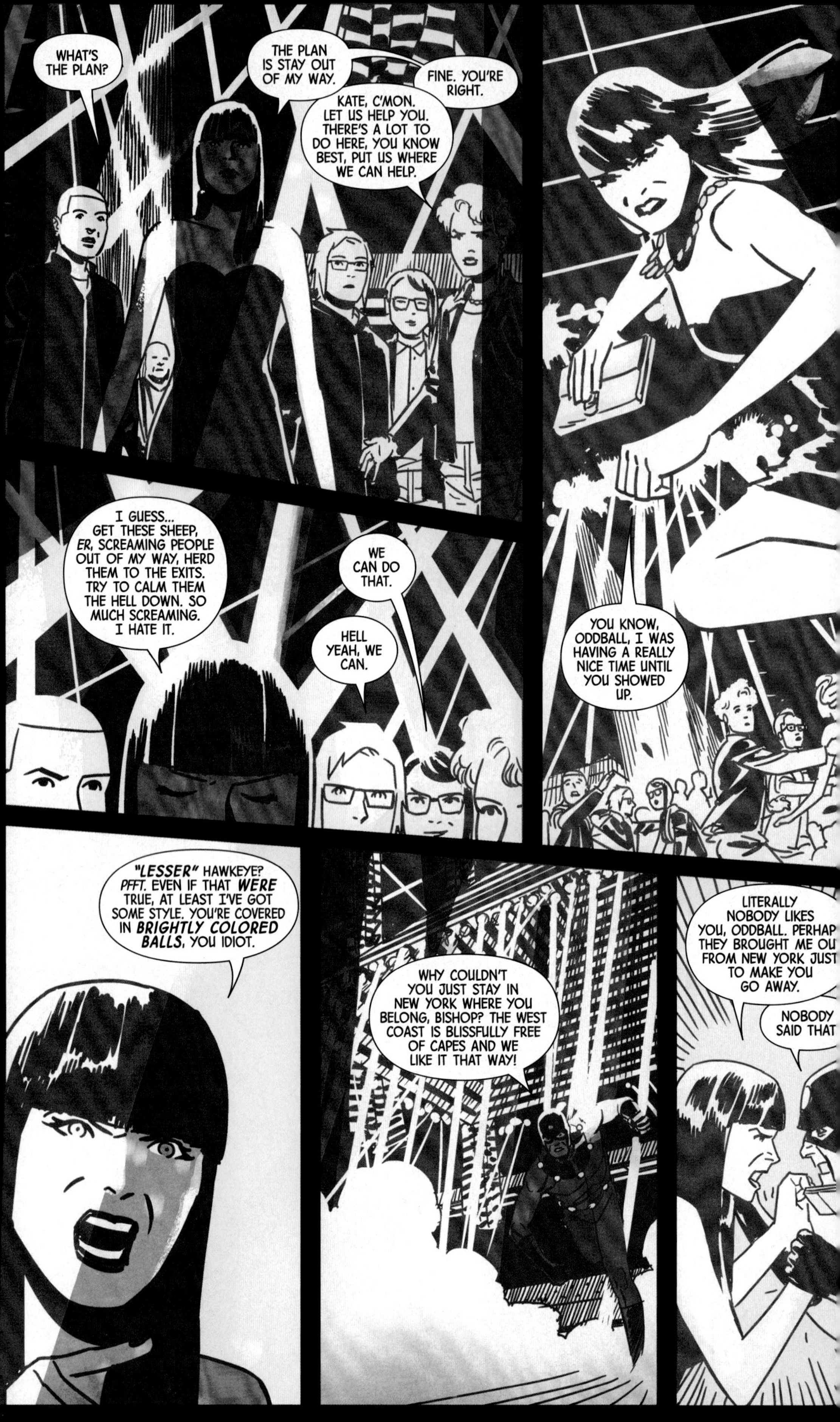
WHAT'S THE PLAN?
THE PLAN IS STAY OUT OF MY WAY.
FINE. YOU'RE RIGHT.
KATE, C'MON. LET US HELP YOU. THERE'S A LOT TO DO HERE, YOU KNOW BEST, PUT US WHERE WE CAN HELP.
I GUESS... GET THESE SHEEP, *ER*, SCREAMING PEOPLE OUT OF MY WAY, HERD THEM TO THE EXITS. TRY TO CALM THEM THE HELL DOWN. SO MUCH SCREAMING. I HATE IT.
WE CAN DO THAT.
HELL YEAH, WE CAN.
YOU KNOW, ODDBALL, I WAS HAVING A REALLY NICE TIME UNTIL YOU SHOWED UP.
"LESSER" HAWKEYE? *PFFT.* EVEN IF THAT **WERE** TRUE, AT LEAST I'VE GOT SOME STYLE. YOU'RE COVERED IN **BRIGHTLY COLORED BALLS**, YOU IDIOT.
WHY COULDN'T YOU JUST STAY IN NEW YORK WHERE YOU BELONG, BISHOP? THE WEST COAST IS BLISSFULLY FREE OF CAPES AND WE LIKE IT THAT WAY!
LITERALLY NOBODY LIKES YOU, ODDBALL. PERHAP THEY BROUGHT ME OU FROM NEW YORK JUST TO MAKE YOU GO AWAY.
NOBODY SAID THAT

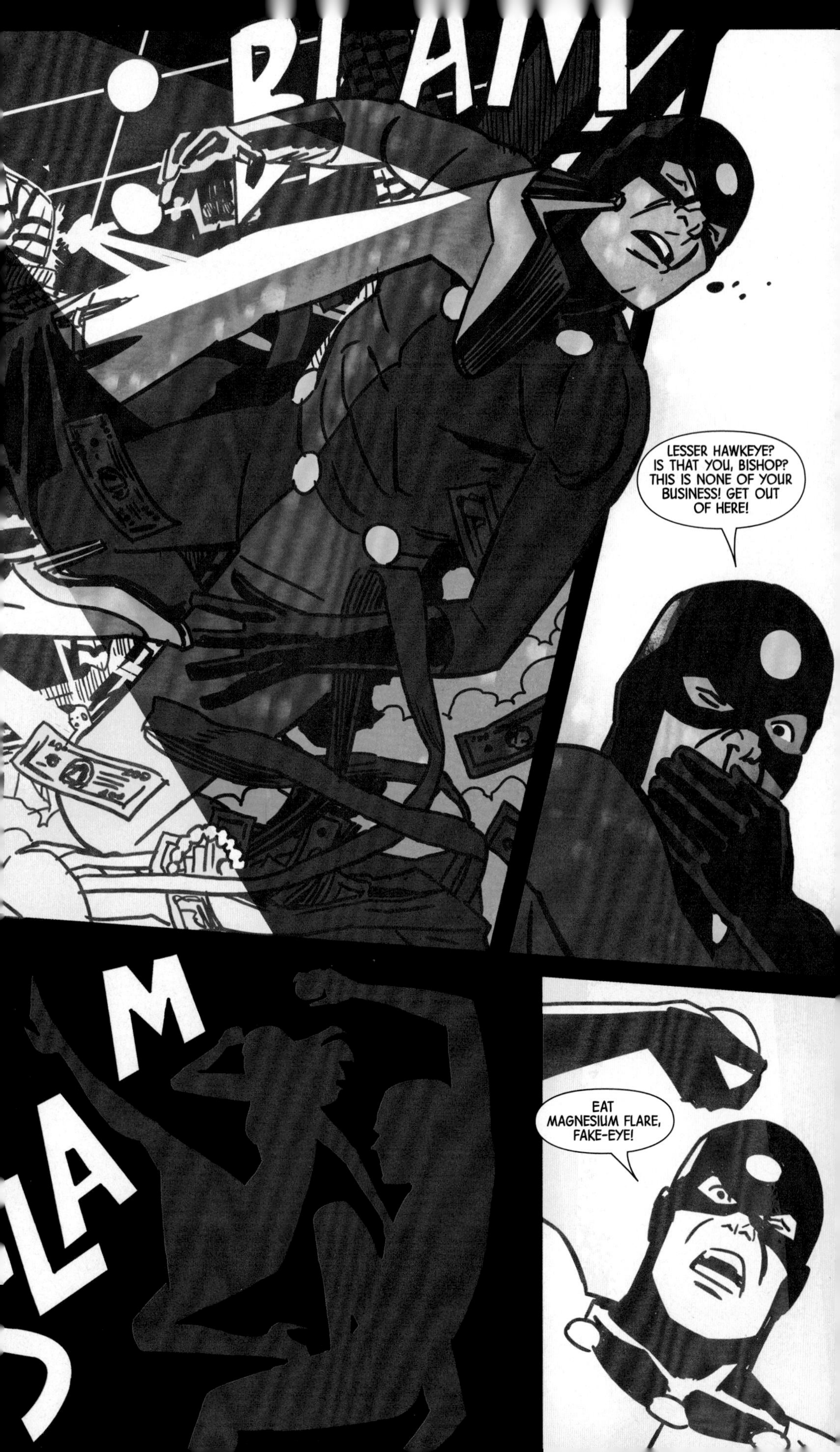
LESSER HAWKEYE? IS THAT YOU, BISHOP? THIS IS NONE OF YOUR BUSINESS! GET OUT OF HERE!
EAT MAGNESIUM FLARE, FAKE-EYE!

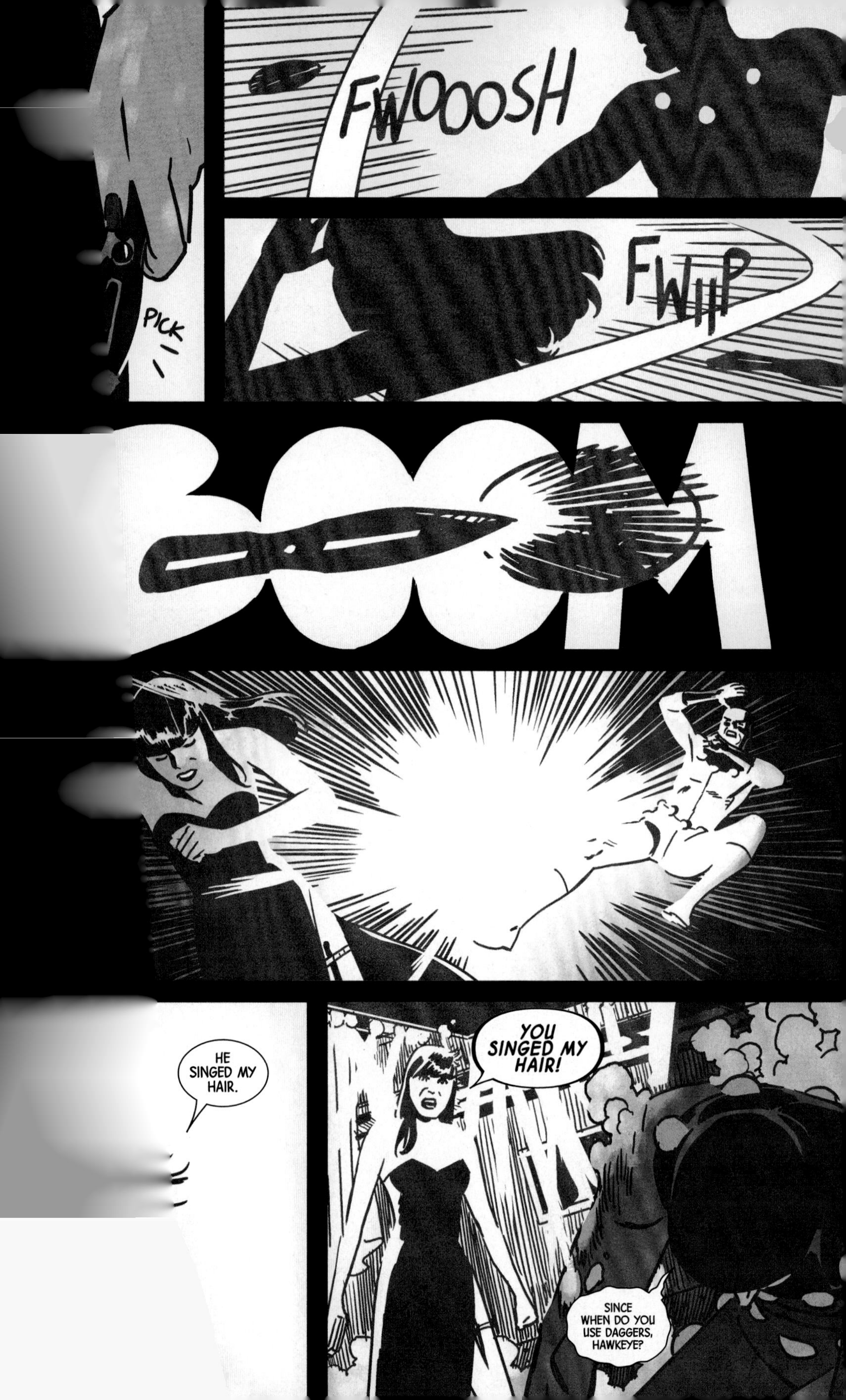
FWOOOSH
PICK
FWIIP
BOOM
HE SINGED MY HAIR.
YOU SINGED MY HAIR!
SINCE WHEN DO YOU USE DAGGERS, HAWKEYE?

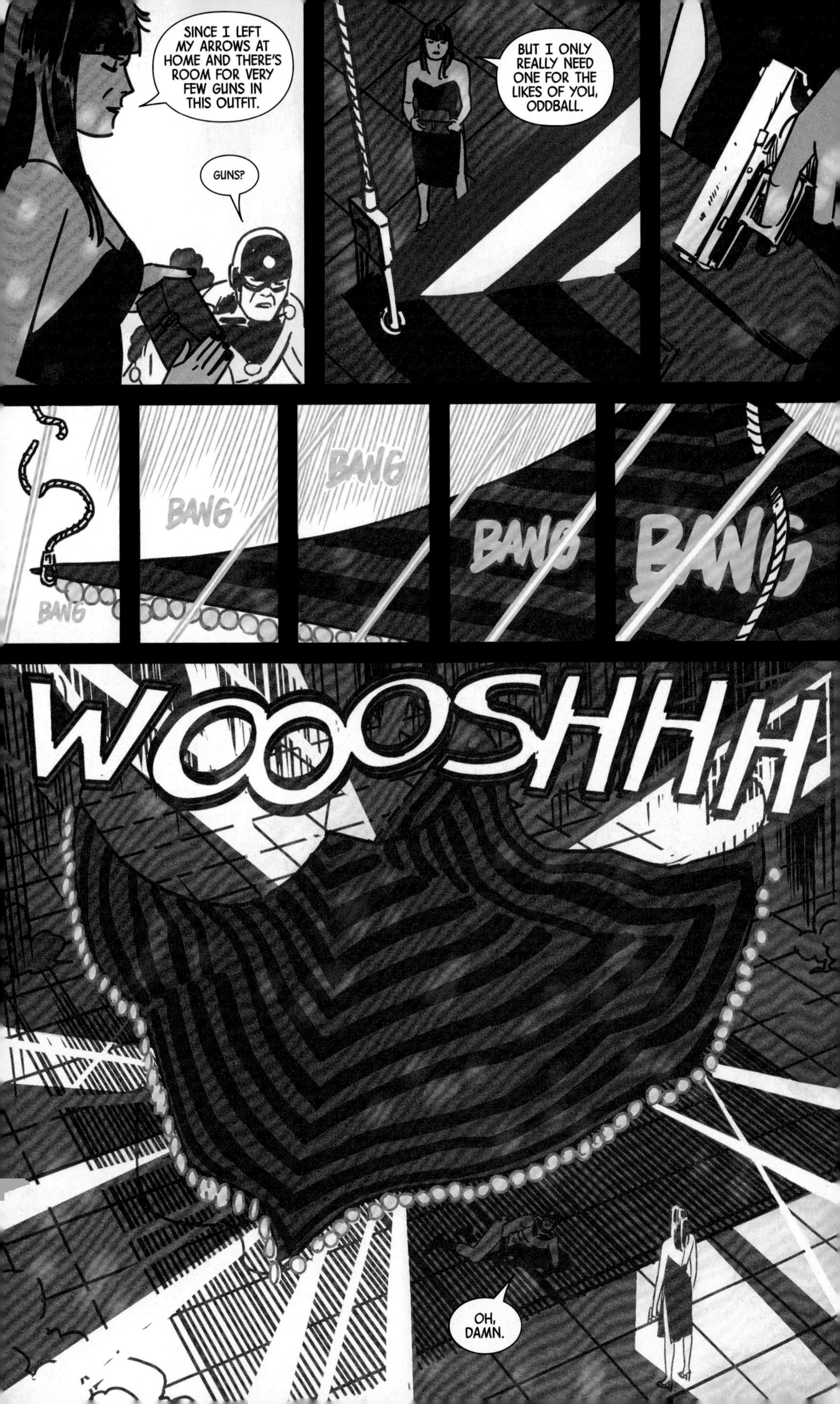
SINCE I LEFT MY ARROWS AT HOME AND THERE'S ROOM FOR VERY FEW GUNS IN THIS OUTFIT.
GUNS?
BUT I ONLY REALLY NEED ONE FOR THE LIKES OF YOU, ODDBALL.
BANG
BANG
BANG
BANG
BANG
WOOOSHHH
OH, DAMN.

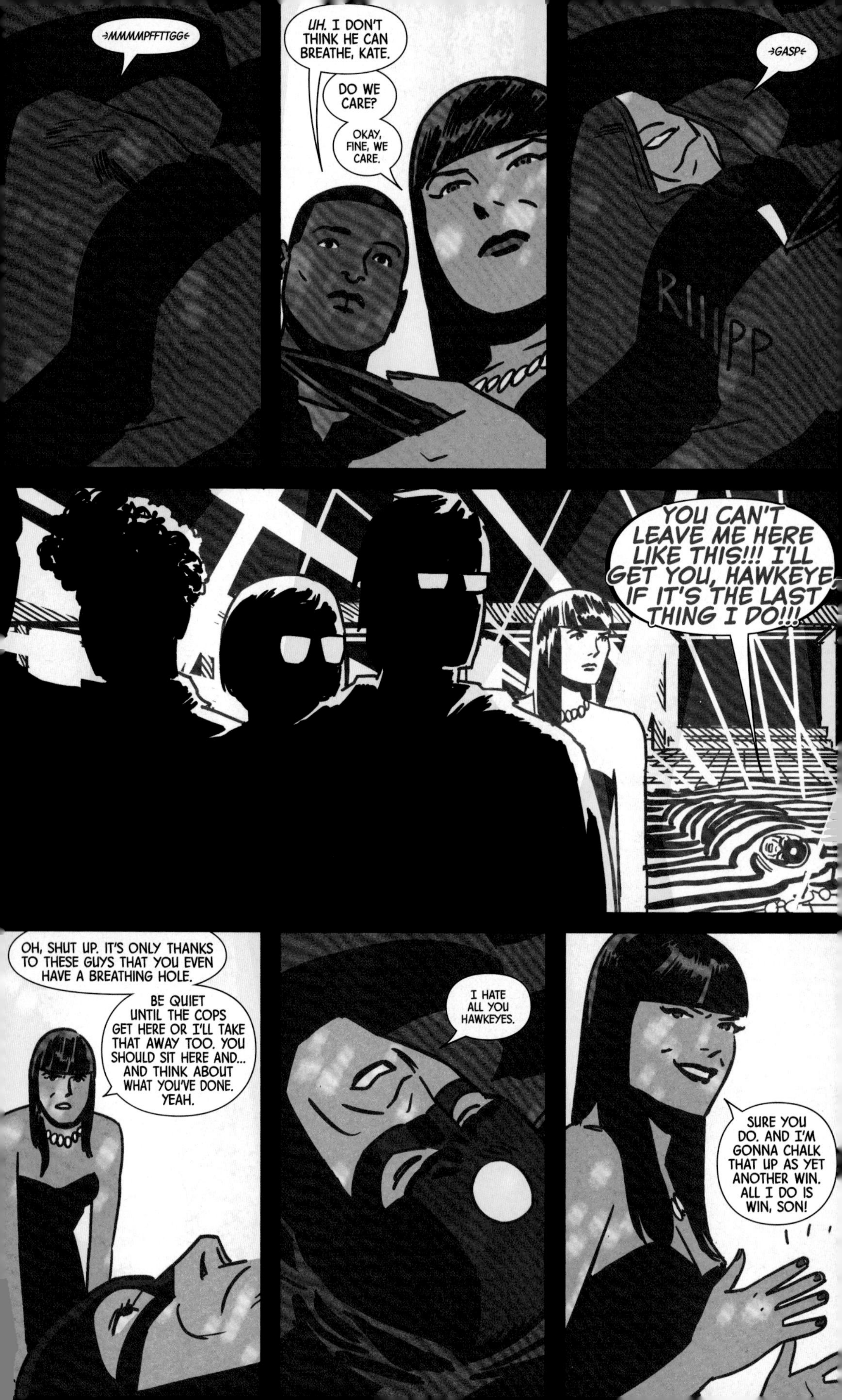
MMMMPFFTTGG
UH. I DON'T THINK HE CAN BREATHE, KATE.
DO WE CARE?
OKAY, FINE, WE CARE.
GASP
RIIIPP
YOU CAN'T LEAVE ME HERE LIKE THIS!!! I'LL GET YOU, HAWKEYE IF IT'S THE LAST THING I DO!!!
OH, SHUT UP. IT'S ONLY THANKS TO THESE GUYS THAT YOU EVEN HAVE A BREATHING HOLE.
BE QUIET UNTIL THE COPS GET HERE OR I'LL TAKE THAT AWAY TOO. YOU SHOULD SIT HERE AND... AND THINK ABOUT WHAT YOU'VE DONE. YEAH.
I HATE ALL YOU HAWKEYES.
SURE YOU DO. AND I'M GONNA CHALK THAT UP AS YET ANOTHER WIN. ALL I DO IS WIN, SON!

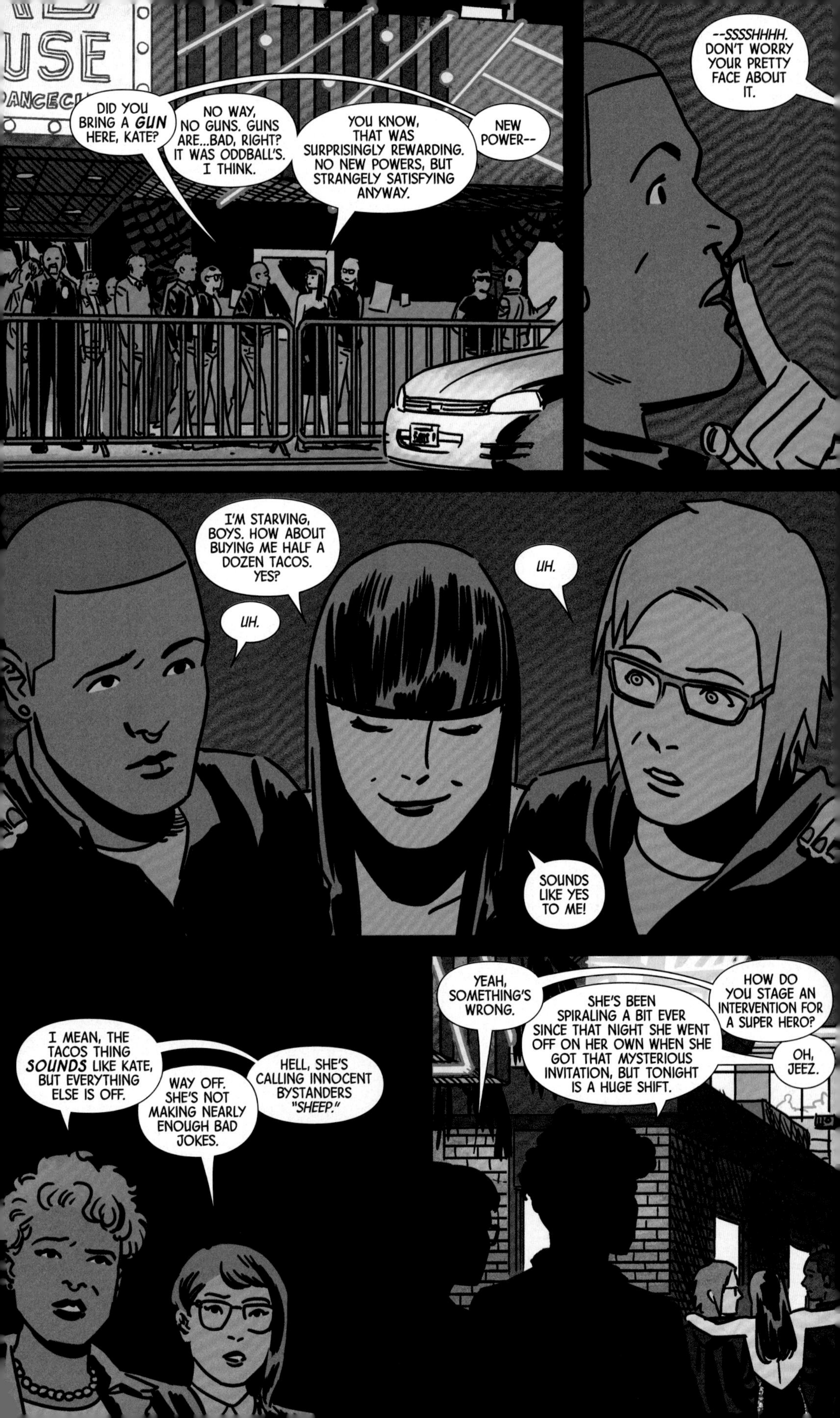
USE
DANCECL
DID YOU BRING A GUN HERE, KATE?
NO WAY, NO GUNS. GUNS ARE...BAD, RIGHT? IT WAS ODDBALL'S. I THINK.
YOU KNOW, THAT WAS SURPRISINGLY REWARDING. NO NEW POWERS, BUT STRANGELY SATISFYING ANYWAY.
NEW POWER--
--SSSSHHHH. DON'T WORRY YOUR PRETTY FACE ABOUT IT.
I'M STARVING, BOYS. HOW ABOUT BUYING ME HALF A DOZEN TACOS. YES?
UH.
UH.
SOUNDS LIKE YES TO ME!
I MEAN, THE TACOS THING SOUNDS LIKE KATE, BUT EVERYTHING ELSE IS OFF.
WAY OFF. SHE'S NOT MAKING NEARLY ENOUGH BAD JOKES.
HELL, SHE'S CALLING INNOCENT BYSTANDERS "SHEEP."
YEAH, SOMETHING'S WRONG.
SHE'S BEEN SPIRALING A BIT EVER SINCE THAT NIGHT SHE WENT OFF ON HER OWN WHEN SHE GOT THAT MYSTERIOUS INVITATION, BUT TONIGHT IS A HUGE SHIFT.
HOW DO YOU STAGE AN INTERVENTION FOR A SUPER HERO?
OH, JEEZ.

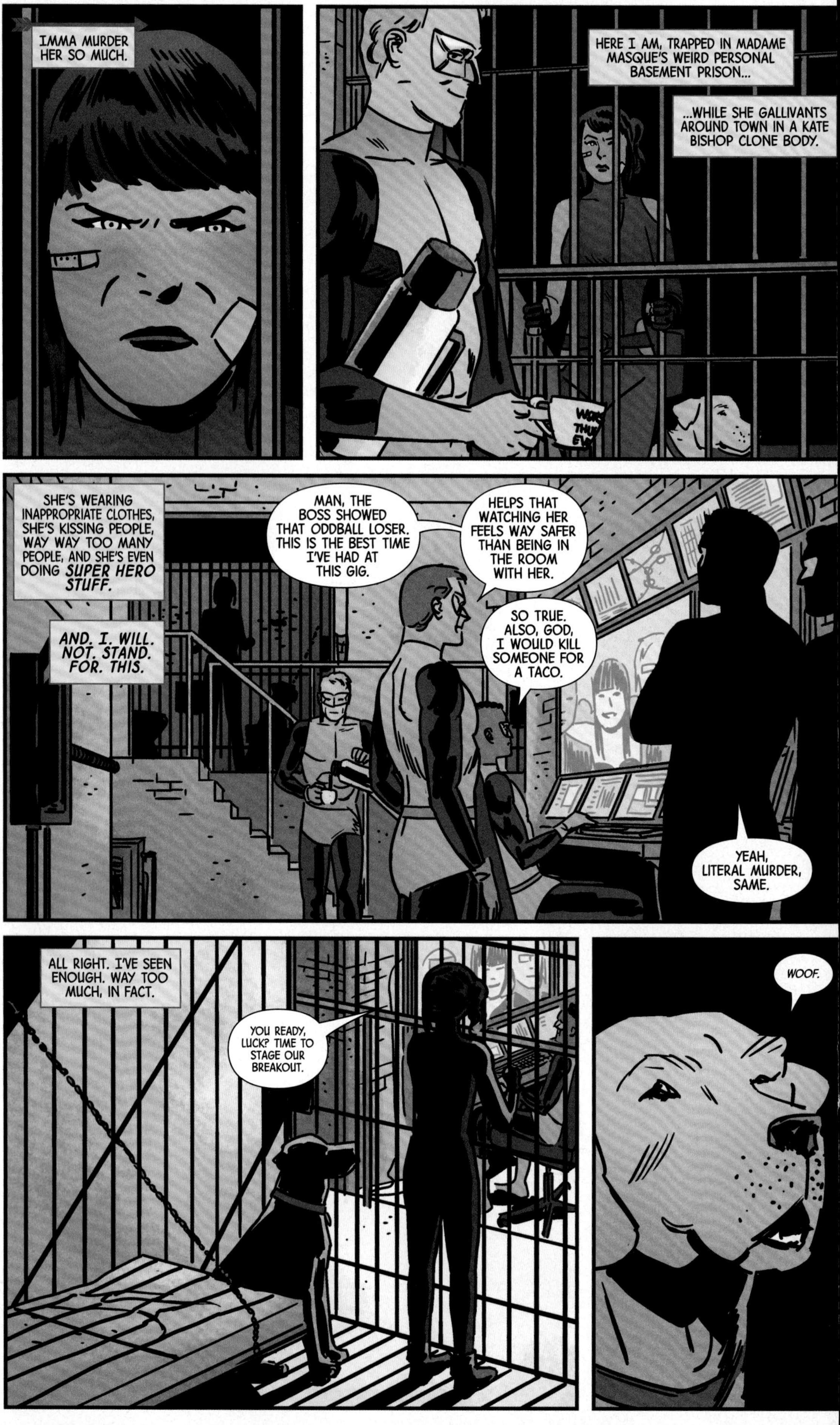
IMMA MURDER HER SO MUCH.
HERE I AM, TRAPPED IN MADAME MASQUE'S WEIRD PERSONAL BASEMENT PRISON...
...WHILE SHE GALLIVANTS AROUND TOWN IN A KATE BISHOP CLONE BODY.
SHE'S WEARING INAPPROPRIATE CLOTHES, SHE'S KISSING PEOPLE, WAY WAY TOO MANY PEOPLE, AND SHE'S EVEN DOING SUPER HERO STUFF.
AND. I. WILL. NOT. STAND. FOR. THIS.
MAN, THE BOSS SHOWED THAT ODDBALL LOSER. THIS IS THE BEST TIME I'VE HAD AT THIS GIG.
HELPS THAT WATCHING HER FEELS WAY SAFER THAN BEING IN THE ROOM WITH HER.
SO TRUE. ALSO, GOD, I WOULD KILL SOMEONE FOR A TACO.
YEAH, LITERAL MURDER, SAME.
ALL RIGHT. I'VE SEEN ENOUGH. WAY TOO MUCH, IN FACT.
YOU READY, LUCK? TIME TO STAGE OUR BREAKOUT.
WOOF.

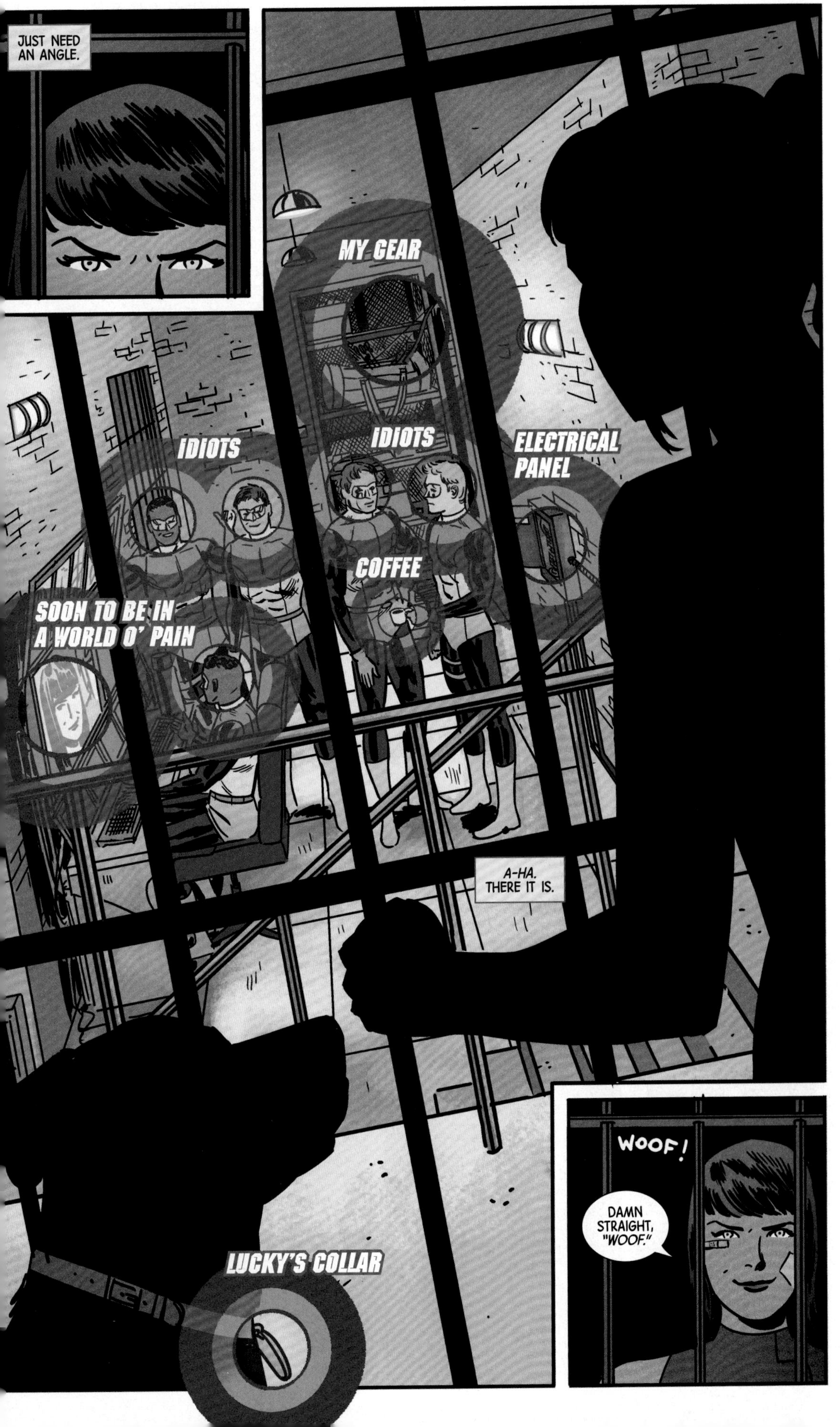

JUST NEED AN ANGLE.
MY GEAR
IDIOTS
IDIOTS
ELECTRICAL PANEL
COFFEE
SOON TO BE IN A WORLD O' PAIN
A-HA. THERE IT IS.
LUCKY'S COLLAR
WOOF!
DAMN STRAIGHT, "WOOF."

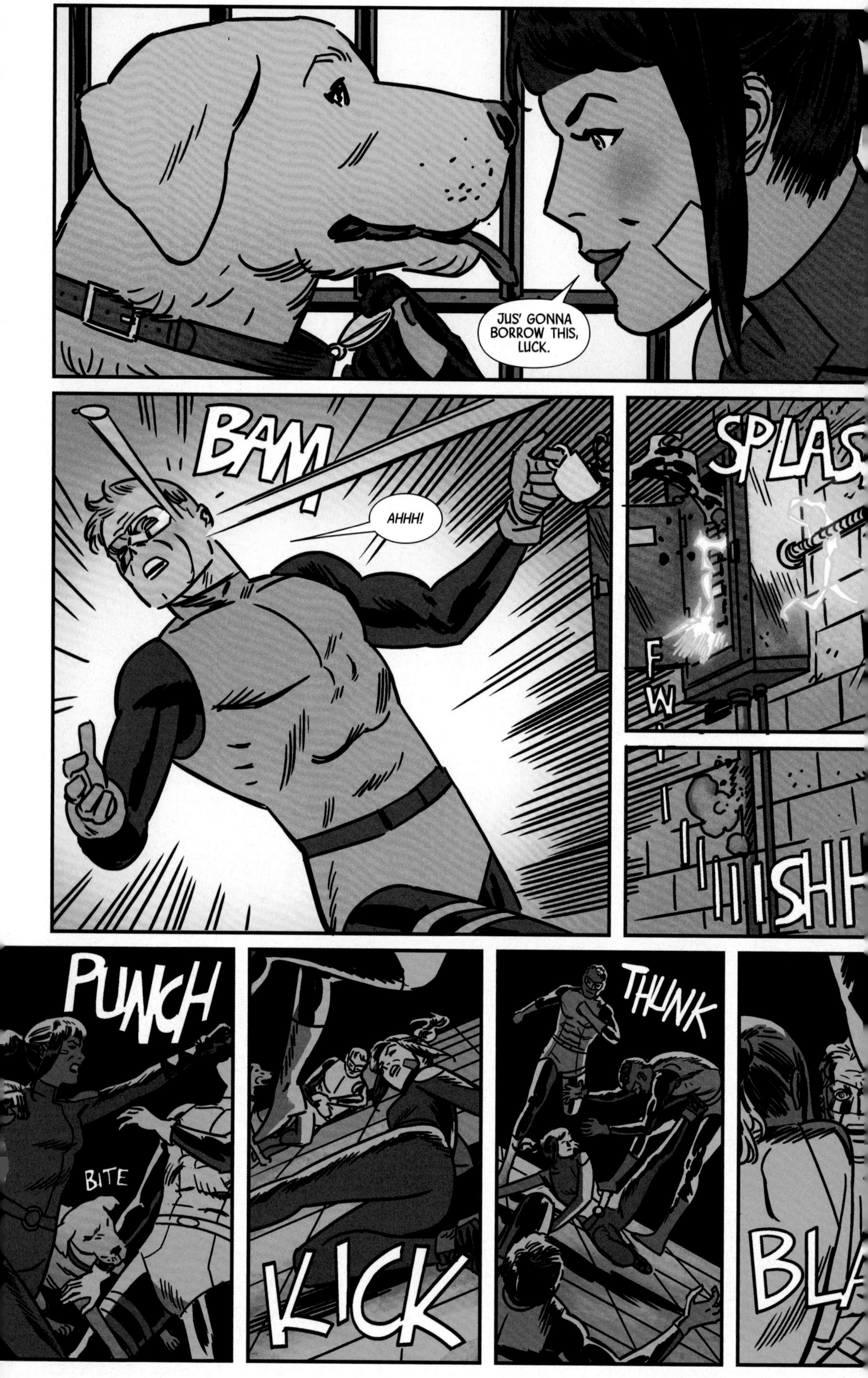
JUS' GONNA BORROW THIS, LUCK.
BAM
AHHH!
SPLAS
FWIIIIIISHH
PUNCH
BITE
KICK
THUNK
BLA

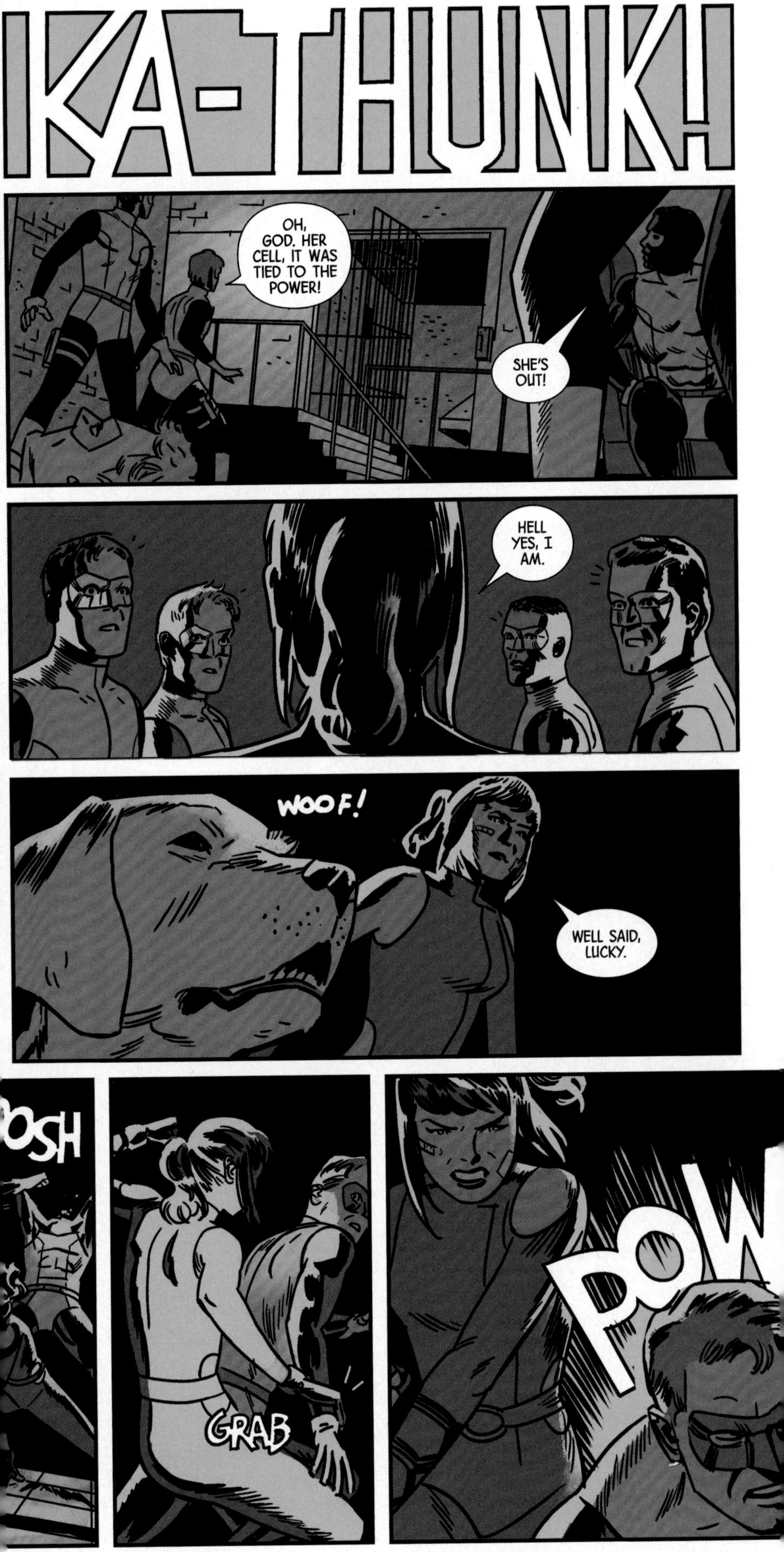
KA-THUNK!
OH, GOD. HER CELL, IT WAS TIED TO THE POWER!
SHE'S OUT!
HELL YES, I AM.
WOOF!
WELL SAID, LUCKY.
OSH
GRAB
POW

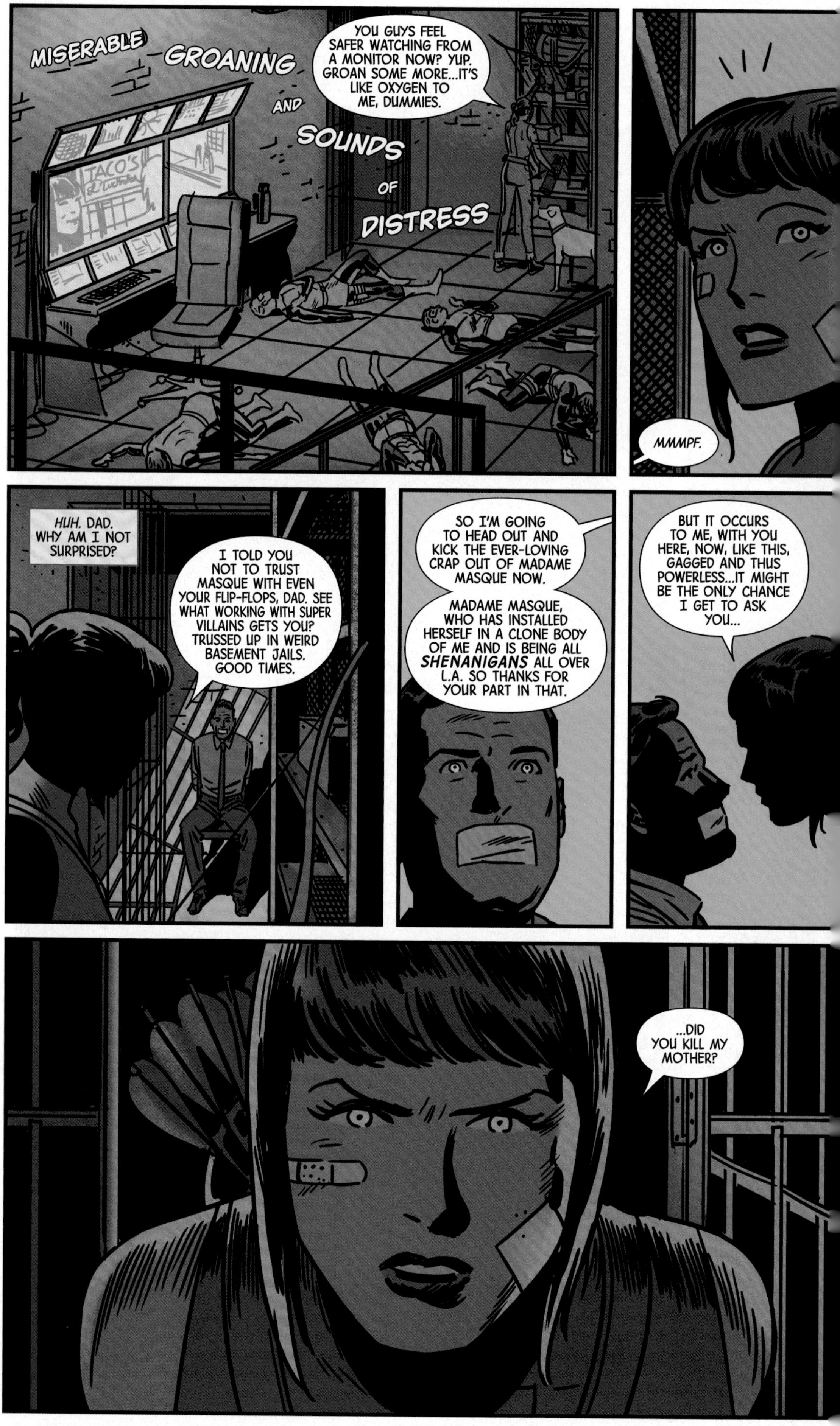
MISERABLE GROANING AND SOUNDS OF DISTRESS
YOU GUYS FEEL SAFER WATCHING FROM A MONITOR NOW? YUP. GROAN SOME MORE...IT'S LIKE OXYGEN TO ME, DUMMIES.
TACO'S
MMMPF.
HUH. DAD. WHY AM I NOT SURPRISED?
I TOLD YOU NOT TO TRUST MASQUE WITH EVEN YOUR FLIP-FLOPS, DAD. SEE WHAT WORKING WITH SUPER VILLAINS GETS YOU? TRUSSED UP IN WEIRD BASEMENT JAILS. GOOD TIMES.
SO I'M GOING TO HEAD OUT AND KICK THE EVER-LOVING CRAP OUT OF MADAME MASQUE NOW.
MADAME MASQUE, WHO HAS INSTALLED HERSELF IN A CLONE BODY OF ME AND IS BEING ALL SHENANIGANS ALL OVER L.A. SO THANKS FOR YOUR PART IN THAT.
BUT IT OCCURS TO ME, WITH YOU HERE, NOW, LIKE THIS, GAGGED AND THUS POWERLESS...IT MIGHT BE THE ONLY CHANCE I GET TO ASK YOU...
...DID YOU KILL MY MOTHER?

HAWK
INVESTIGATIONS

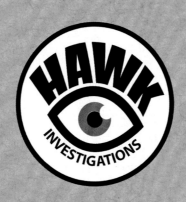

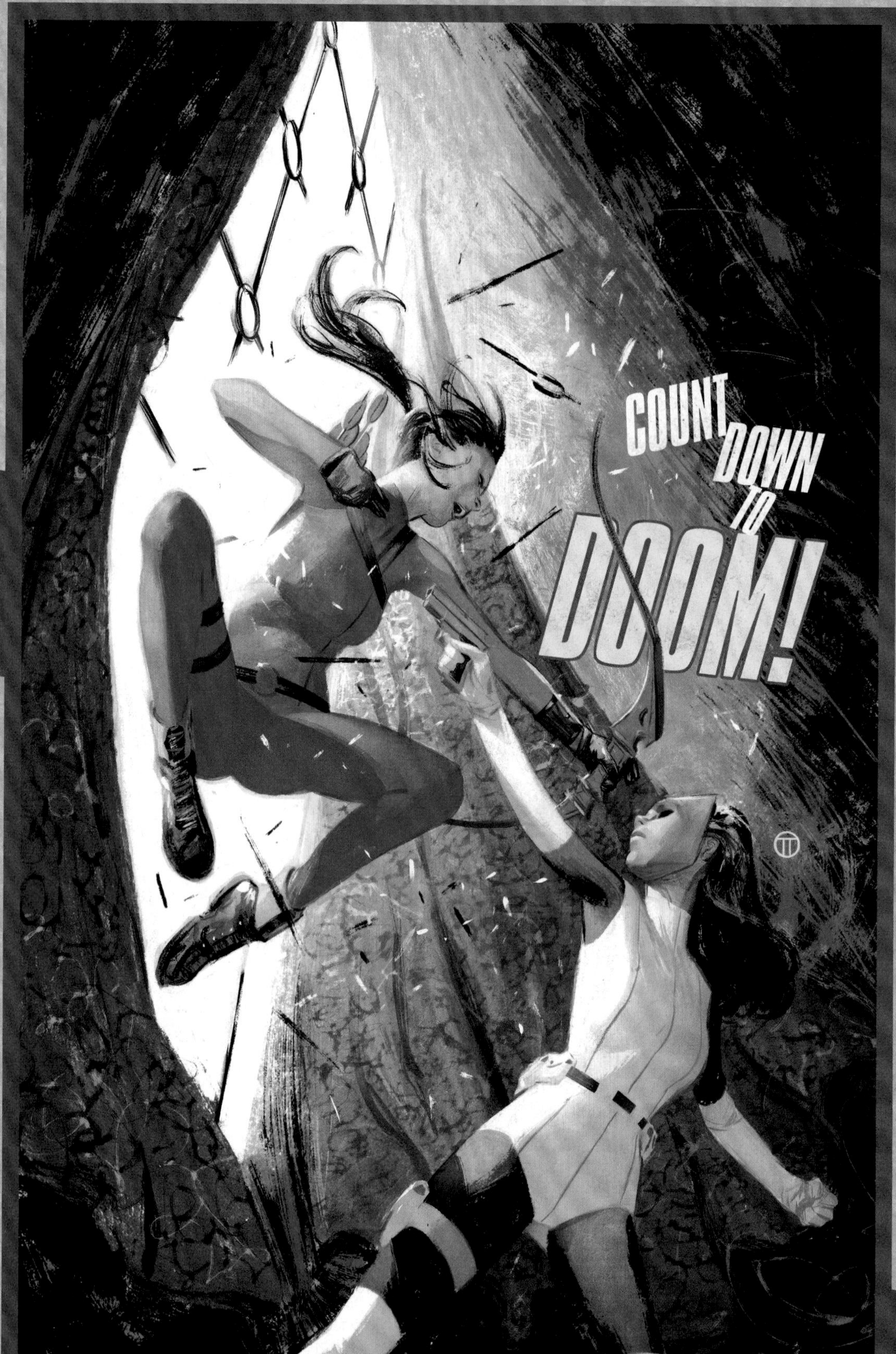
COUNT DOWN TO DOOM!

11

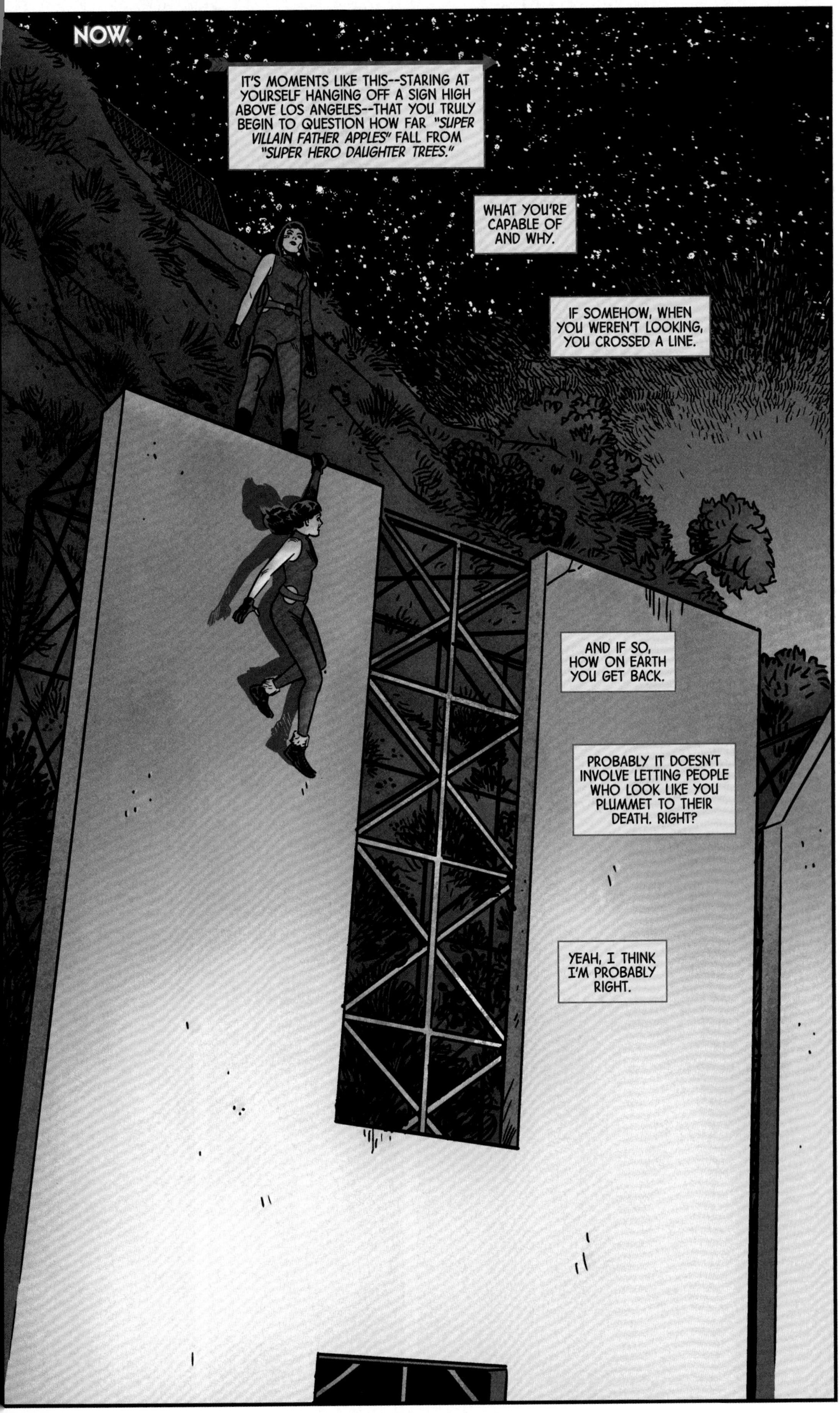
NOW.
IT'S MOMENTS LIKE THIS--STARING AT YOURSELF HANGING OFF A SIGN HIGH ABOVE LOS ANGELES--THAT YOU TRULY BEGIN TO QUESTION HOW FAR "SUPER VILLAIN FATHER APPLES" FALL FROM "SUPER HERO DAUGHTER TREES."
WHAT YOU'RE CAPABLE OF AND WHY.
IF SOMEHOW, WHEN YOU WEREN'T LOOKING, YOU CROSSED A LINE.
AND IF SO, HOW ON EARTH YOU GET BACK.
PROBABLY IT DOESN'T INVOLVE LETTING PEOPLE WHO LOOK LIKE YOU PLUMMET TO THEIR DEATH. RIGHT?
YEAH, I THINK I'M PROBABLY RIGHT.

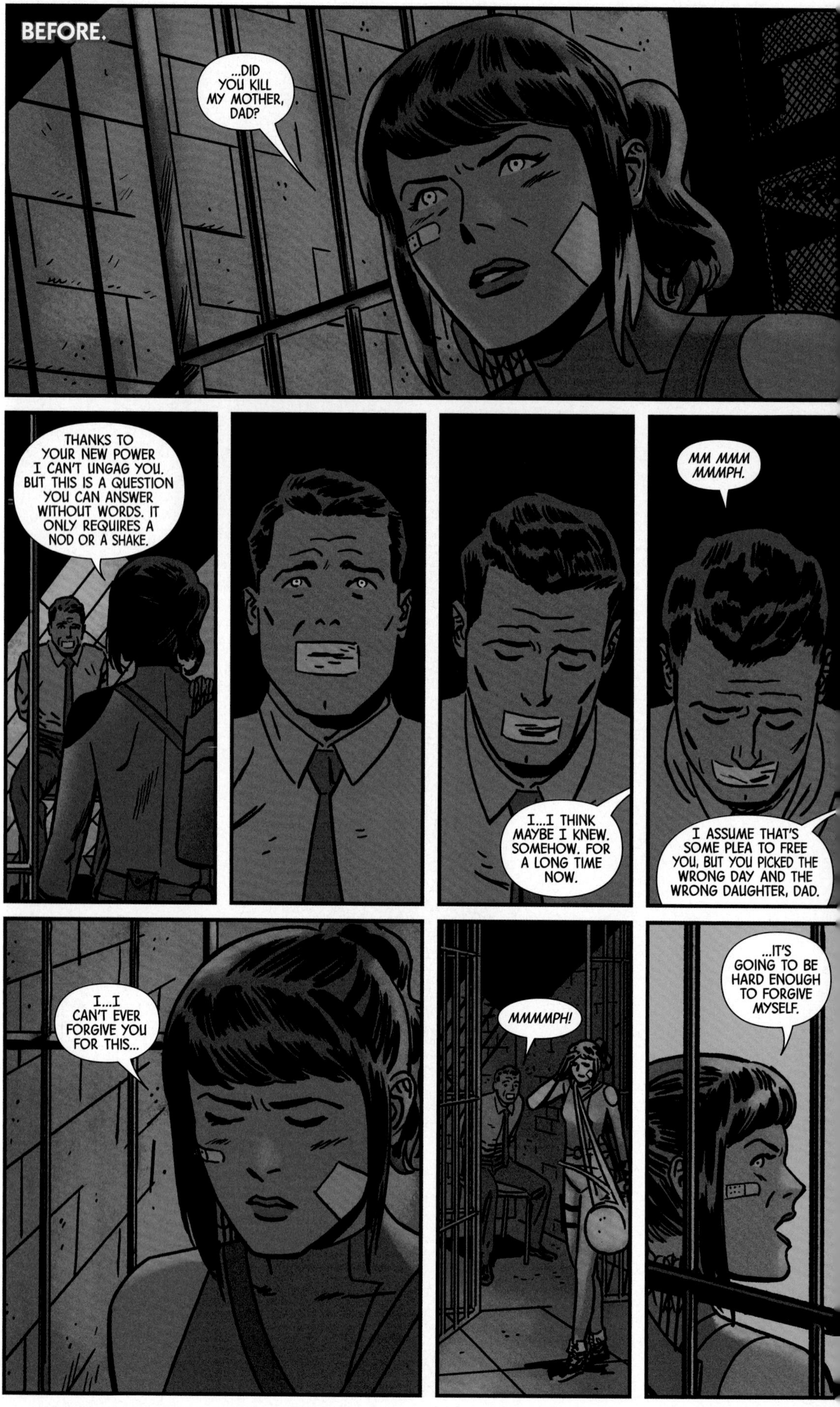
BEFORE.
...DID YOU KILL MY MOTHER, DAD?
THANKS TO YOUR NEW POWER I CAN'T UNGAG YOU. BUT THIS IS A QUESTION YOU CAN ANSWER WITHOUT WORDS. IT ONLY REQUIRES A NOD OR A SHAKE.
I...I THINK MAYBE I KNEW. SOMEHOW. FOR A LONG TIME NOW.
MM MMM MMMPH.
I ASSUME THAT'S SOME PLEA TO FREE YOU, BUT YOU PICKED THE WRONG DAY AND THE WRONG DAUGHTER, DAD.
I...I CAN'T EVER FORGIVE YOU FOR THIS...
MMMMPH!
...IT'S GOING TO BE HARD ENOUGH TO FORGIVE MYSELF.

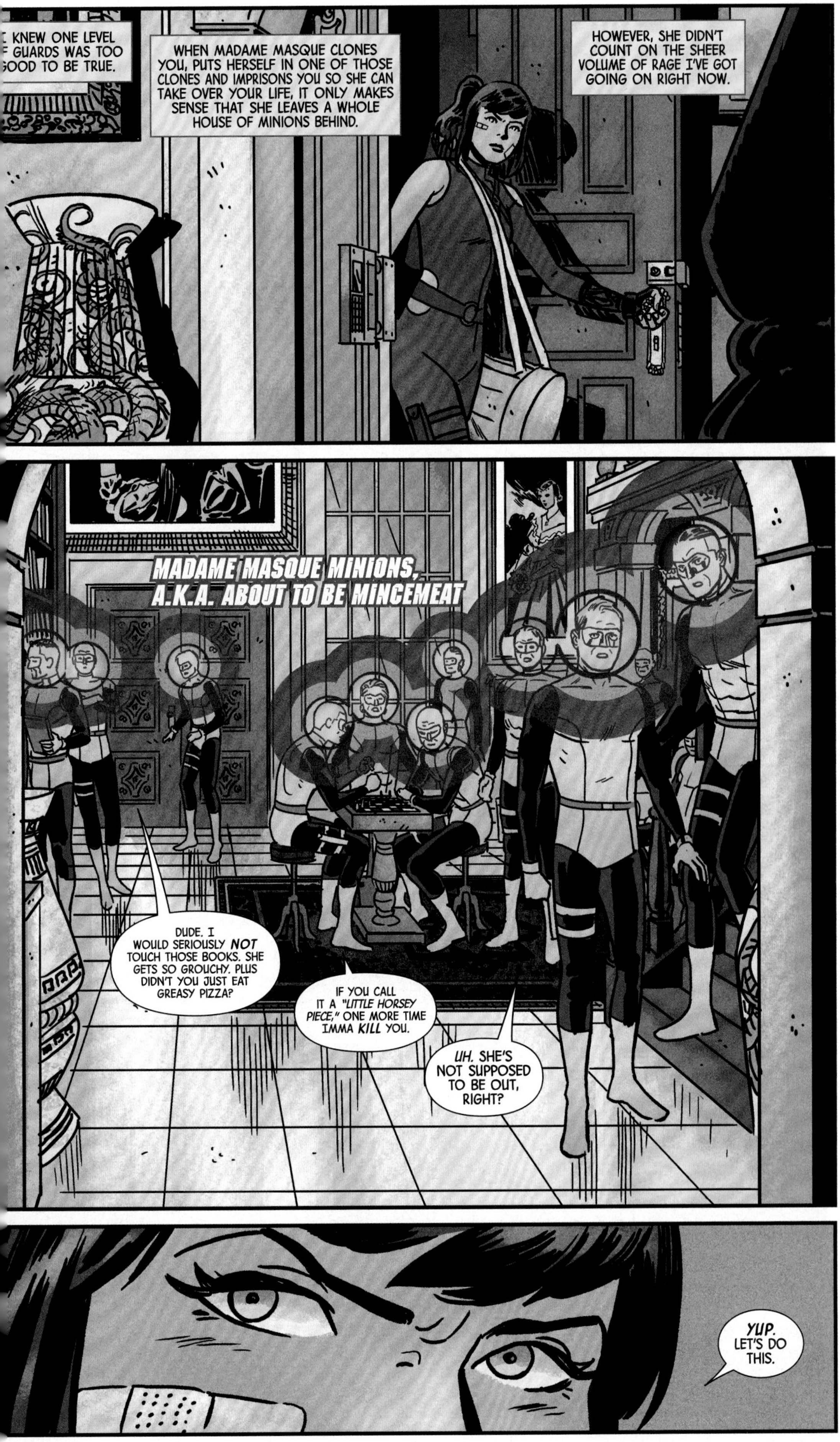
I KNEW ONE LEVEL OF GUARDS WAS TOO GOOD TO BE TRUE.
WHEN MADAME MASQUE CLONES YOU, PUTS HERSELF IN ONE OF THOSE CLONES AND IMPRISONS YOU SO SHE CAN TAKE OVER YOUR LIFE, IT ONLY MAKES SENSE THAT SHE LEAVES A WHOLE HOUSE OF MINIONS BEHIND.
HOWEVER, SHE DIDN'T COUNT ON THE SHEER VOLUME OF RAGE I'VE GOT GOING ON RIGHT NOW.
MADAME MASQUE MINIONS, A.K.A. ABOUT TO BE MINCEMEAT
DUDE. I WOULD SERIOUSLY NOT TOUCH THOSE BOOKS. SHE GETS SO GROUCHY. PLUS DIDN'T YOU JUST EAT GREASY PIZZA?
IF YOU CALL IT A "LITTLE HORSEY PIECE," ONE MORE TIME IMMA KILL YOU.
UH. SHE'S NOT SUPPOSED TO BE OUT, RIGHT?
YUP. LET'S DO THIS.

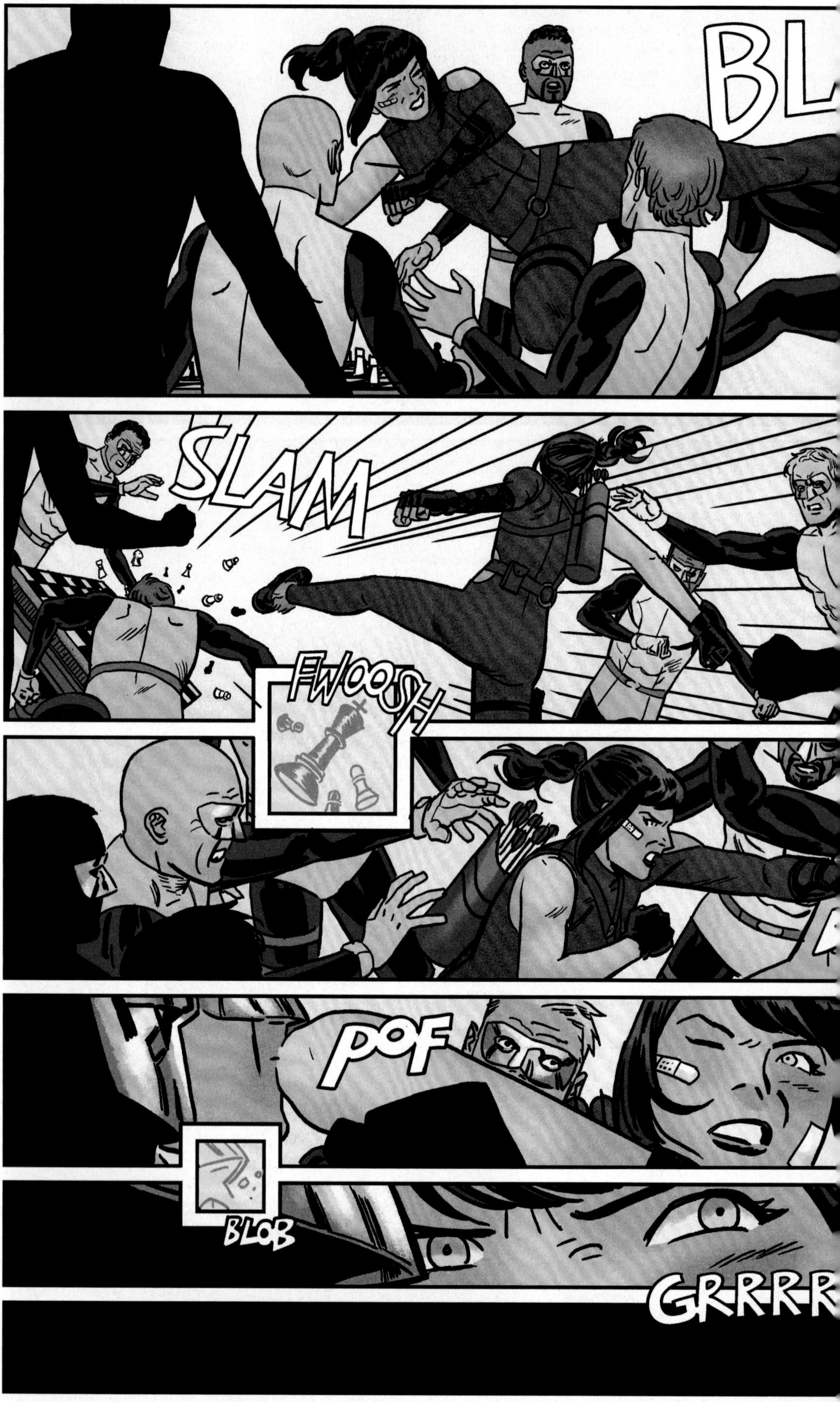
BL
SLAM
FWOOSH
POF
BLOB
GRRRR

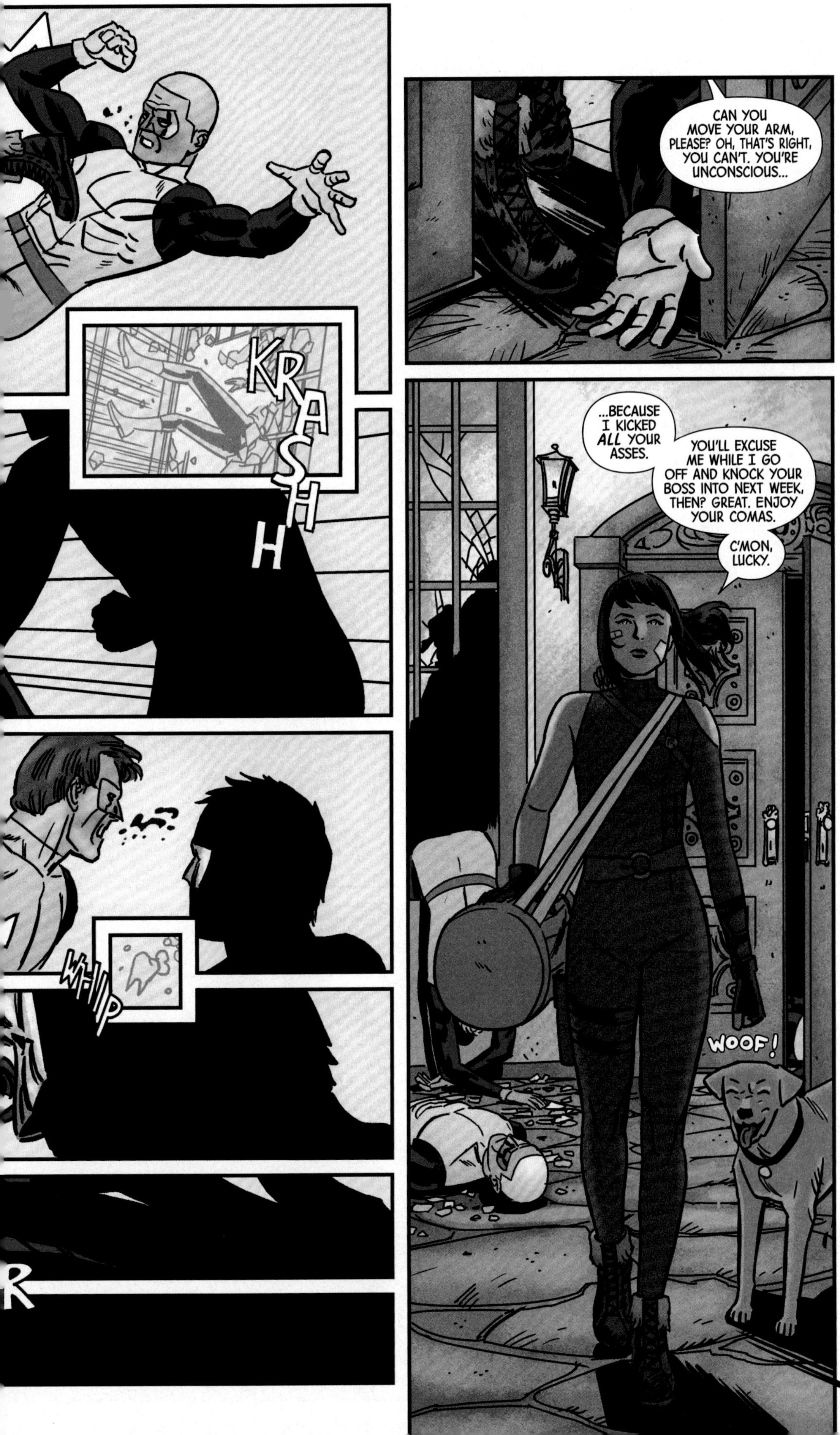
KRASHH
WHIP
CAN YOU MOVE YOUR ARM, PLEASE? OH, THAT'S RIGHT, YOU CAN'T. YOU'RE UNCONSCIOUS...
...BECAUSE I KICKED ALL YOUR ASSES.
YOU'LL EXCUSE ME WHILE I GO OFF AND KNOCK YOUR BOSS INTO NEXT WEEK, THEN? GREAT. ENJOY YOUR COMAS.
C'MON, LUCKY.
WOOF!

HOLLYWOOD.
STILL BEFORE, BUT LATER.

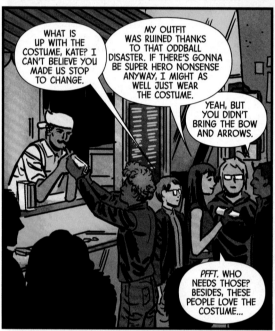

WHAT IS UP WITH THE COSTUME, KATE? I CAN'T BELIEVE YOU MADE US STOP TO CHANGE.

MY OUTFIT WAS RUINED THANKS TO THAT ODDBALL DISASTER. IF THERE'S GONNA BE SUPER HERO NONSENSE ANYWAY, I MIGHT AS WELL JUST WEAR THE COSTUME.

YEAH, BUT YOU DIDN'T BRING THE BOW AND ARROWS.

PFFT. WHO NEEDS THOSE? BESIDES, THESE PEOPLE LOVE THE COSTUME...

...JUST LOOK AT THEM! THEY'RE EATING IT UP!

HELLO, MY FACE. HAVE SOME VERY SERIOUS BRUISING!

BLAM

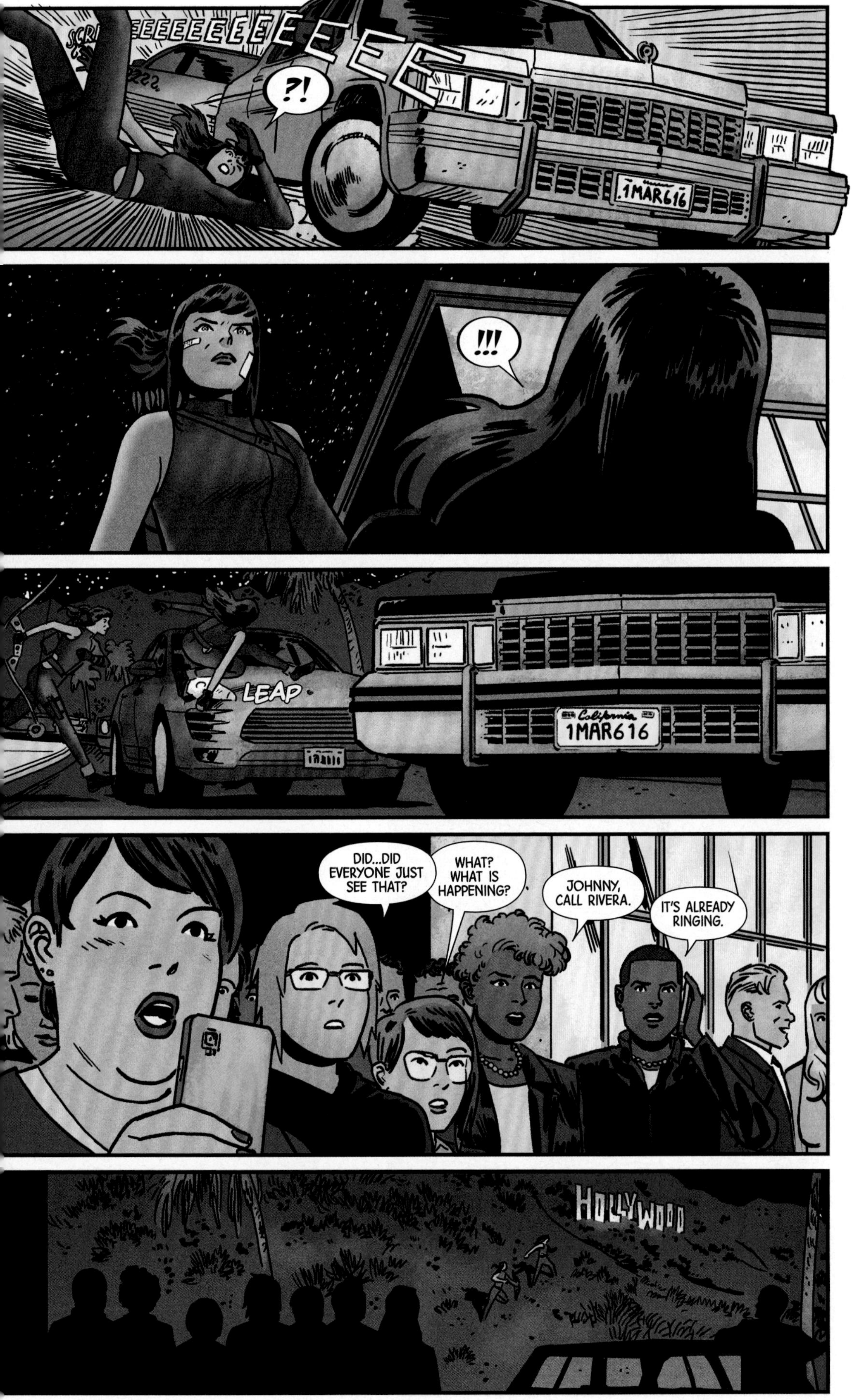
SCREEEEEEEEEEEEEEE
?!
1MAR616
!!!
LEAP
California
1MAR616
DID...DID EVERYONE JUST SEE THAT?
WHAT? WHAT IS HAPPENING?
JOHNNY, CALL RIVERA.
IT'S ALREADY RINGING.
HOLLYWOOD

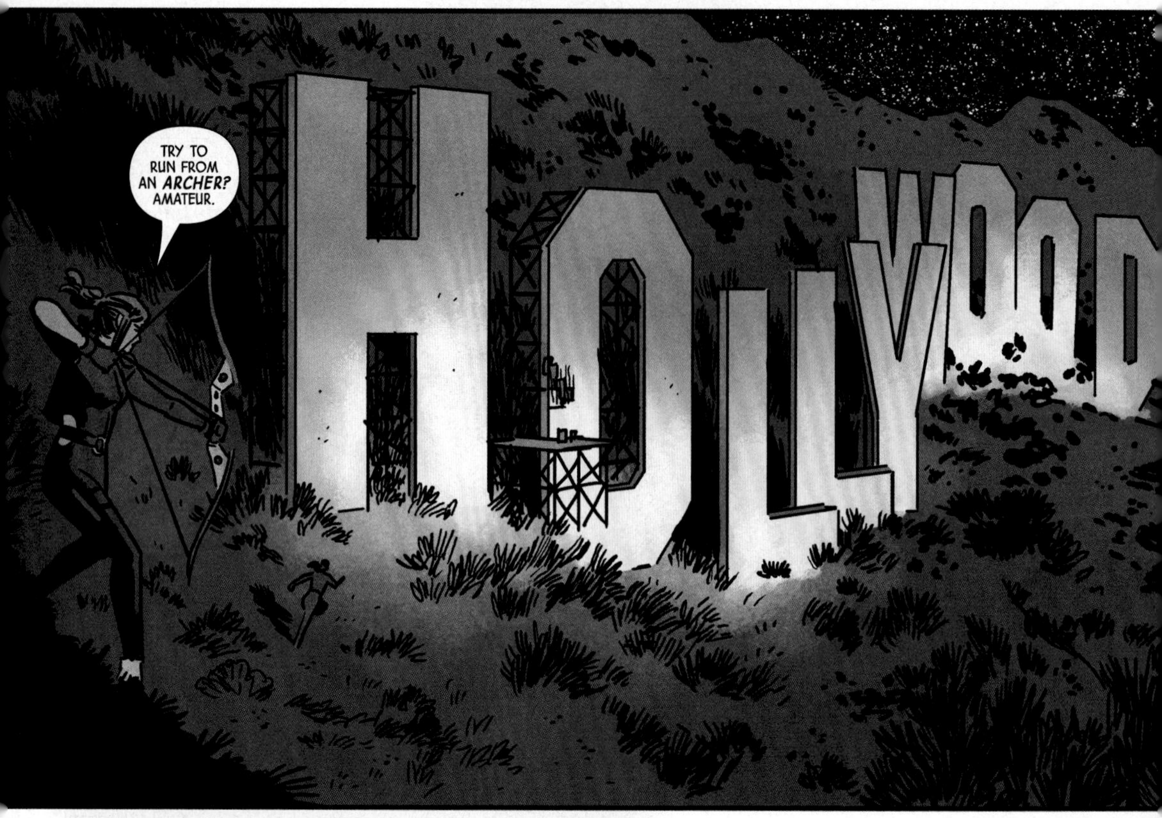
TRY TO RUN FROM AN ARCHER? AMATEUR.

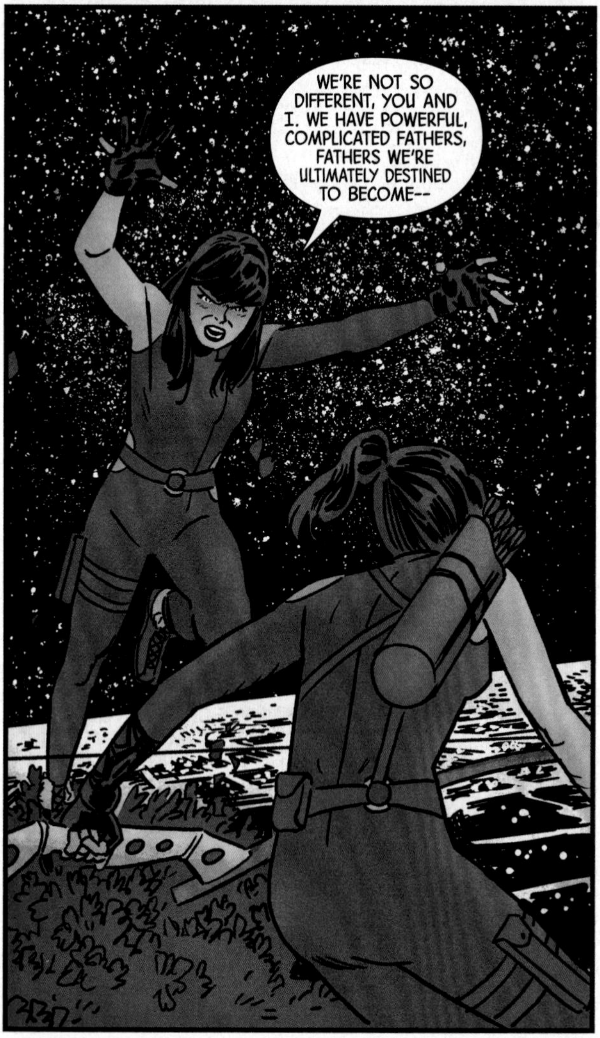
WE'RE NOT SO DIFFERENT, YOU AND I. WE HAVE POWERFUL, COMPLICATED FATHERS, FATHERS WE'RE ULTIMATELY DESTINED TO BECOME--

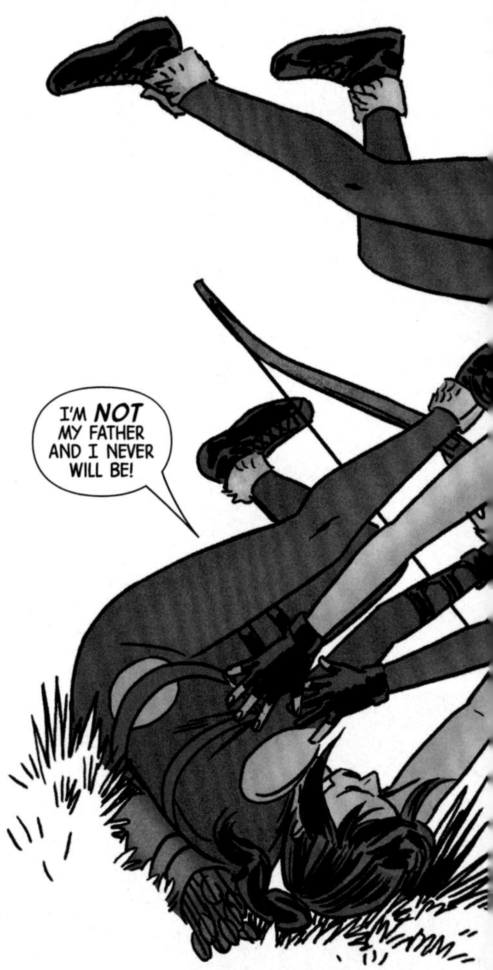
I'M NOT MY FATHER AND I NEVER WILL BE!

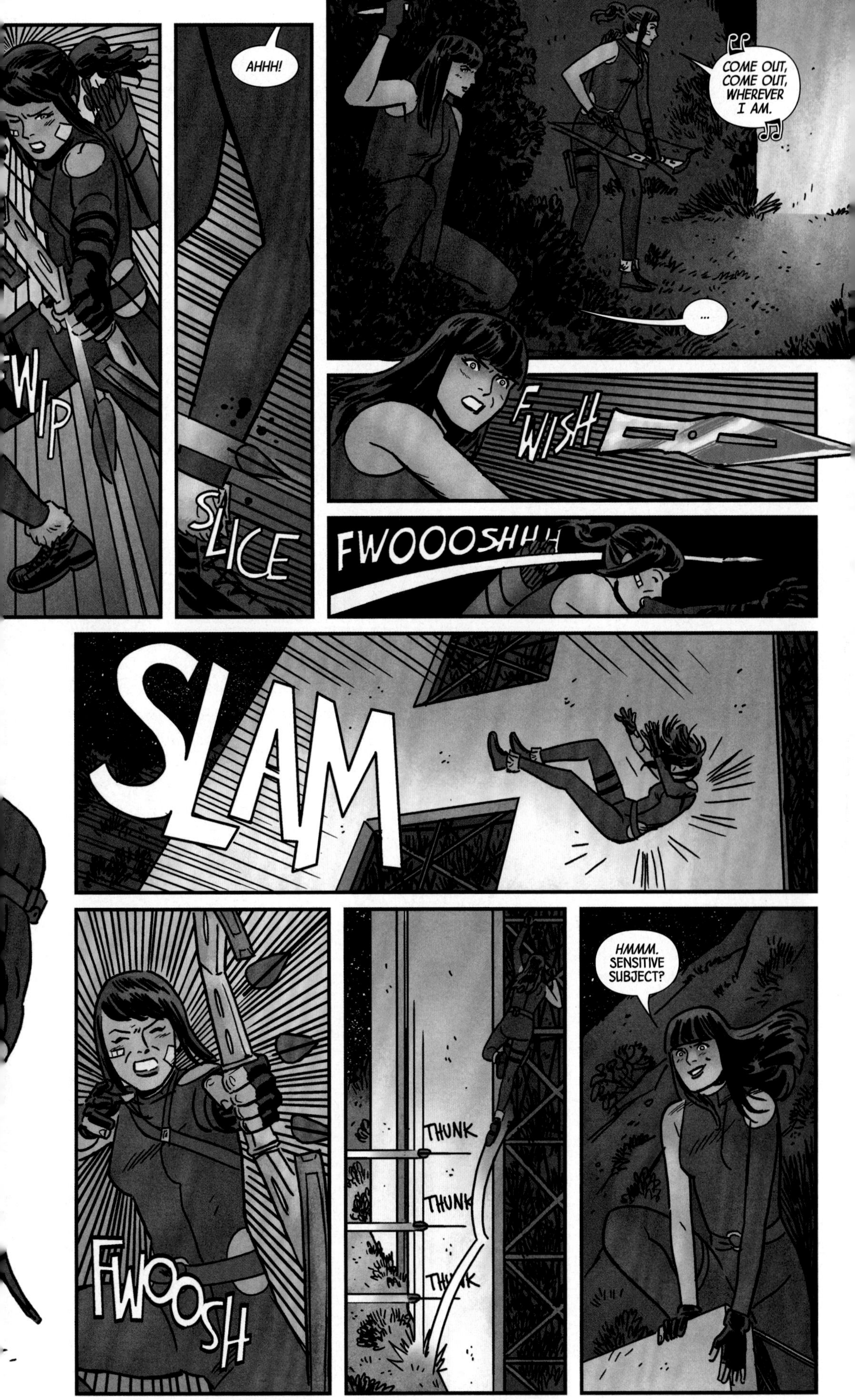

WIP
AHHH!
SLICE
COME OUT, COME OUT, WHEREVER I AM.
...
FWISH
FWOOOSHHH
SLAM
FWOOSH
THUNK
THUNK
THUNK
HMMM. SENSITIVE SUBJECT?

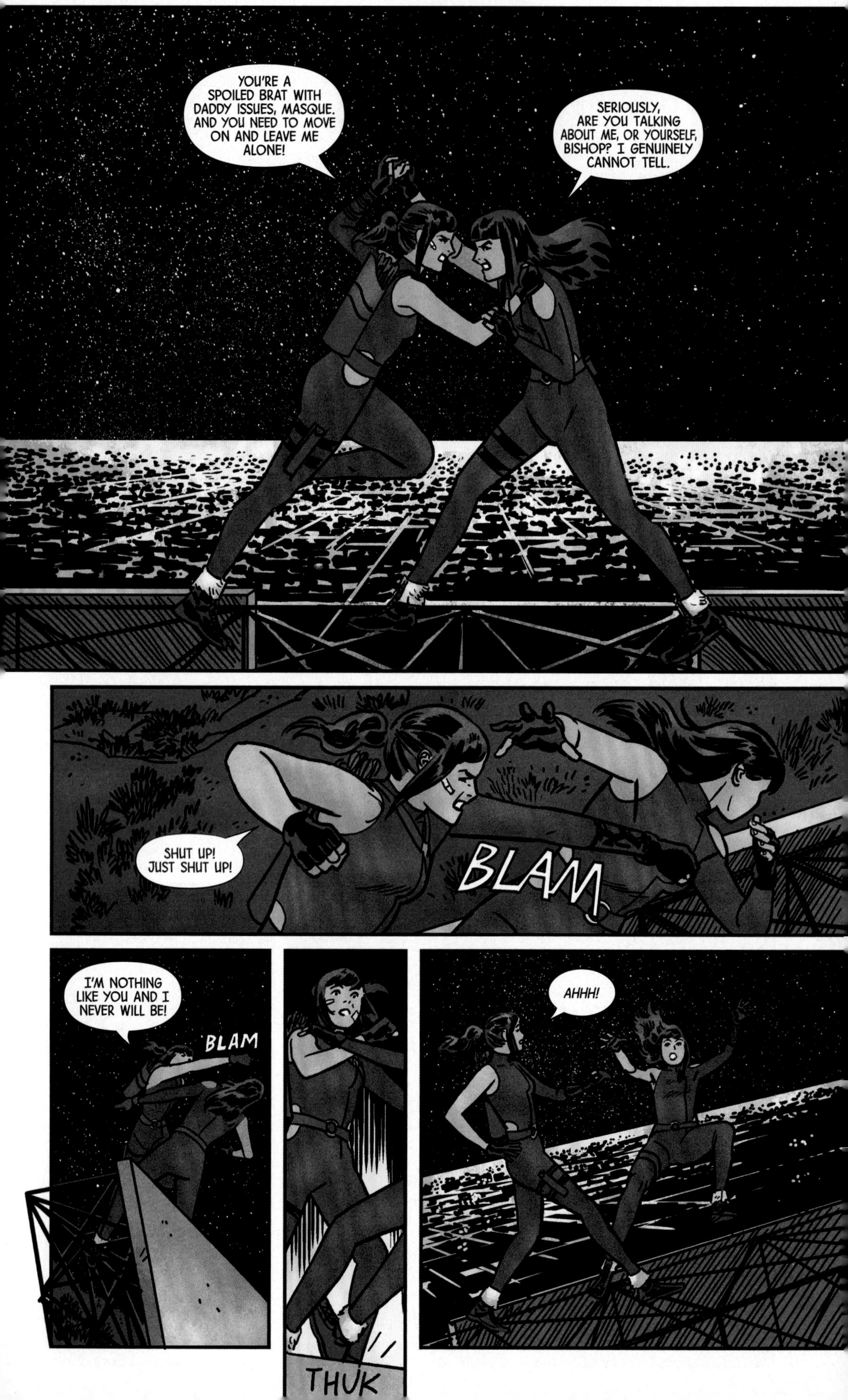
YOU'RE A SPOILED BRAT WITH DADDY ISSUES, MASQUE. AND YOU NEED TO MOVE ON AND LEAVE ME ALONE!
SERIOUSLY, ARE YOU TALKING ABOUT ME, OR YOURSELF, BISHOP? I GENUINELY CANNOT TELL.
SHUT UP! JUST SHUT UP!
BLAM
I'M NOTHING LIKE YOU AND I NEVER WILL BE!
BLAM
THUK
AHHH!

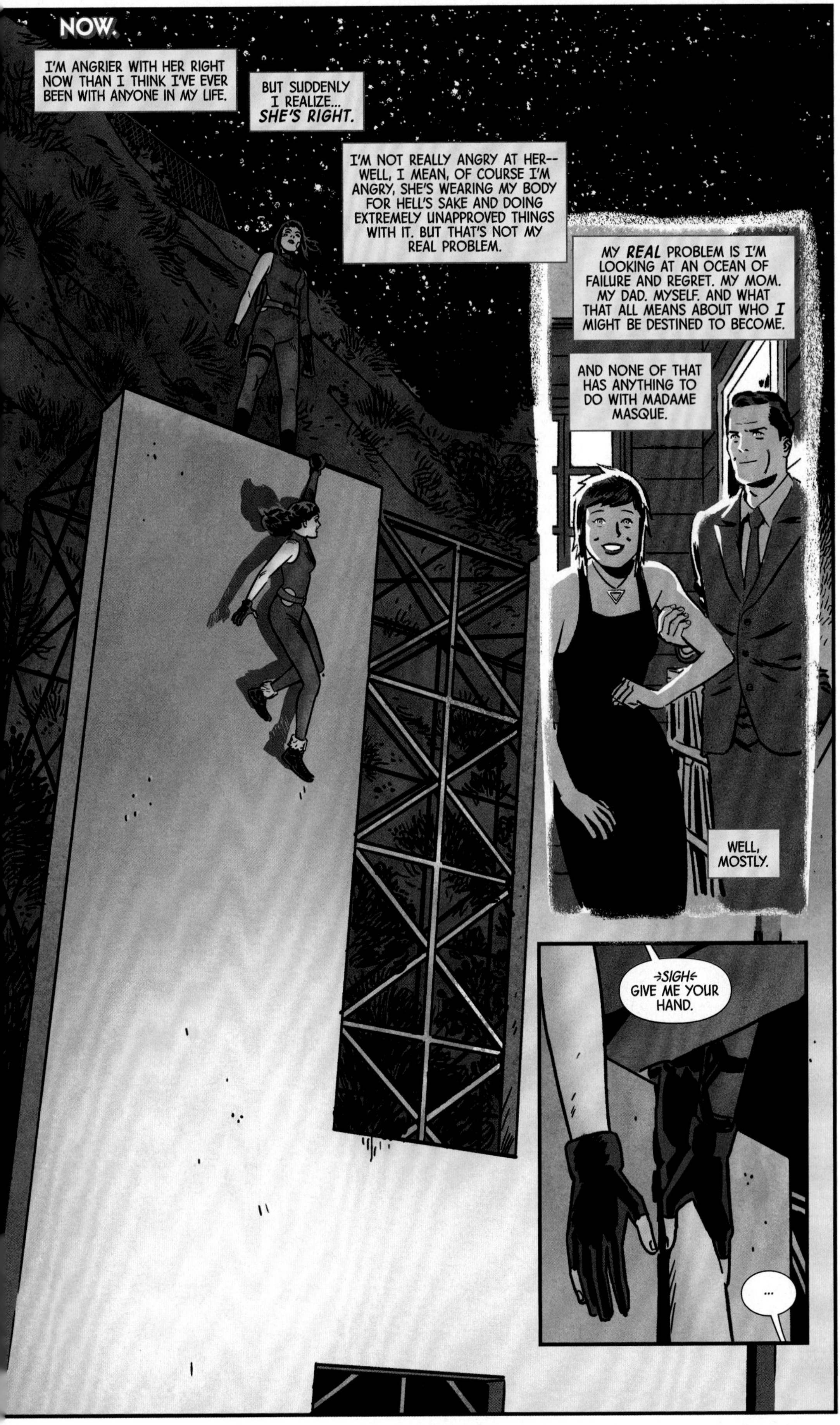

NOW.
I'M ANGRIER WITH HER RIGHT NOW THAN I THINK I'VE EVER BEEN WITH ANYONE IN MY LIFE.
BUT SUDDENLY I REALIZE... SHE'S RIGHT.
I'M NOT REALLY ANGRY AT HER-- WELL, I MEAN, OF COURSE I'M ANGRY, SHE'S WEARING MY BODY FOR HELL'S SAKE AND DOING EXTREMELY UNAPPROVED THINGS WITH IT. BUT THAT'S NOT MY REAL PROBLEM.
MY REAL PROBLEM IS I'M LOOKING AT AN OCEAN OF FAILURE AND REGRET. MY MOM. MY DAD. MYSELF. AND WHAT THAT ALL MEANS ABOUT WHO I MIGHT BE DESTINED TO BECOME.
AND NONE OF THAT HAS ANYTHING TO DO WITH MADAME MASQUE.
WELL, MOSTLY.
>SIGH< GIVE ME YOUR HAND.
...

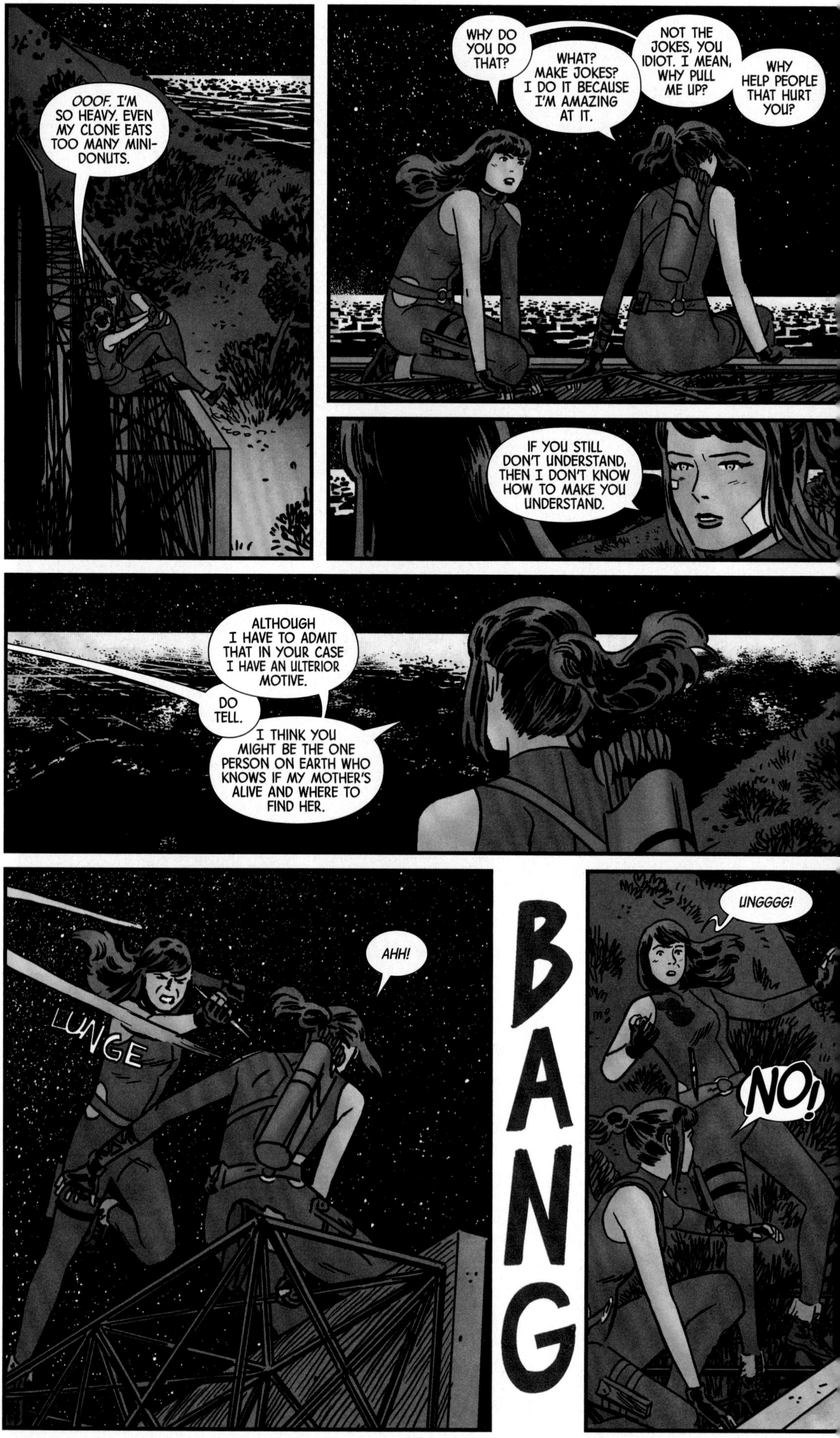
OOOF. I'M SO HEAVY. EVEN MY CLONE EATS TOO MANY MINI-DONUTS.
WHY DO YOU DO THAT?
WHAT? MAKE JOKES? I DO IT BECAUSE I'M AMAZING AT IT.
NOT THE JOKES, YOU IDIOT. I MEAN, WHY PULL ME UP?
WHY HELP PEOPLE THAT HURT YOU?
IF YOU STILL DON'T UNDERSTAND, THEN I DON'T KNOW HOW TO MAKE YOU UNDERSTAND.
ALTHOUGH I HAVE TO ADMIT THAT IN YOUR CASE I HAVE AN ULTERIOR MOTIVE.
DO TELL.
I THINK YOU MIGHT BE THE ONE PERSON ON EARTH WHO KNOWS IF MY MOTHER'S ALIVE AND WHERE TO FIND HER.
LUNGE
AHH!
BANG
UNGGGG!
NO!

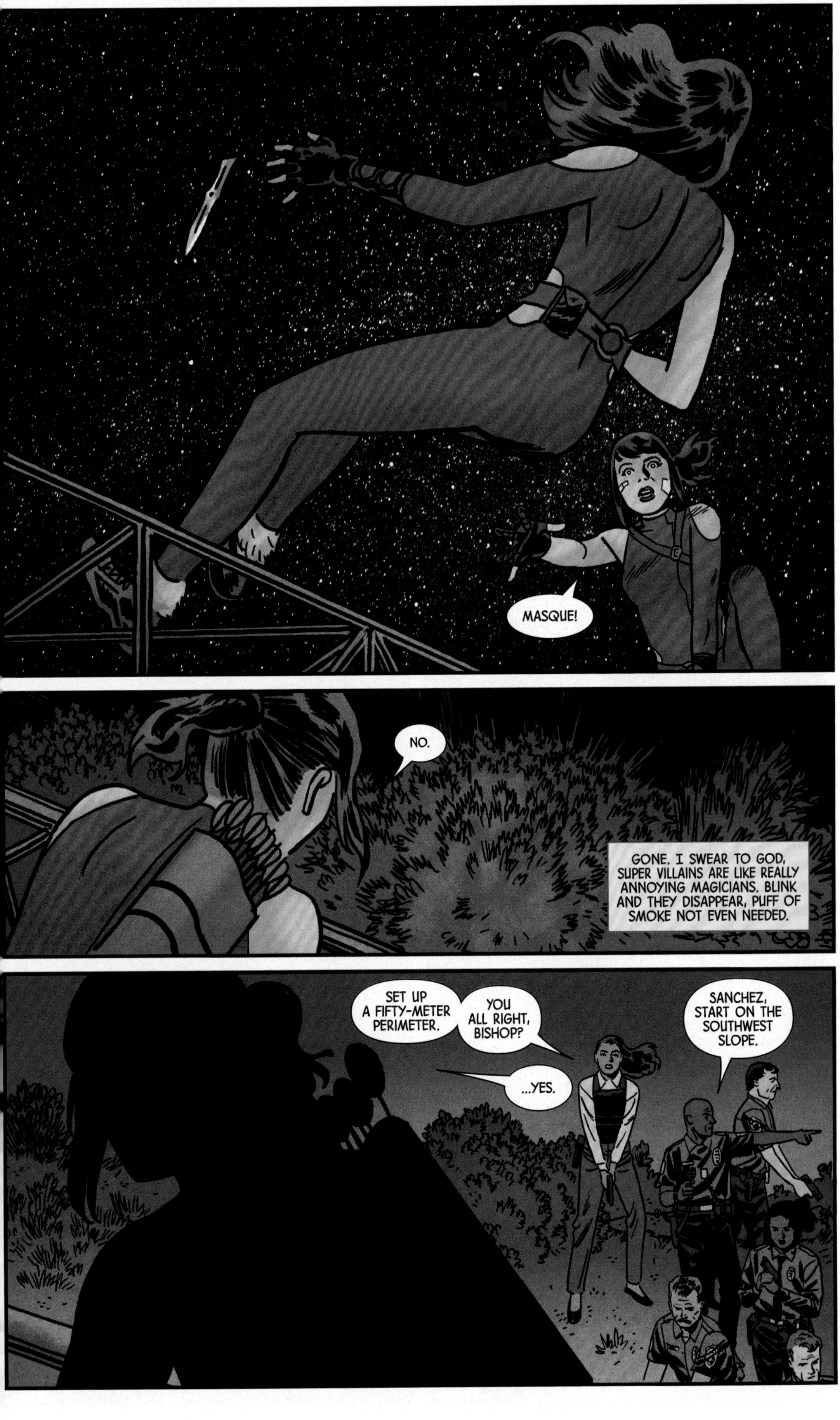
MASQUE!
NO.
GONE. I SWEAR TO GOD, SUPER VILLAINS ARE LIKE REALLY ANNOYING MAGICIANS. BLINK AND THEY DISAPPEAR, PUFF OF SMOKE NOT EVEN NEEDED.
SET UP A FIFTY-METER PERIMETER.
YOU ALL RIGHT, BISHOP?
...YES.
SANCHEZ, START ON THE SOUTHWEST SLOPE.

WHAT THE HELL IS GOING ON HERE, BISHOP?

IT'S A SUPER VILLAIN CALLED MADAME MASQUE. SHE'S PUT HERSELF IN A CLONE OF MY BODY. THINKS SHE CAN GET SUPER-POWERS THAT WAY.

CAN SHE?

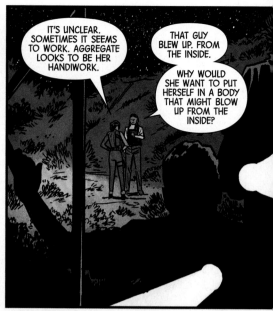

IT'S UNCLEAR. SOMETIMES IT SEEMS TO WORK. AGGREGATE LOOKS TO BE HER HANDIWORK.

THAT GUY BLEW UP. FROM THE INSIDE.

WHY WOULD SHE WANT TO PUT HERSELF IN A BODY THAT MIGHT BLOW UP FROM THE INSIDE?

I'D LIKE AN ANSWER TO THAT MYSELF. IT *MIGHT* BE THAT *SHE* BLEW THAT BODY UP, SOME KIND OF SELF-DESTRUCT SHE INSTALLED?

MAYBE SHE WAS MONITORING HIM AND THOUGHT HE MIGHT GIVE HER UP? I DON'T KNOW.

HEY...HOW DID YOU KNOW WHICH ONE WAS ME?

JUST TOOK A GUESS, GOT LUCKY.

WOOF. THAT'S A DANGEROUS LITTLE GAME.

ARE YOU KIDDING, BISHOP? I'VE NEVER SEEN YOU WITHOUT, LIKE, 75 INJURIES ON YOUR FACE...PRETTY EASY TO TELL YOU TWO APART.

HEY NOW.

I'M GONNA GO DOWN THERE AND HELP WITH THE SEARCH.

SHE WON'T BE THERE.

YES, WELL, I LOVE WASTING MY TIME.

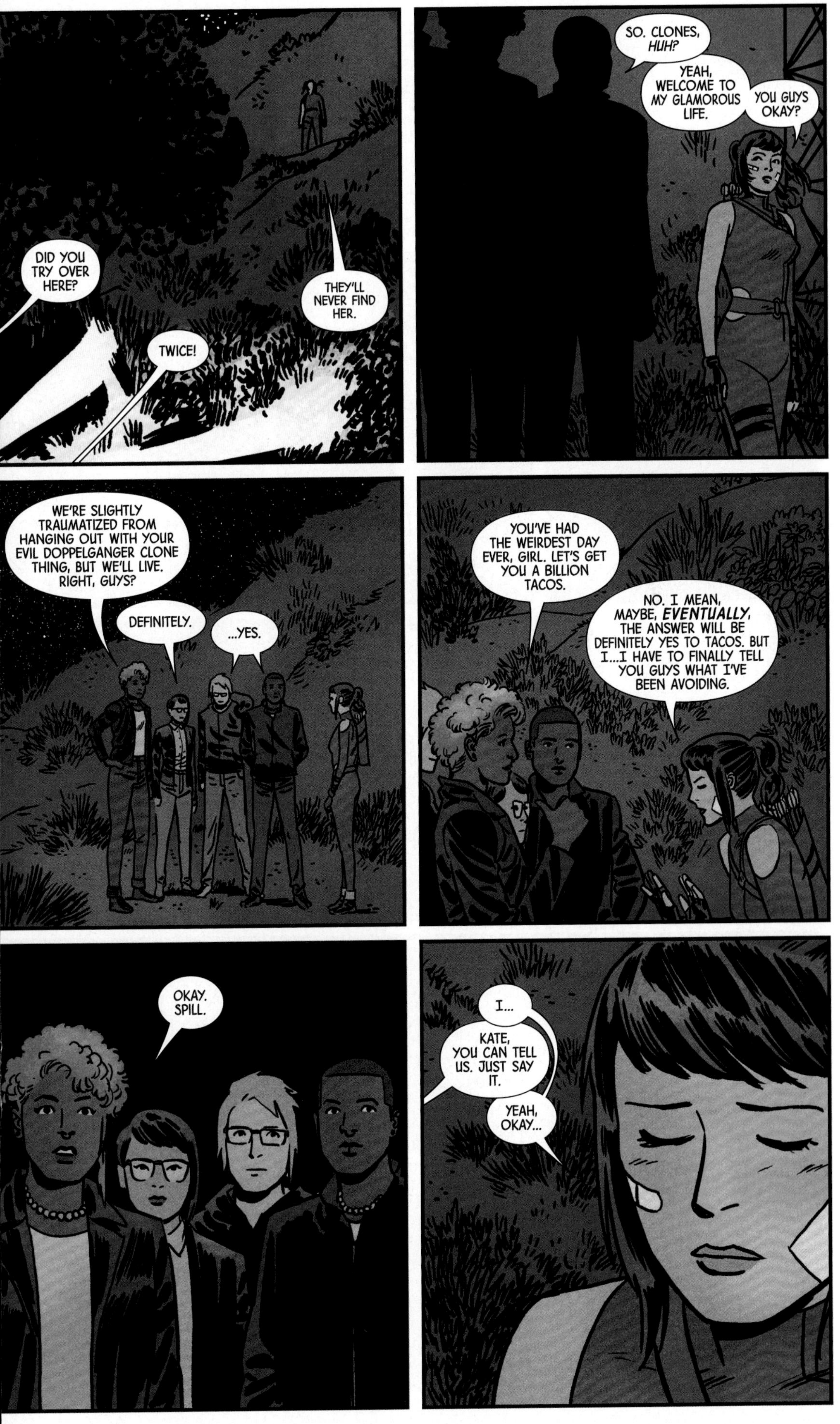
DID YOU TRY OVER HERE?
TWICE!
THEY'LL NEVER FIND HER.
SO. CLONES, *HUH?*
YEAH, WELCOME TO MY GLAMOROUS LIFE.
YOU GUYS OKAY?
WE'RE SLIGHTLY TRAUMATIZED FROM HANGING OUT WITH YOUR EVIL DOPPELGANGER CLONE THING, BUT WE'LL LIVE. RIGHT, GUYS?
DEFINITELY.
...YES.
YOU'VE HAD THE WEIRDEST DAY EVER, GIRL. LET'S GET YOU A BILLION TACOS.
NO. I MEAN, MAYBE, ***EVENTUALLY,*** THE ANSWER WILL BE DEFINITELY YES TO TACOS. BUT I...I HAVE TO FINALLY TELL YOU GUYS WHAT I'VE BEEN AVOIDING.
OKAY. SPILL.
I...
KATE, YOU CAN TELL US. JUST SAY IT.
YEAH, OKAY...

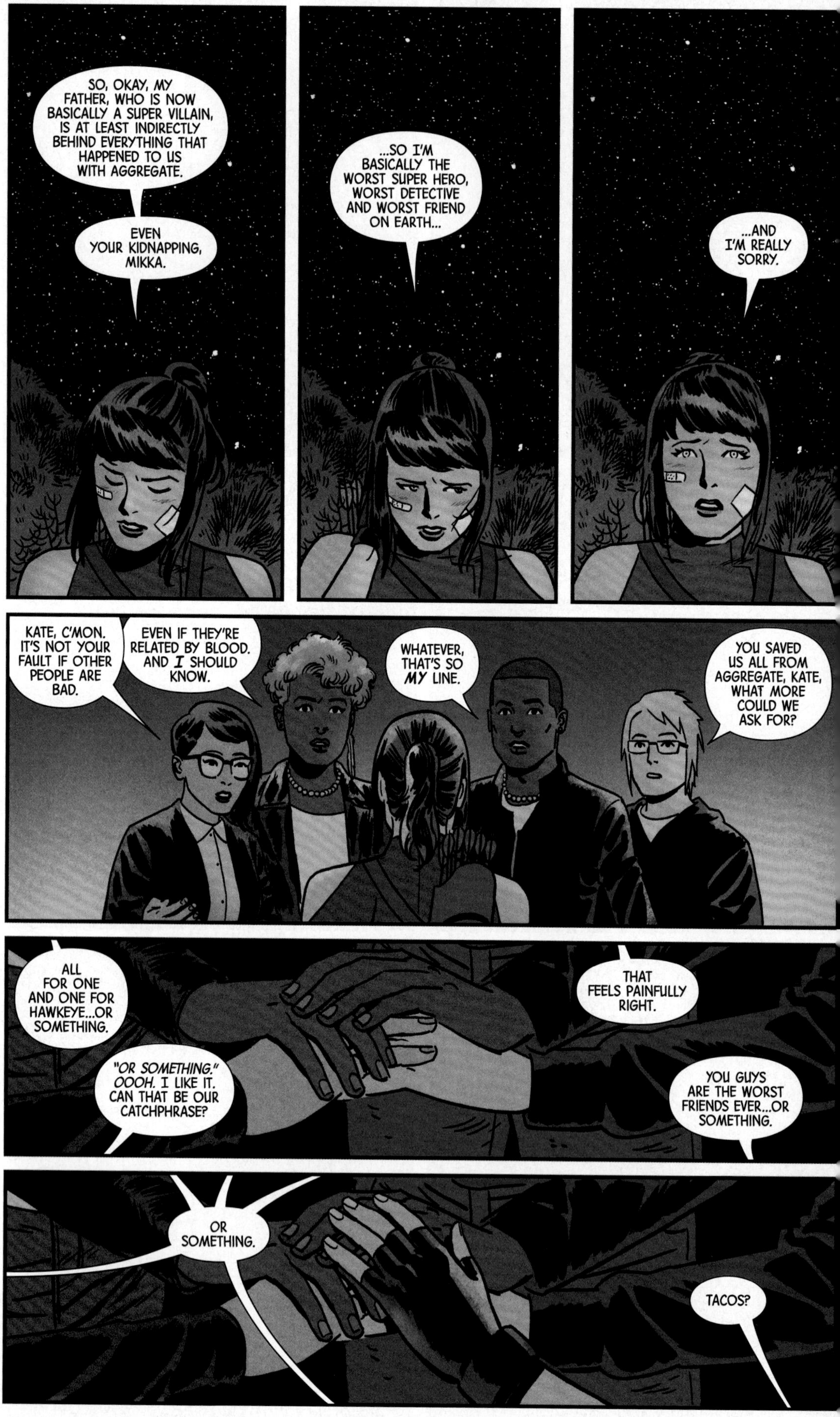
SO, OKAY, MY FATHER, WHO IS NOW BASICALLY A SUPER VILLAIN, IS AT LEAST INDIRECTLY BEHIND EVERYTHING THAT HAPPENED TO US WITH AGGREGATE.
EVEN YOUR KIDNAPPING, MIKKA.
...SO I'M BASICALLY THE WORST SUPER HERO, WORST DETECTIVE AND WORST FRIEND ON EARTH...
...AND I'M REALLY SORRY.
KATE, C'MON. IT'S NOT YOUR FAULT IF OTHER PEOPLE ARE BAD.
EVEN IF THEY'RE RELATED BY BLOOD. AND *I* SHOULD KNOW.
WHATEVER, THAT'S SO *MY* LINE.
YOU SAVED US ALL FROM AGGREGATE, KATE, WHAT MORE COULD WE ASK FOR?
ALL FOR ONE AND ONE FOR HAWKEYE...OR SOMETHING.
THAT FEELS PAINFULLY RIGHT.
"OR SOMETHING." OOOH. I LIKE IT. CAN THAT BE OUR CATCHPHRASE?
YOU GUYS ARE THE WORST FRIENDS EVER...OR SOMETHING.
OR SOMETHING.
TACOS?

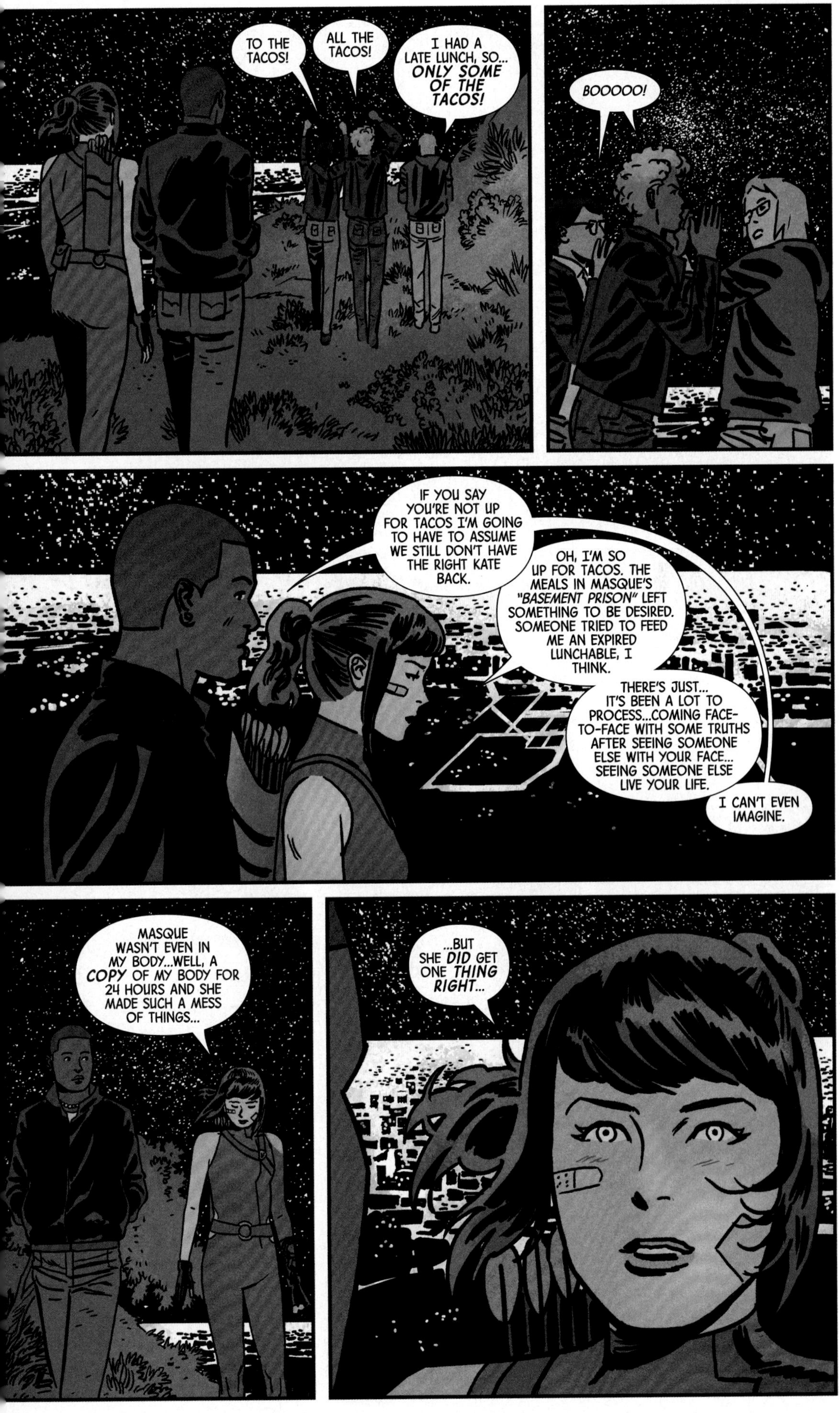
TO THE TACOS!
ALL THE TACOS!
I HAD A LATE LUNCH, SO... ONLY SOME OF THE TACOS!
BOOOOO!
IF YOU SAY YOU'RE NOT UP FOR TACOS I'M GOING TO HAVE TO ASSUME WE STILL DON'T HAVE THE RIGHT KATE BACK.
OH, I'M SO UP FOR TACOS. THE MEALS IN MASQUE'S "BASEMENT PRISON" LEFT SOMETHING TO BE DESIRED. SOMEONE TRIED TO FEED ME AN EXPIRED LUNCHABLE, I THINK.
THERE'S JUST... IT'S BEEN A LOT TO PROCESS...COMING FACE-TO-FACE WITH SOME TRUTHS AFTER SEEING SOMEONE ELSE WITH YOUR FACE... SEEING SOMEONE ELSE LIVE YOUR LIFE.
I CAN'T EVEN IMAGINE.
MASQUE WASN'T EVEN IN MY BODY...WELL, A COPY OF MY BODY FOR 24 HOURS AND SHE MADE SUCH A MESS OF THINGS...
...BUT SHE DID GET ONE THING RIGHT...

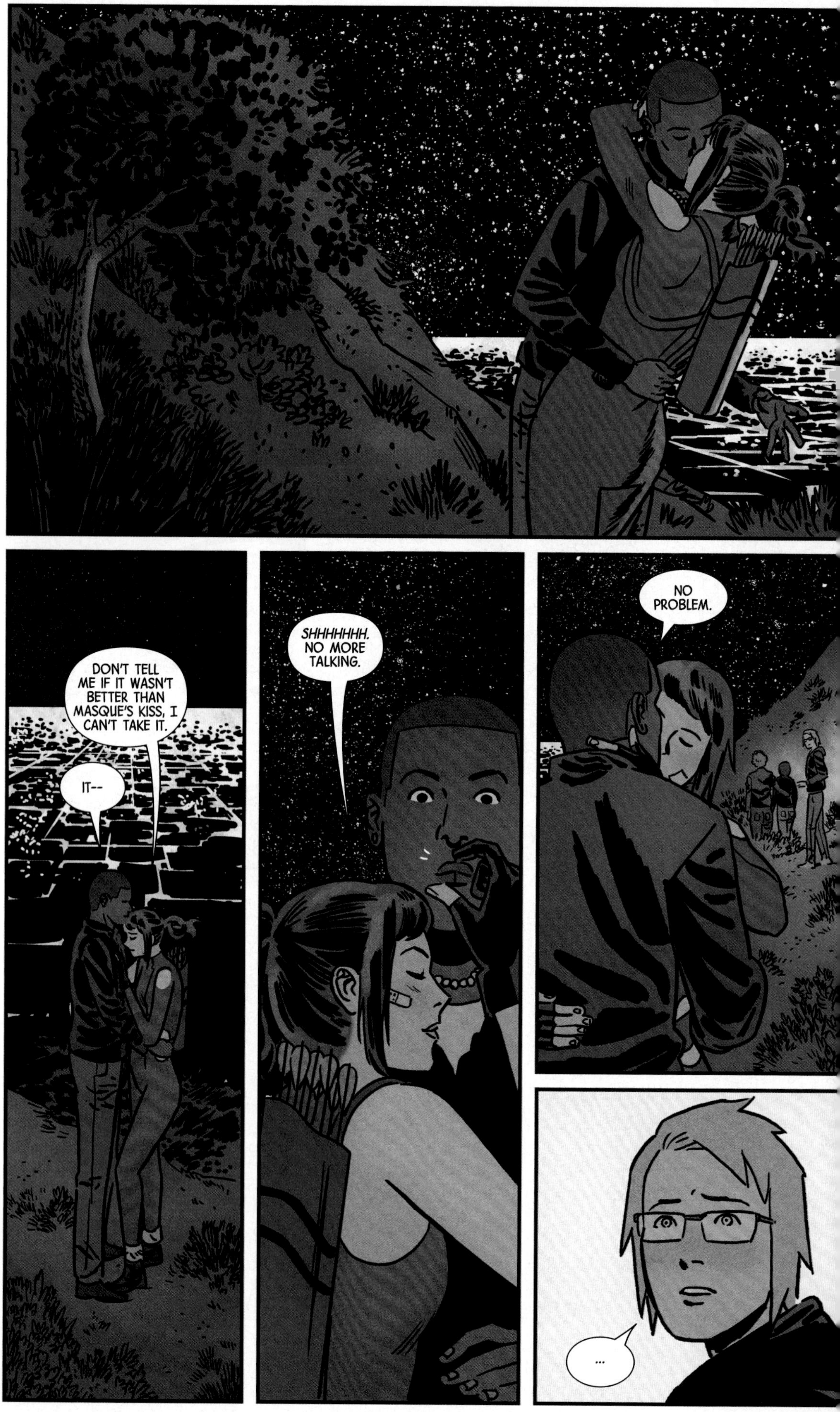
DON'T TELL ME IF IT WASN'T BETTER THAN MASQUE'S KISS, I CAN'T TAKE IT.
IT--
SHHHHHHH. NO MORE TALKING.
NO PROBLEM.
...

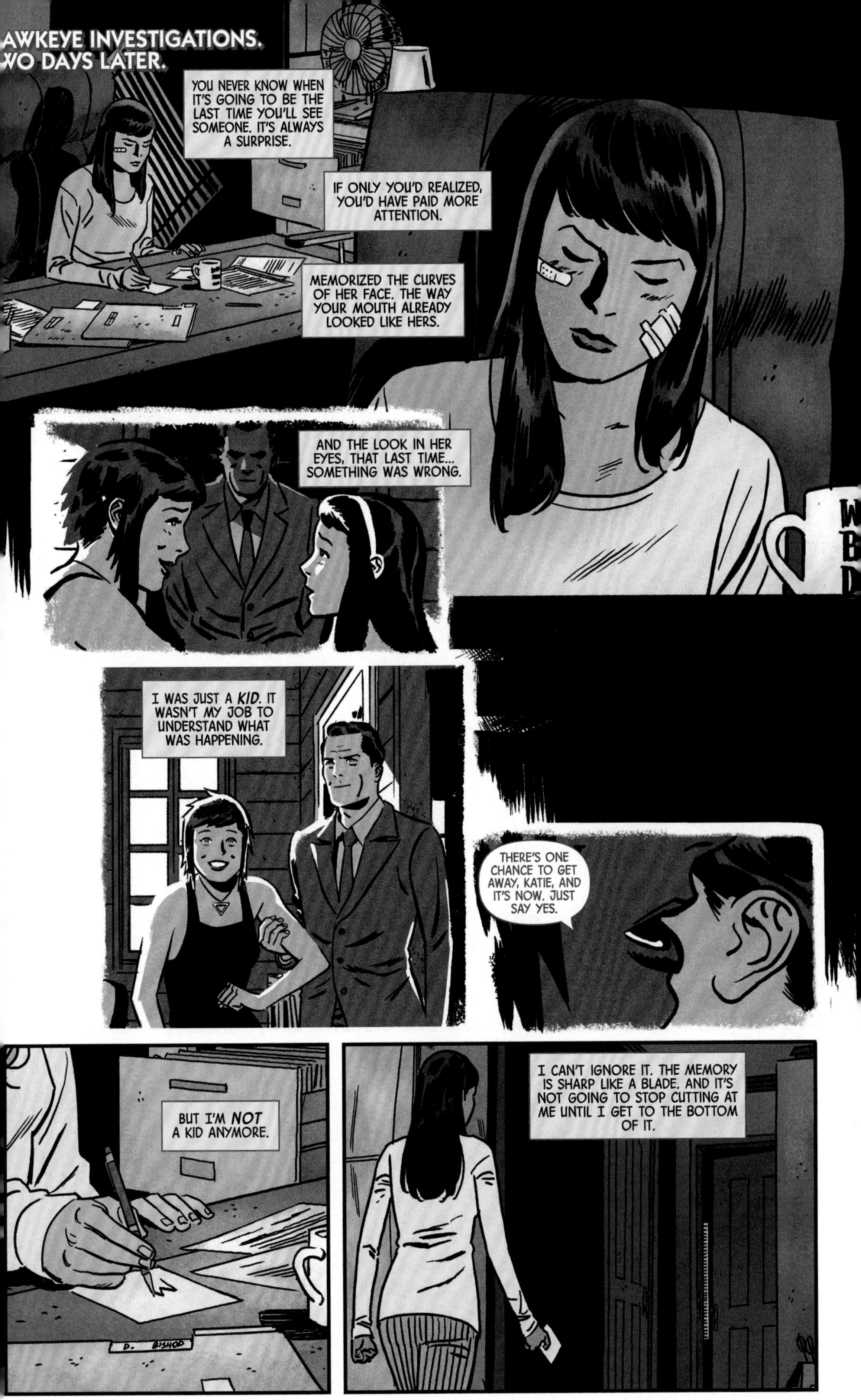
AWKEYE INVESTIGATIONS.
WO DAYS LATER.
YOU NEVER KNOW WHEN IT'S GOING TO BE THE LAST TIME YOU'LL SEE SOMEONE. IT'S ALWAYS A SURPRISE.
IF ONLY YOU'D REALIZED, YOU'D HAVE PAID MORE ATTENTION.
MEMORIZED THE CURVES OF HER FACE. THE WAY YOUR MOUTH ALREADY LOOKED LIKE HERS.
AND THE LOOK IN HER EYES, THAT LAST TIME... SOMETHING WAS WRONG.
I WAS JUST A KID. IT WASN'T MY JOB TO UNDERSTAND WHAT WAS HAPPENING.
THERE'S ONE CHANCE TO GET AWAY, KATIE, AND IT'S NOW. JUST SAY YES.
BUT I'M NOT A KID ANYMORE.
D. BISHOP
I CAN'T IGNORE IT. THE MEMORY IS SHARP LIKE A BLADE. AND IT'S NOT GOING TO STOP CUTTING AT ME UNTIL I GET TO THE BOTTOM OF IT.

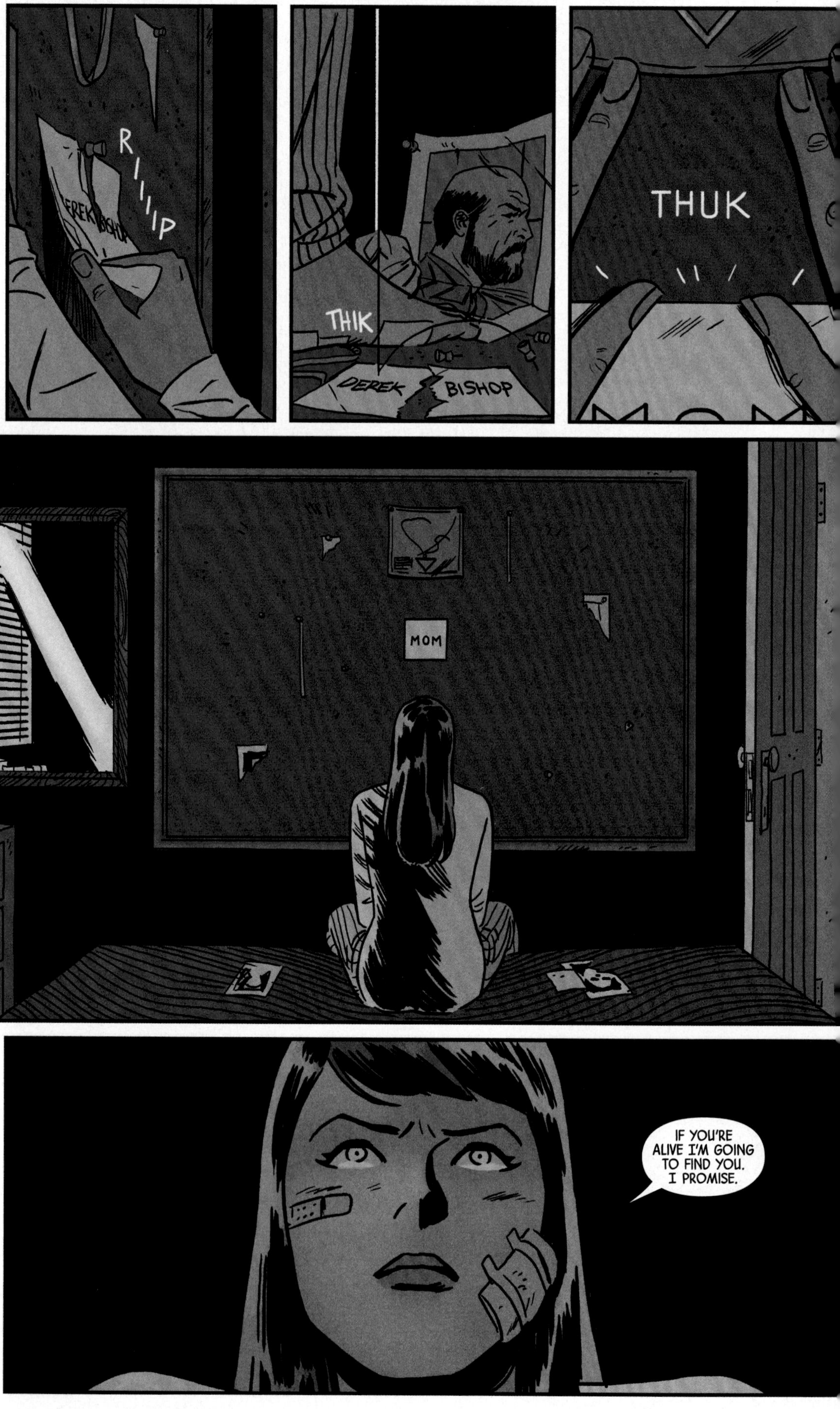

RIIIIP
FREK BISHOP
THIK
DEREK BISHOP
THUK
MOM
IF YOU'RE ALIVE I'M GOING TO FIND YOU. I PROMISE.

hawkeye

HOW TO DRAW HAWKEYE
IN SIX EASY STEPS!

BY CHIP "BOWS AND ARROWS SHOULD BE ILLEGAL" ZDARSKY

Wow! A "sketch variant cover"! I guess you love paying extra for NO art! Well, to prepare you to draw your very own HAWKEYE, here's a fun and informative step-by-step guide!

1

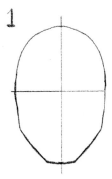

All right! First we start with the outline of the face! Divide into four so you have guides for the next step probably.

2

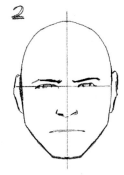

Ah! I was right! Place eyes about halfway up the face, nose halfway of that, and mouth halfway of THAT! Some ears on either side and you've pretty much got a face!

3

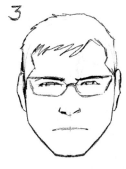

Rough in some hair for Hawkeye and some COOL SHADES. Don't worry too much about accuracy at this stage; you can always refine as you go on.

4

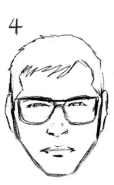

For example: Here I've slimmed the jawline a touch and made their glasses a bit larger. We can start adding details to features here as well!

5

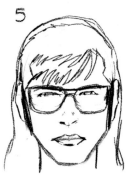

Add more hair here, so it's coming down the sides. You'll need to add the neck at this point so the hair can sit behind it!

6

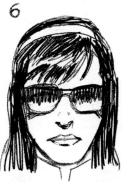

Now to render! At this stage you can choose to—oh. Wait, did ... did I just make HAWKEYE a ... a woman?? D-doctor, am I ... an SJW?? Tell my wife I love

#11 how to draw variant by Chip Zdarsky

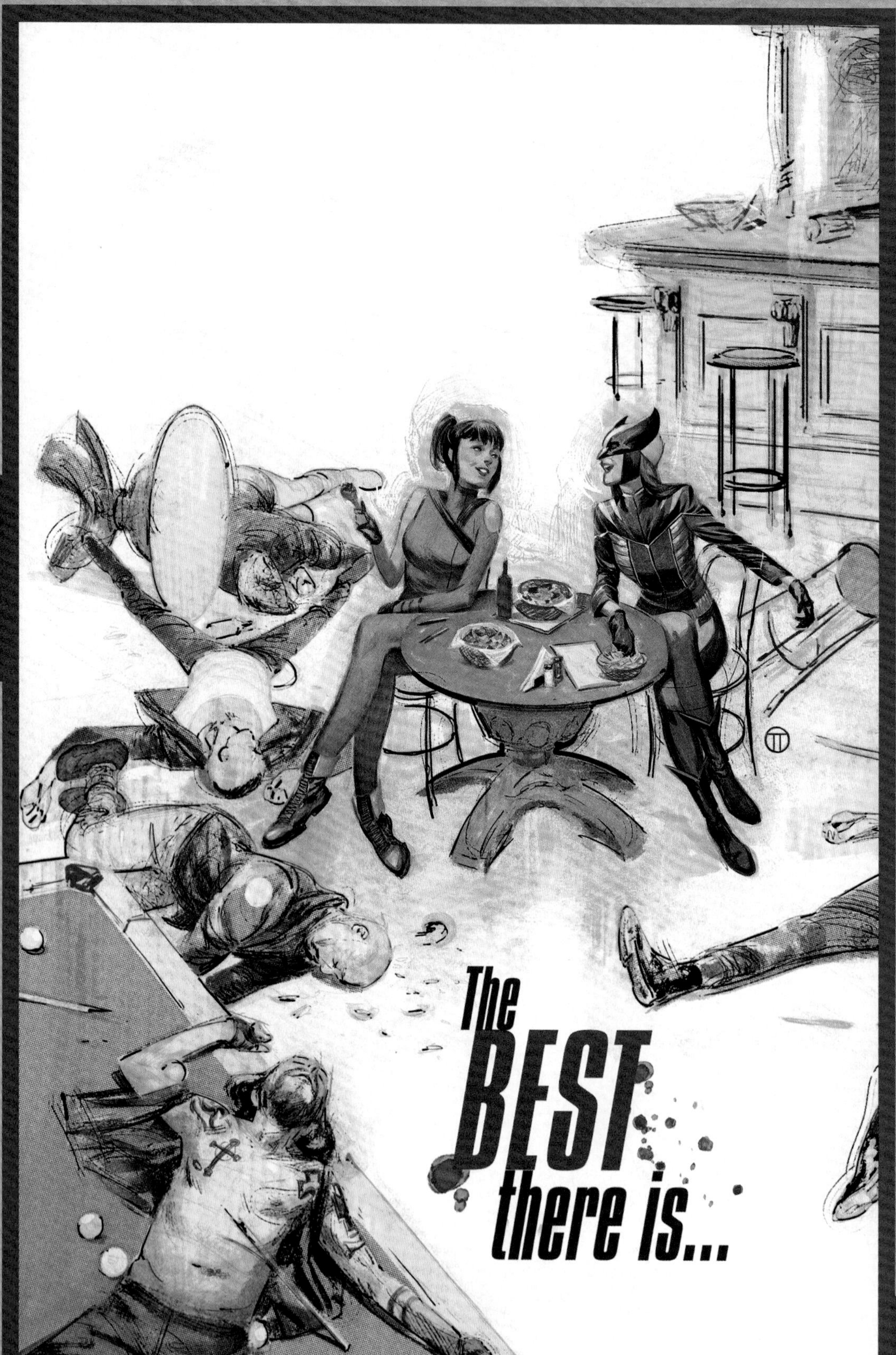
The BEST there is...

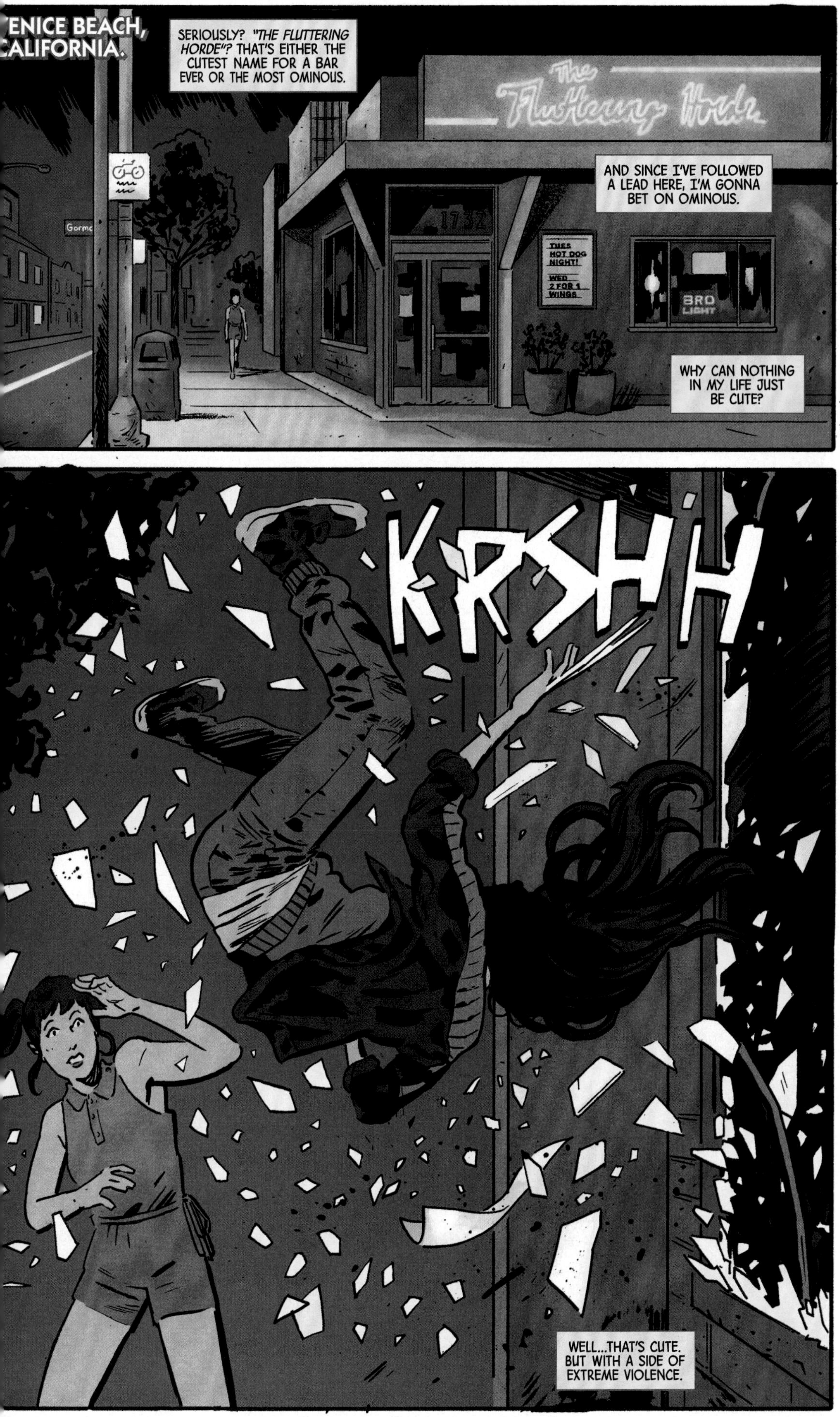
ENICE BEACH, CALIFORNIA.
SERIOUSLY? "THE FLUTTERING HORDE"? THAT'S EITHER THE CUTEST NAME FOR A BAR EVER OR THE MOST OMINOUS.
The Fluttering Horde
Gorma
1732
TUES HOT DOG NIGHT!
WED 2 FOR 1 WINGS
BRO LIGHT
AND SINCE I'VE FOLLOWED A LEAD HERE, I'M GONNA BET ON OMINOUS.
WHY CAN NOTHING IN MY LIFE JUST BE CUTE?
KRSHH
WELL...THAT'S CUTE. BUT WITH A SIDE OF EXTREME VIOLENCE.

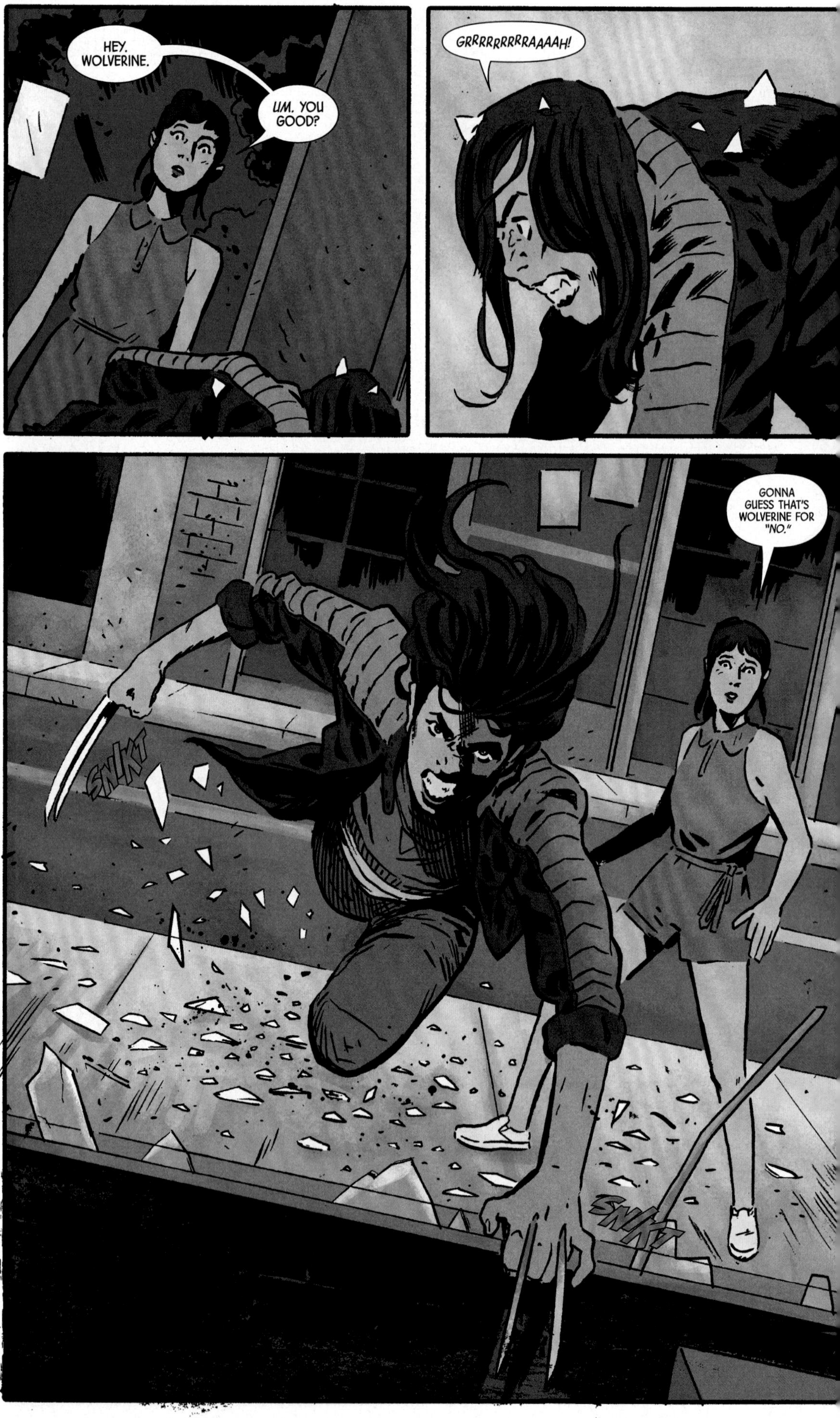
HEY. WOLVERINE.
UM. YOU GOOD?
GRRRRRRRRRAAAAH!
GONNA GUESS THAT'S WOLVERINE FOR "NO."
SNIKT
SNIKT

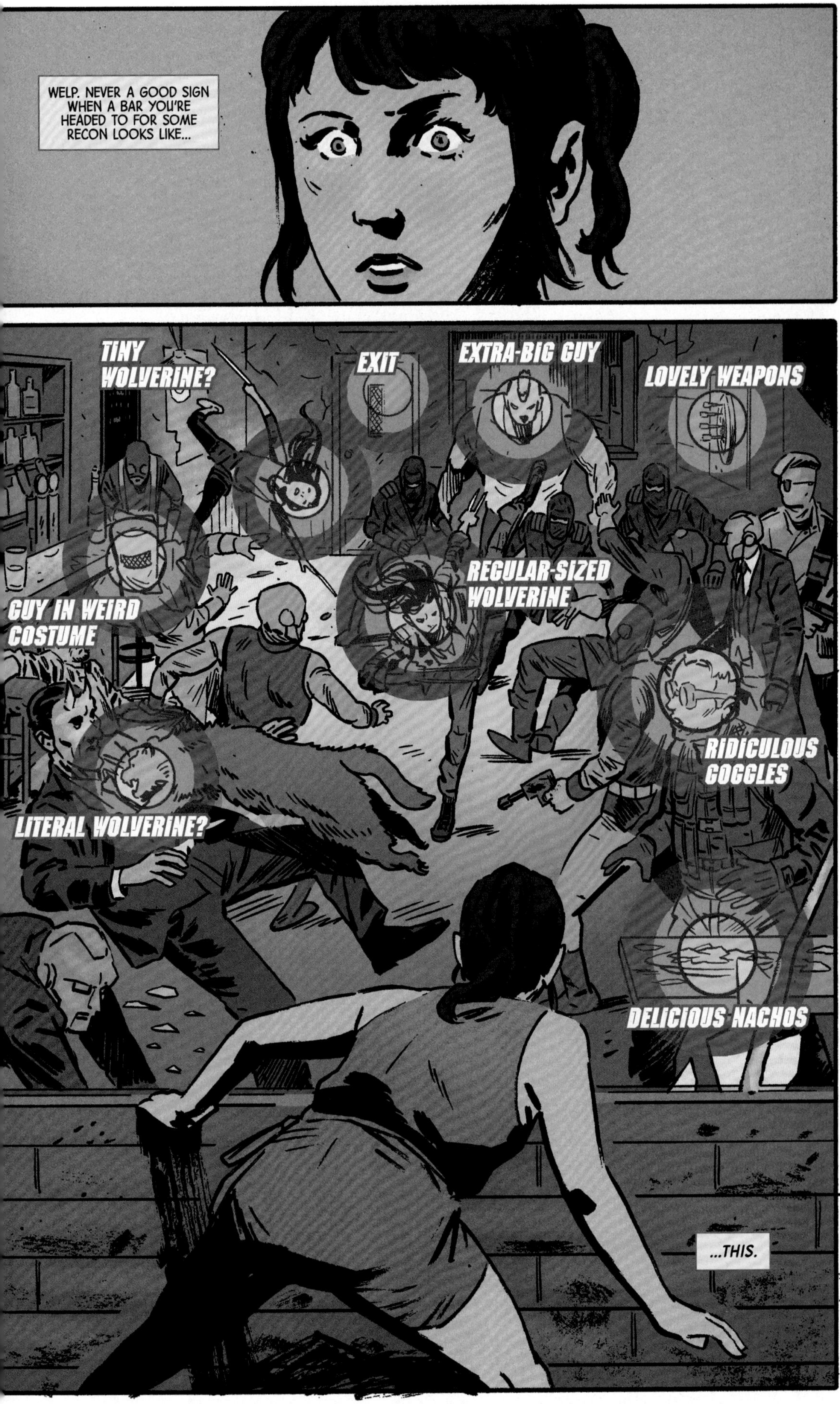
WELP. NEVER A GOOD SIGN WHEN A BAR YOU'RE HEADED TO FOR SOME RECON LOOKS LIKE...
TINY WOLVERINE?
EXIT
EXTRA-BIG GUY
LOVELY WEAPONS
GUY IN WEIRD COSTUME
REGULAR-SIZED WOLVERINE
RIDICULOUS GOGGLES
LITERAL WOLVERINE?
DELICIOUS NACHOS
...THIS.

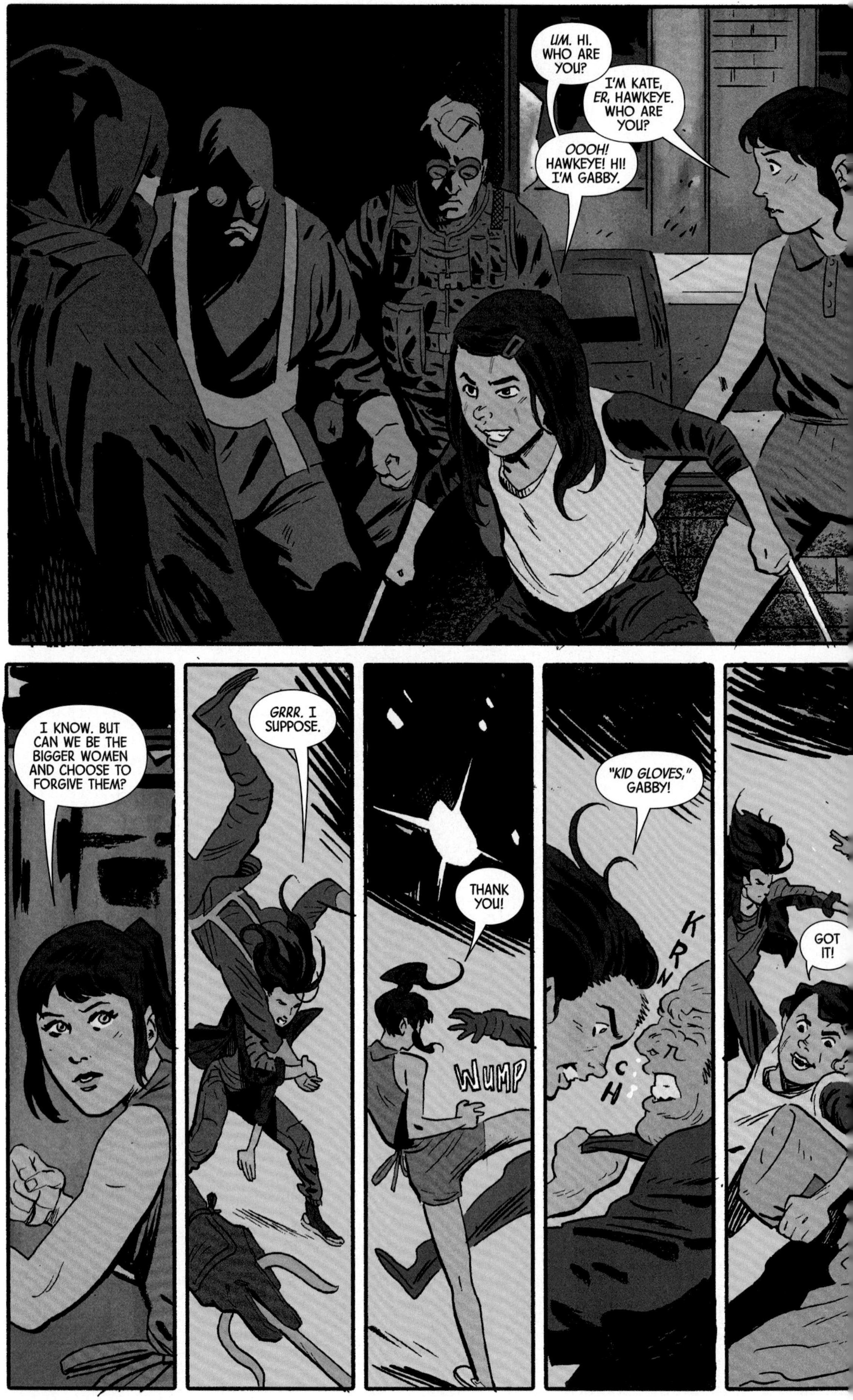
UM. HI. WHO ARE YOU?
I'M KATE, ER, HAWKEYE. WHO ARE YOU?
OOOH! HAWKEYE! HI! I'M GABBY.
I KNOW. BUT CAN WE BE THE BIGGER WOMEN AND CHOOSE TO FORGIVE THEM?
GRRR. I SUPPOSE.
THANK YOU!
WUMP
"KID GLOVES," GABBY!
KRNCH
GOT IT!

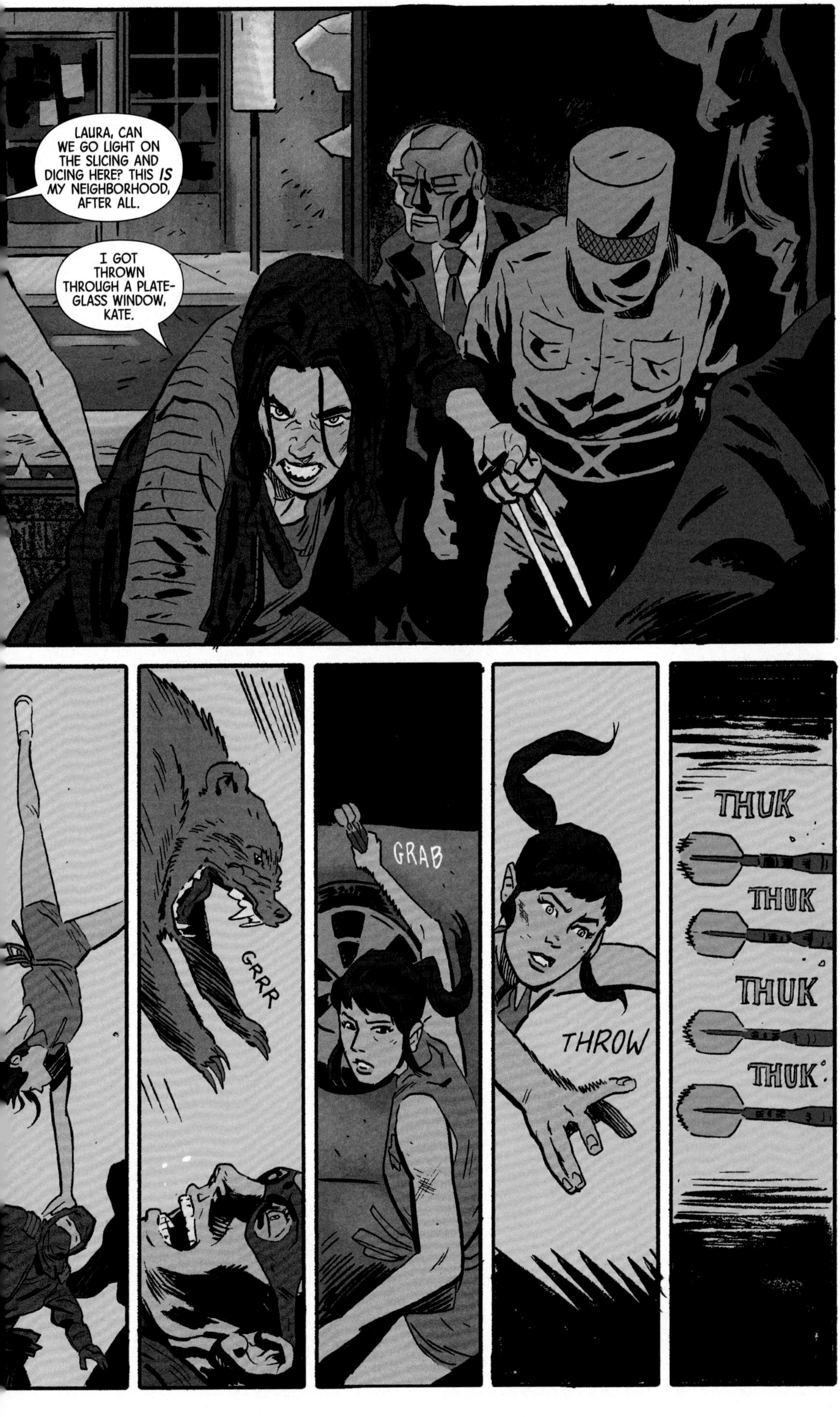

LAURA, CAN WE GO LIGHT ON THE SLICING AND DICING HERE? THIS IS MY NEIGHBORHOOD, AFTER ALL.
I GOT THROWN THROUGH A PLATE-GLASS WINDOW, KATE.
GRRR
GRAB
THROW
THUK
THUK
THUK
THUK

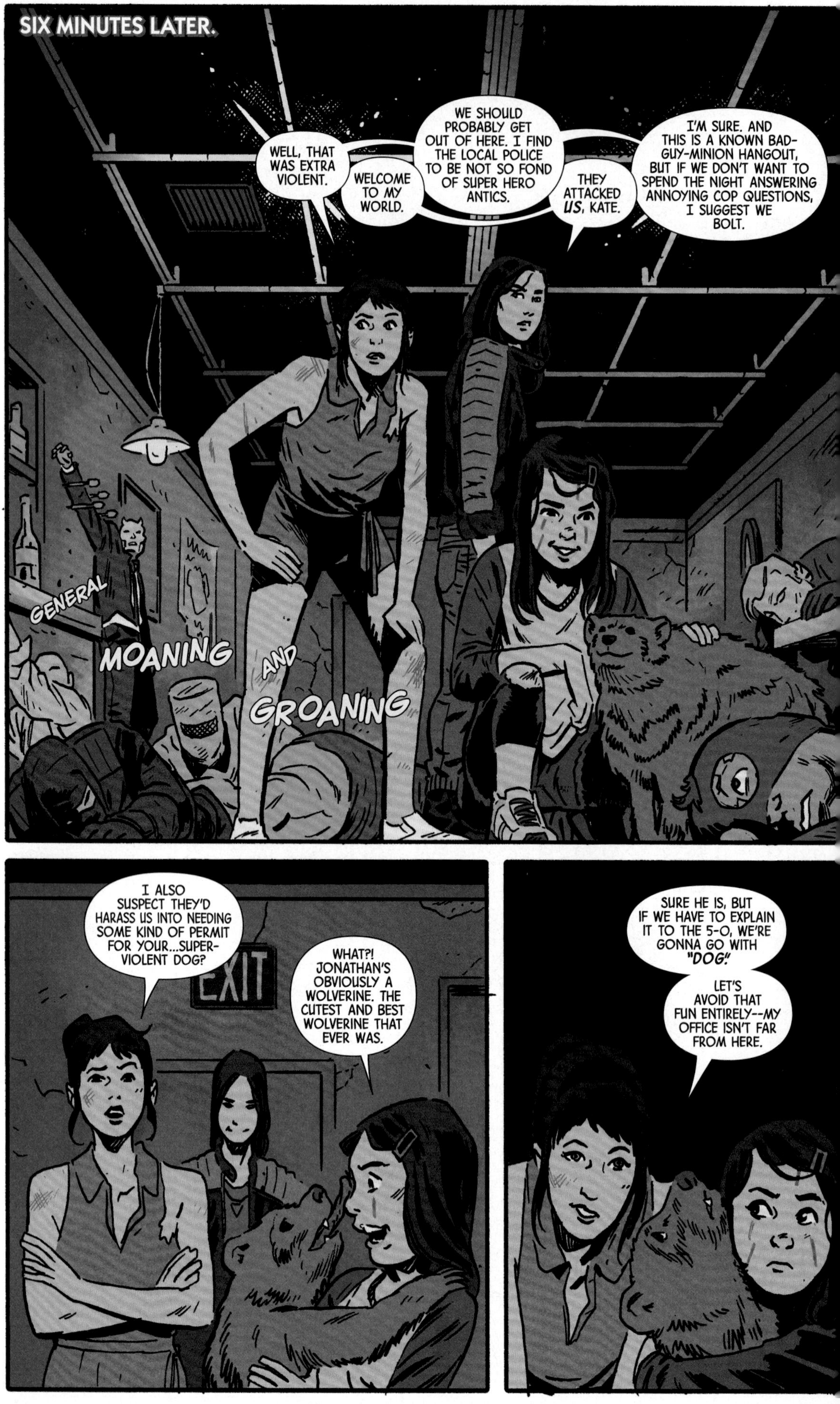
SIX MINUTES LATER.
WELL, THAT WAS EXTRA VIOLENT.
WELCOME TO MY WORLD.
WE SHOULD PROBABLY GET OUT OF HERE. I FIND THE LOCAL POLICE TO BE NOT SO FOND OF SUPER HERO ANTICS.
THEY ATTACKED US, KATE.
I'M SURE. AND THIS IS A KNOWN BAD-GUY-MINION HANGOUT, BUT IF WE DON'T WANT TO SPEND THE NIGHT ANSWERING ANNOYING COP QUESTIONS, I SUGGEST WE BOLT.
GENERAL MOANING AND GROANING
I ALSO SUSPECT THEY'D HARASS US INTO NEEDING SOME KIND OF PERMIT FOR YOUR...SUPER-VIOLENT DOG?
EXIT
WHAT?! JONATHAN'S OBVIOUSLY A WOLVERINE. THE CUTEST AND BEST WOLVERINE THAT EVER WAS.
SURE HE IS, BUT IF WE HAVE TO EXPLAIN IT TO THE 5-O, WE'RE GONNA GO WITH "DOG."
LET'S AVOID THAT FUN ENTIRELY--MY OFFICE ISN'T FAR FROM HERE.

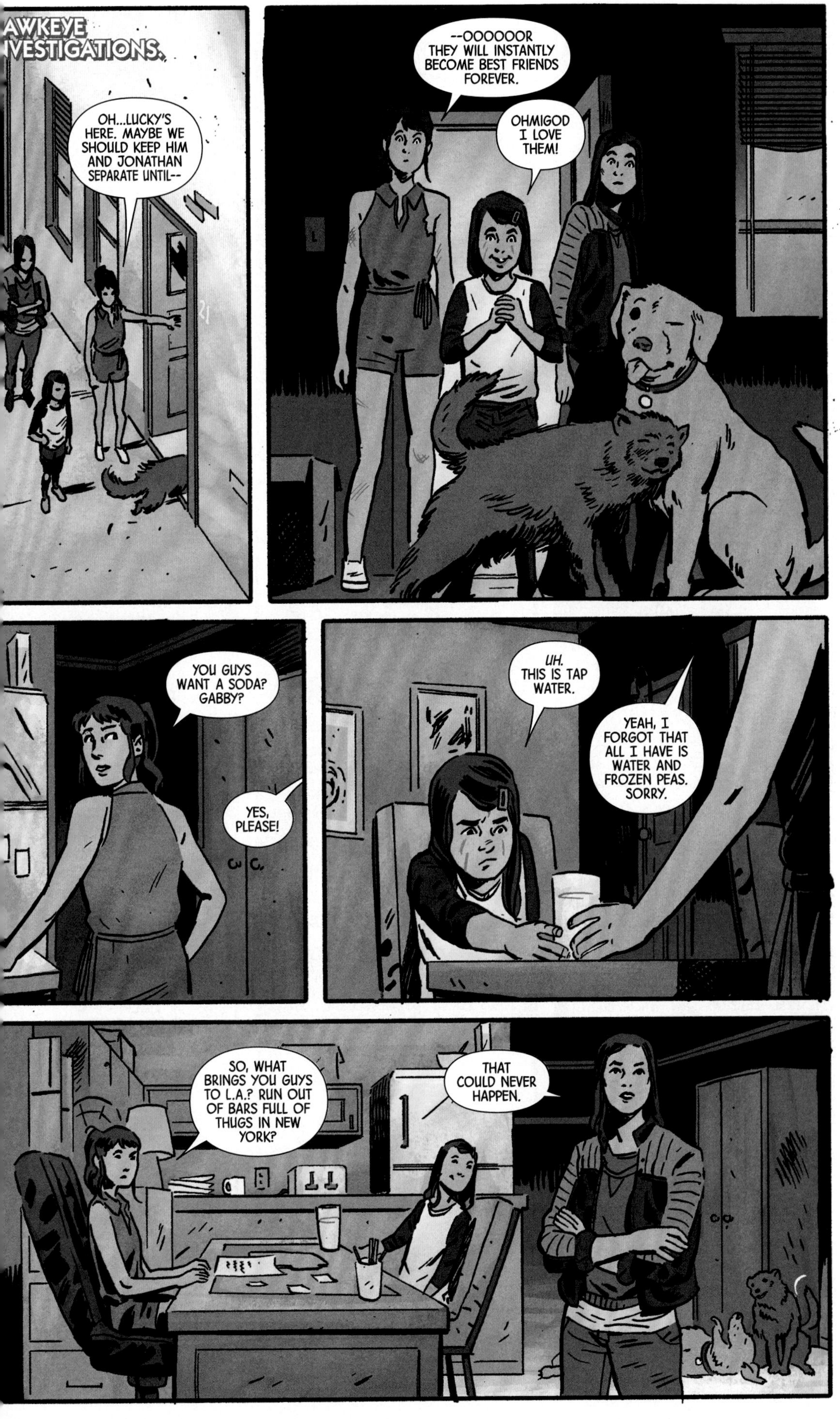
AWKEYE
VESTIGATIONS.
OH...LUCKY'S HERE. MAYBE WE SHOULD KEEP HIM AND JONATHAN SEPARATE UNTIL--
--OOOOOOR THEY WILL INSTANTLY BECOME BEST FRIENDS FOREVER.
OHMIGOD I LOVE THEM!
YOU GUYS WANT A SODA? GABBY?
YES, PLEASE!
UH. THIS IS TAP WATER.
YEAH, I FORGOT THAT ALL I HAVE IS WATER AND FROZEN PEAS. SORRY.
SO, WHAT BRINGS YOU GUYS TO L.A.? RUN OUT OF BARS FULL OF THUGS IN NEW YORK?
THAT COULD NEVER HAPPEN.

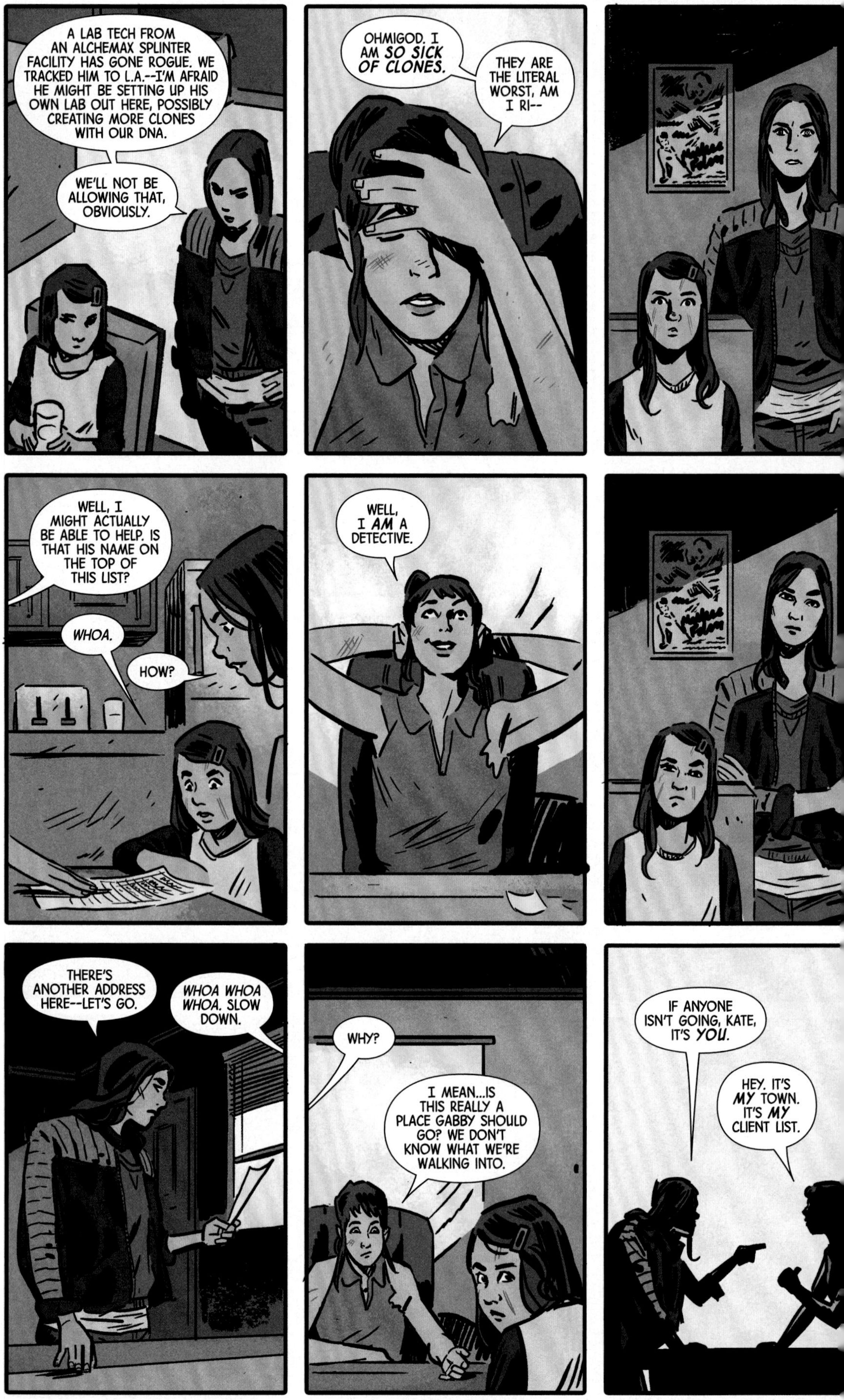
A LAB TECH FROM AN ALCHEMAX SPLINTER FACILITY HAS GONE ROGUE. WE TRACKED HIM TO L.A.--I'M AFRAID HE MIGHT BE SETTING UP HIS OWN LAB OUT HERE, POSSIBLY CREATING MORE CLONES WITH OUR DNA.
WE'LL NOT BE ALLOWING THAT, OBVIOUSLY.
OHMIGOD. I AM SO SICK OF CLONES.
THEY ARE THE LITERAL WORST, AM I RI--
WELL, I MIGHT ACTUALLY BE ABLE TO HELP. IS THAT HIS NAME ON THE TOP OF THIS LIST?
WHOA.
HOW?
WELL, I AM A DETECTIVE.
THERE'S ANOTHER ADDRESS HERE--LET'S GO.
WHOA WHOA WHOA. SLOW DOWN.
WHY?
I MEAN...IS THIS REALLY A PLACE GABBY SHOULD GO? WE DON'T KNOW WHAT WE'RE WALKING INTO.
IF ANYONE ISN'T GOING, KATE, IT'S YOU.
HEY. IT'S MY TOWN. IT'S MY CLIENT LIST.

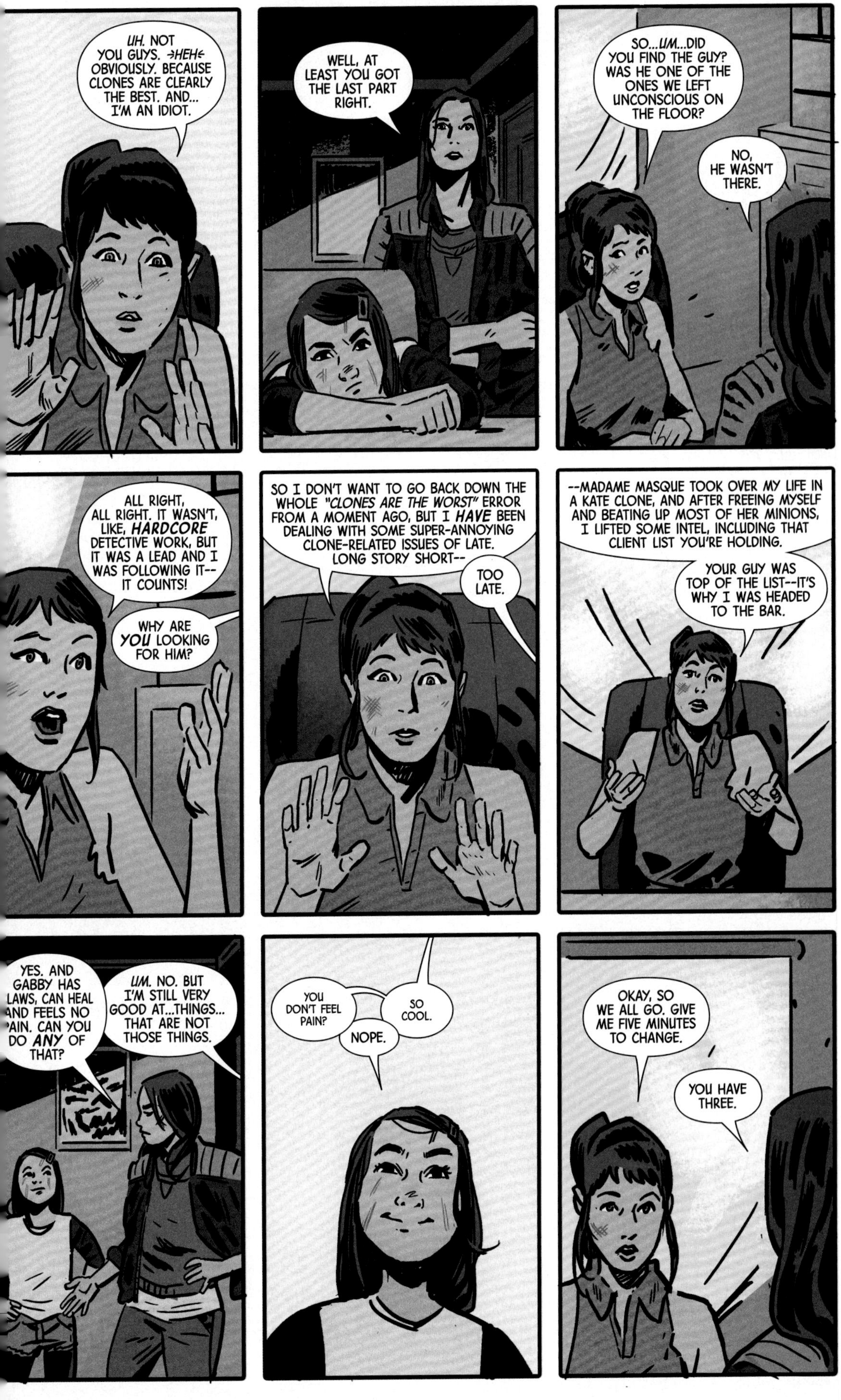
UH. NOT YOU GUYS. ⇛HEH⇚ OBVIOUSLY. BECAUSE CLONES ARE CLEARLY THE BEST. AND... I'M AN IDIOT.
WELL, AT LEAST YOU GOT THE LAST PART RIGHT.
SO...UM...DID YOU FIND THE GUY? WAS HE ONE OF THE ONES WE LEFT UNCONSCIOUS ON THE FLOOR?
NO, HE WASN'T THERE.
ALL RIGHT, ALL RIGHT. IT WASN'T, LIKE, HARDCORE DETECTIVE WORK, BUT IT WAS A LEAD AND I WAS FOLLOWING IT-- IT COUNTS!
WHY ARE YOU LOOKING FOR HIM?
SO I DON'T WANT TO GO BACK DOWN THE WHOLE "CLONES ARE THE WORST" ERROR FROM A MOMENT AGO, BUT I HAVE BEEN DEALING WITH SOME SUPER-ANNOYING CLONE-RELATED ISSUES OF LATE. LONG STORY SHORT--
TOO LATE.
--MADAME MASQUE TOOK OVER MY LIFE IN A KATE CLONE, AND AFTER FREEING MYSELF AND BEATING UP MOST OF HER MINIONS, I LIFTED SOME INTEL, INCLUDING THAT CLIENT LIST YOU'RE HOLDING.
YOUR GUY WAS TOP OF THE LIST--IT'S WHY I WAS HEADED TO THE BAR.
YES. AND GABBY HAS LAWS, CAN HEAL AND FEELS NO PAIN. CAN YOU DO ANY OF THAT?
UM. NO. BUT I'M STILL VERY GOOD AT...THINGS... THAT ARE NOT THOSE THINGS.
YOU DON'T FEEL PAIN?
SO COOL.
NOPE.
OKAY, SO WE ALL GO. GIVE ME FIVE MINUTES TO CHANGE.
YOU HAVE THREE.

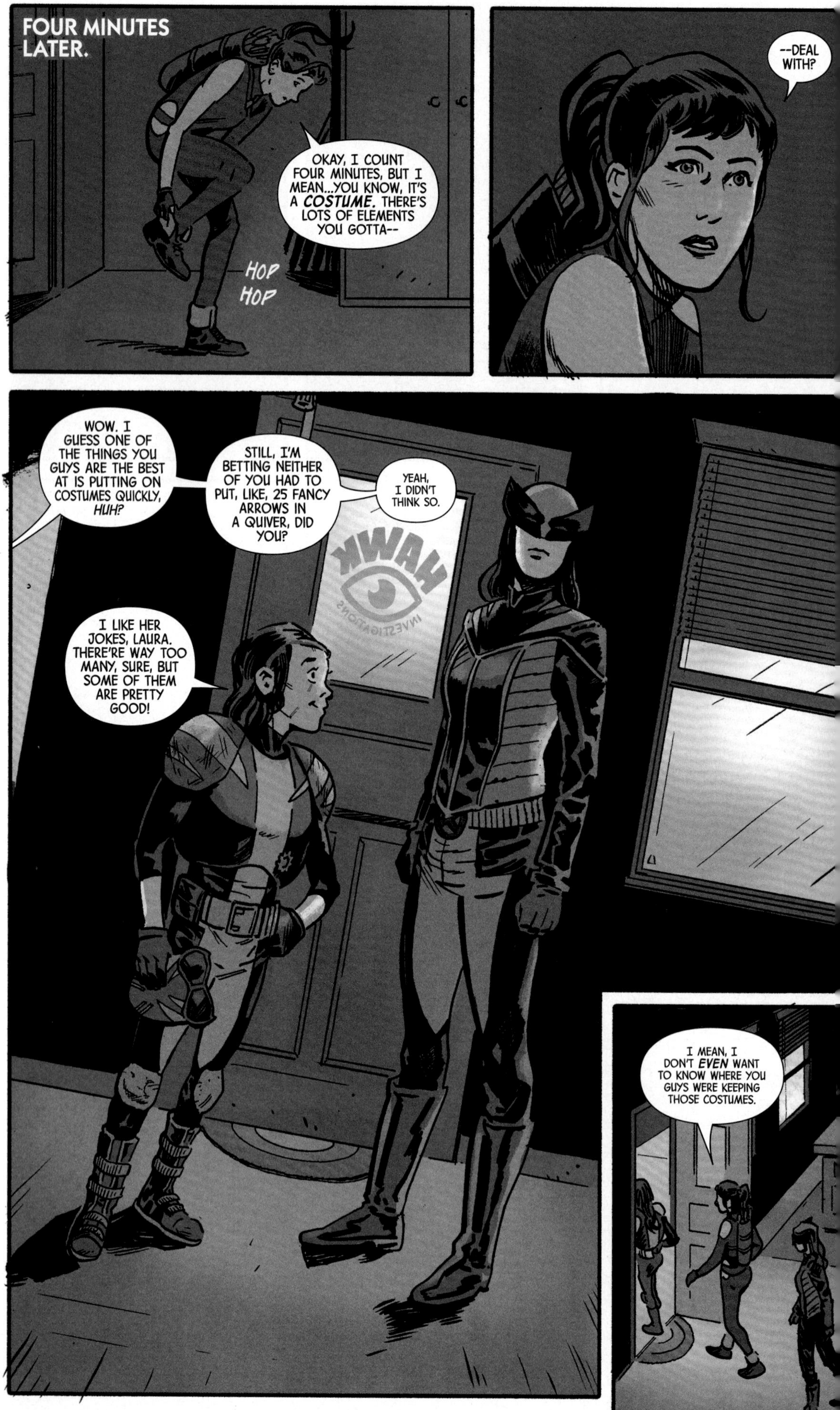
FOUR MINUTES LATER.
OKAY, I COUNT FOUR MINUTES, BUT I MEAN...YOU KNOW, IT'S A COSTUME. THERE'S LOTS OF ELEMENTS YOU GOTTA--
HOP HOP
--DEAL WITH?
WOW. I GUESS ONE OF THE THINGS YOU GUYS ARE THE BEST AT IS PUTTING ON COSTUMES QUICKLY, HUH?
STILL, I'M BETTING NEITHER OF YOU HAD TO PUT, LIKE, 25 FANCY ARROWS IN A QUIVER, DID YOU?
YEAH, I DIDN'T THINK SO.
HAWK INVESTIGATIONS
I LIKE HER JOKES, LAURA. THERE'RE WAY TOO MANY, SURE, BUT SOME OF THEM ARE PRETTY GOOD!
I MEAN, I DON'T EVEN WANT TO KNOW WHERE YOU GUYS WERE KEEPING THOSE COSTUMES.

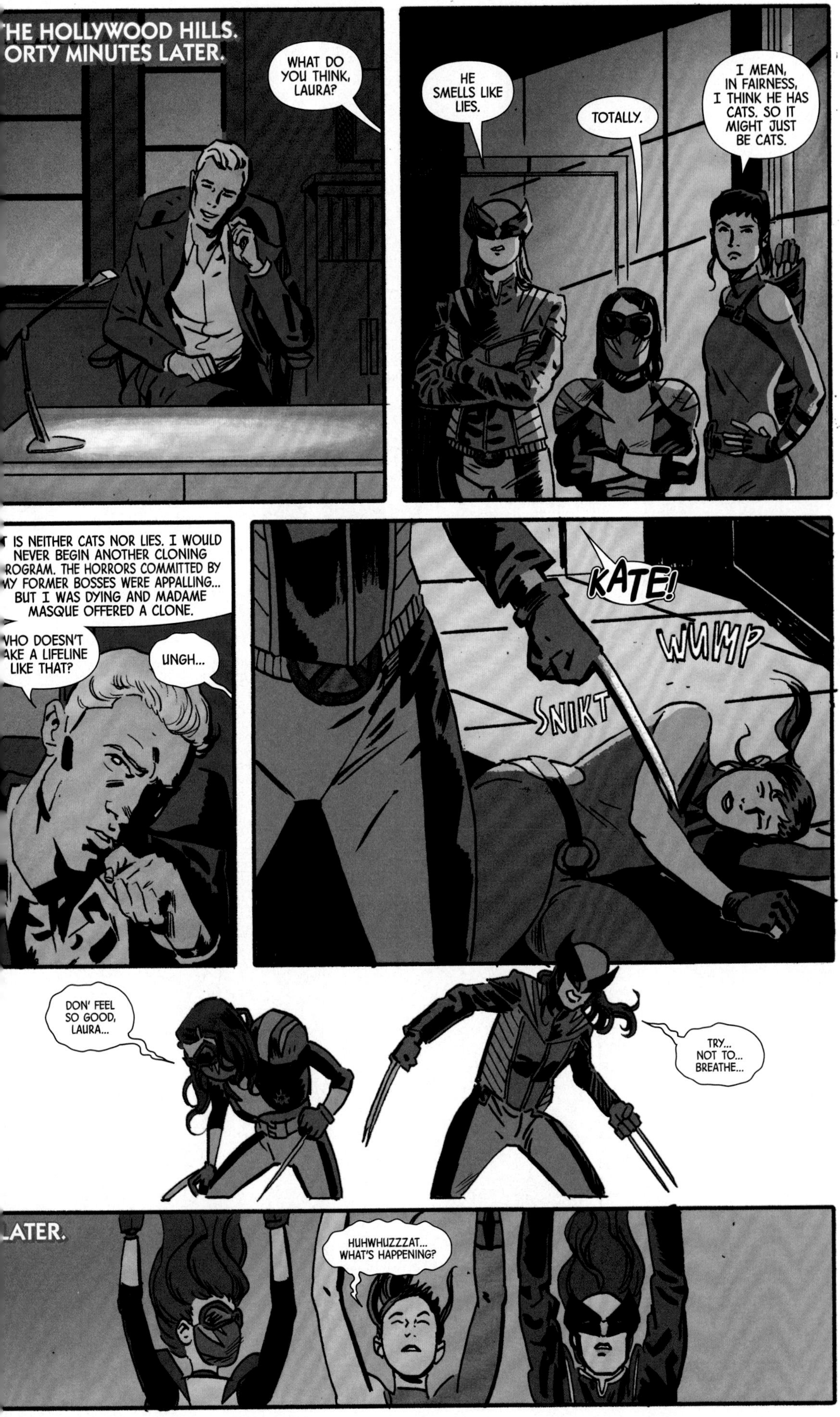

'HE HOLLYWOOD HILLS. ORTY MINUTES LATER.
WHAT DO YOU THINK, LAURA?
HE SMELLS LIKE LIES.
TOTALLY.
I MEAN, IN FAIRNESS, I THINK HE HAS CATS. SO IT MIGHT JUST BE CATS.
T IS NEITHER CATS NOR LIES. I WOULD NEVER BEGIN ANOTHER CLONING ROGRAM. THE HORRORS COMMITTED BY MY FORMER BOSSES WERE APPALLING... BUT I WAS DYING AND MADAME MASQUE OFFERED A CLONE.
WHO DOESN'T AKE A LIFELINE LIKE THAT?
UNGH...
KATE!
WUMP
SNIKT
DON' FEEL SO GOOD, LAURA...
TRY... NOT TO... BREATHE...
LATER.
HUHWHUZZZAT... WHAT'S HAPPENING?

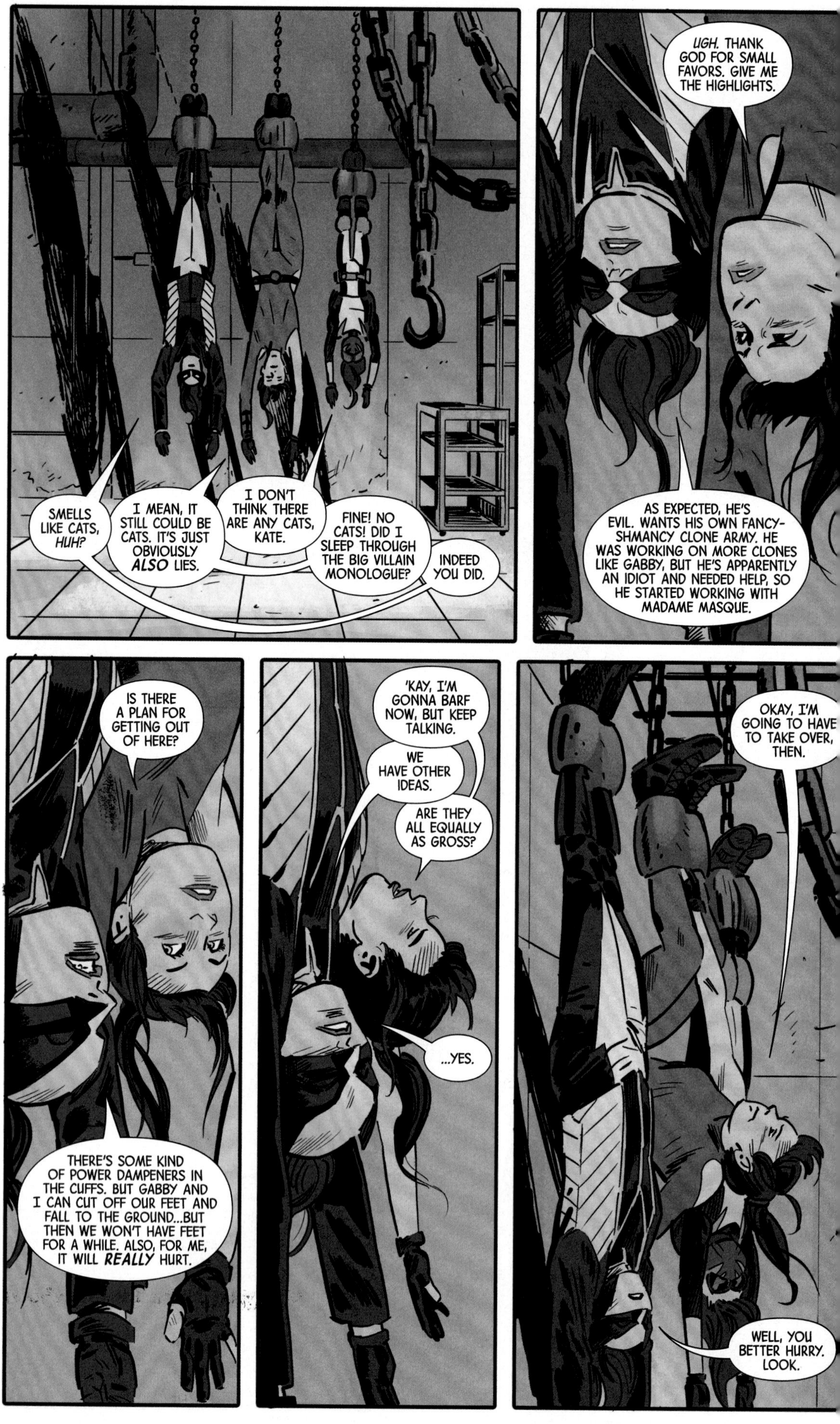
SMELLS LIKE CATS, *HUH?*
I MEAN, IT STILL COULD BE CATS. IT'S JUST OBVIOUSLY **ALSO** LIES.
I DON'T THINK THERE ARE ANY CATS, KATE.
FINE! NO CATS! DID I SLEEP THROUGH THE BIG VILLAIN MONOLOGUE?
INDEED YOU DID.
UGH. THANK GOD FOR SMALL FAVORS. GIVE ME THE HIGHLIGHTS.
AS EXPECTED, HE'S EVIL. WANTS HIS OWN FANCY-SHMANCY CLONE ARMY. HE WAS WORKING ON MORE CLONES LIKE GABBY, BUT HE'S APPARENTLY AN IDIOT AND NEEDED HELP, SO HE STARTED WORKING WITH MADAME MASQUE.
IS THERE A PLAN FOR GETTING OUT OF HERE?
THERE'S SOME KIND OF POWER DAMPENERS IN THE CUFFS. BUT GABBY AND I CAN CUT OFF OUR FEET AND FALL TO THE GROUND...BUT THEN WE WON'T HAVE FEET FOR A WHILE. ALSO, FOR ME, IT WILL **REALLY** HURT.
'KAY, I'M GONNA BARF NOW, BUT KEEP TALKING.
WE HAVE OTHER IDEAS.
ARE THEY ALL EQUALLY AS GROSS?
...YES.
OKAY, I'M GOING TO HAVE TO TAKE OVER, THEN.
WELL, YOU BETTER HURRY. LOOK.

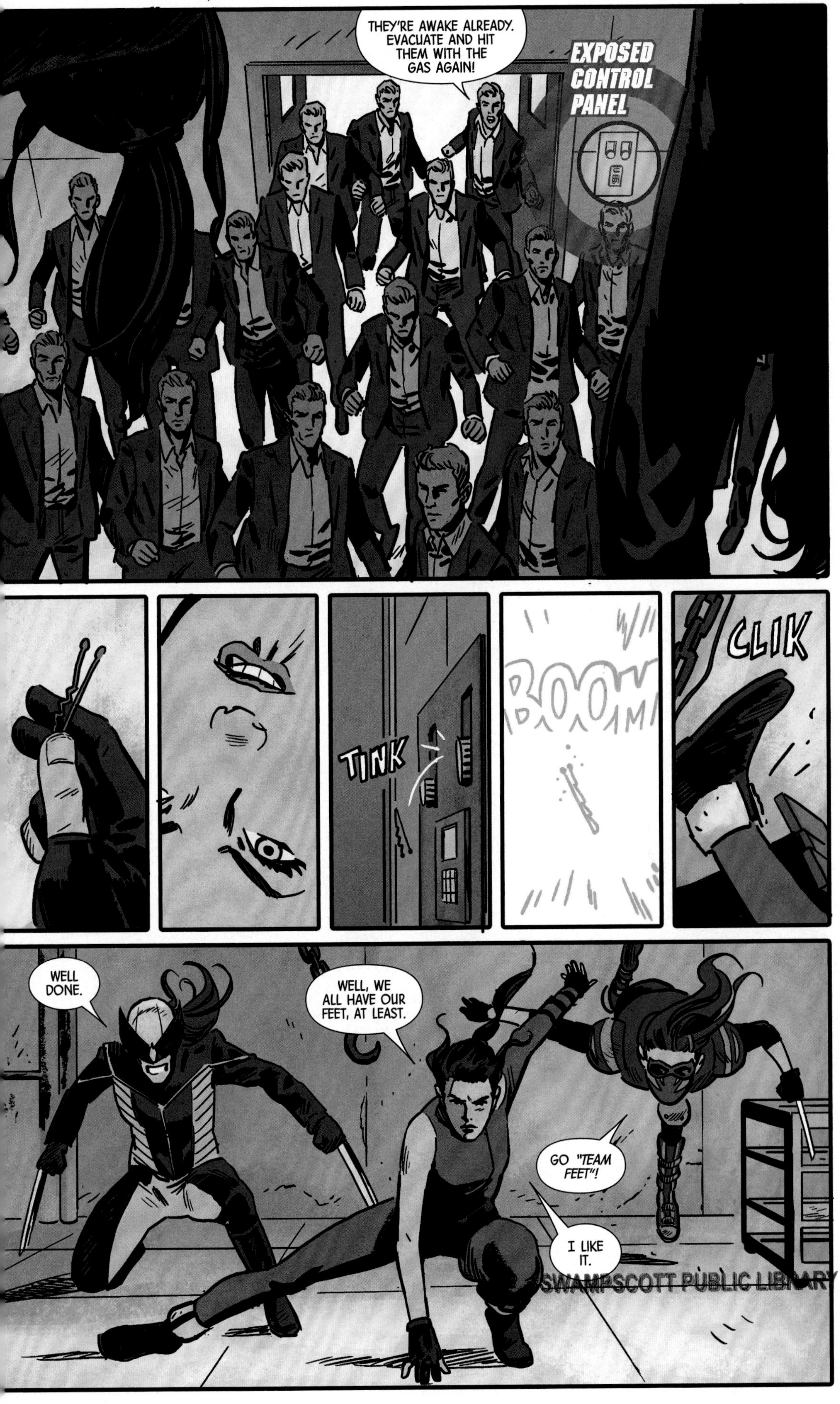
THEY'RE AWAKE ALREADY. EVACUATE AND HIT THEM WITH THE GAS AGAIN!
EXPOSED CONTROL PANEL
TINK
BOOM
CLIK
WELL DONE.
WELL, WE ALL HAVE OUR FEET, AT LEAST.
GO "TEAM FEET"!
I LIKE IT.

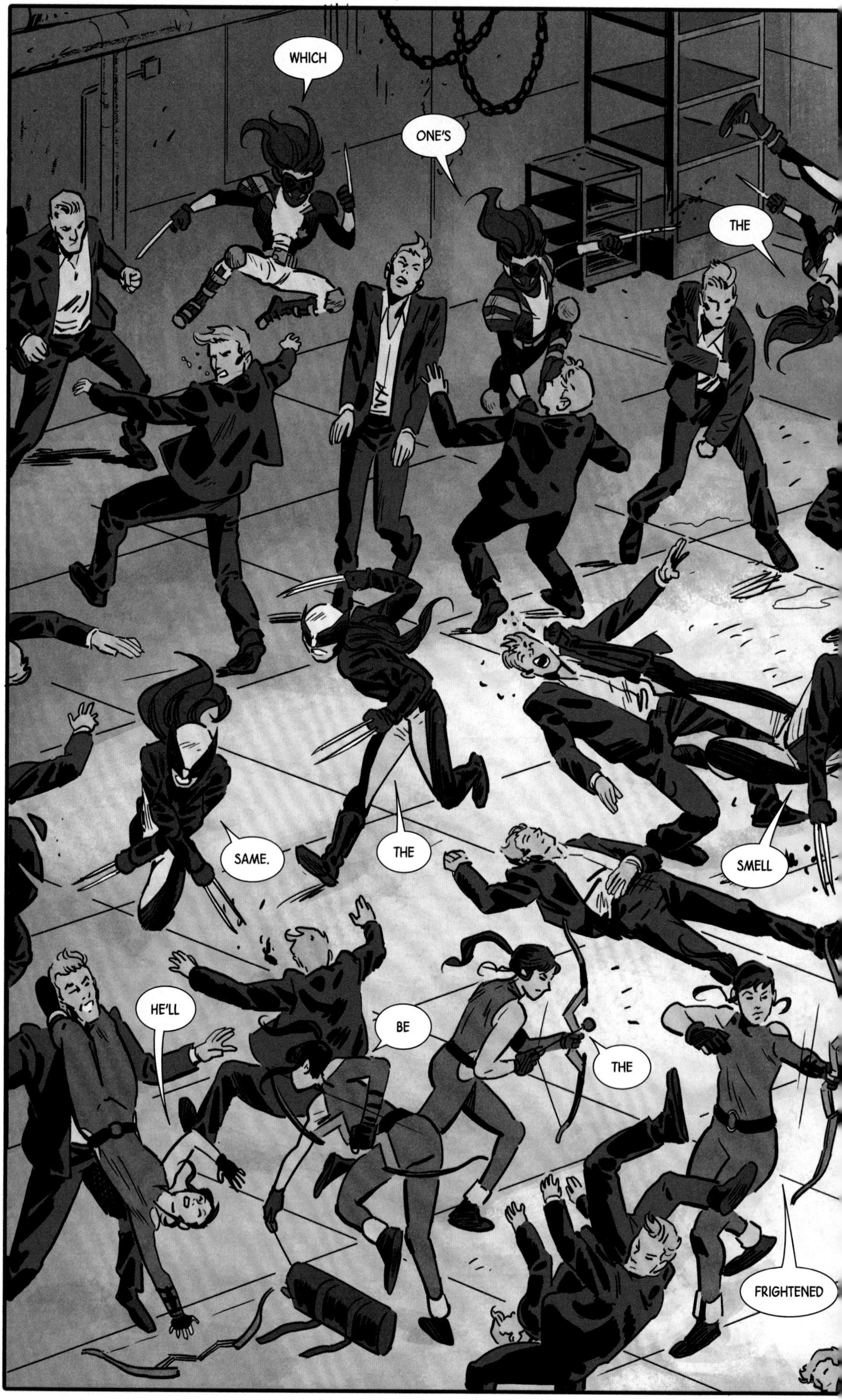
WHICH
ONE'S
THE
SAME.
THE
SMELL
HE'LL
BE
THE
FRIGHTENED

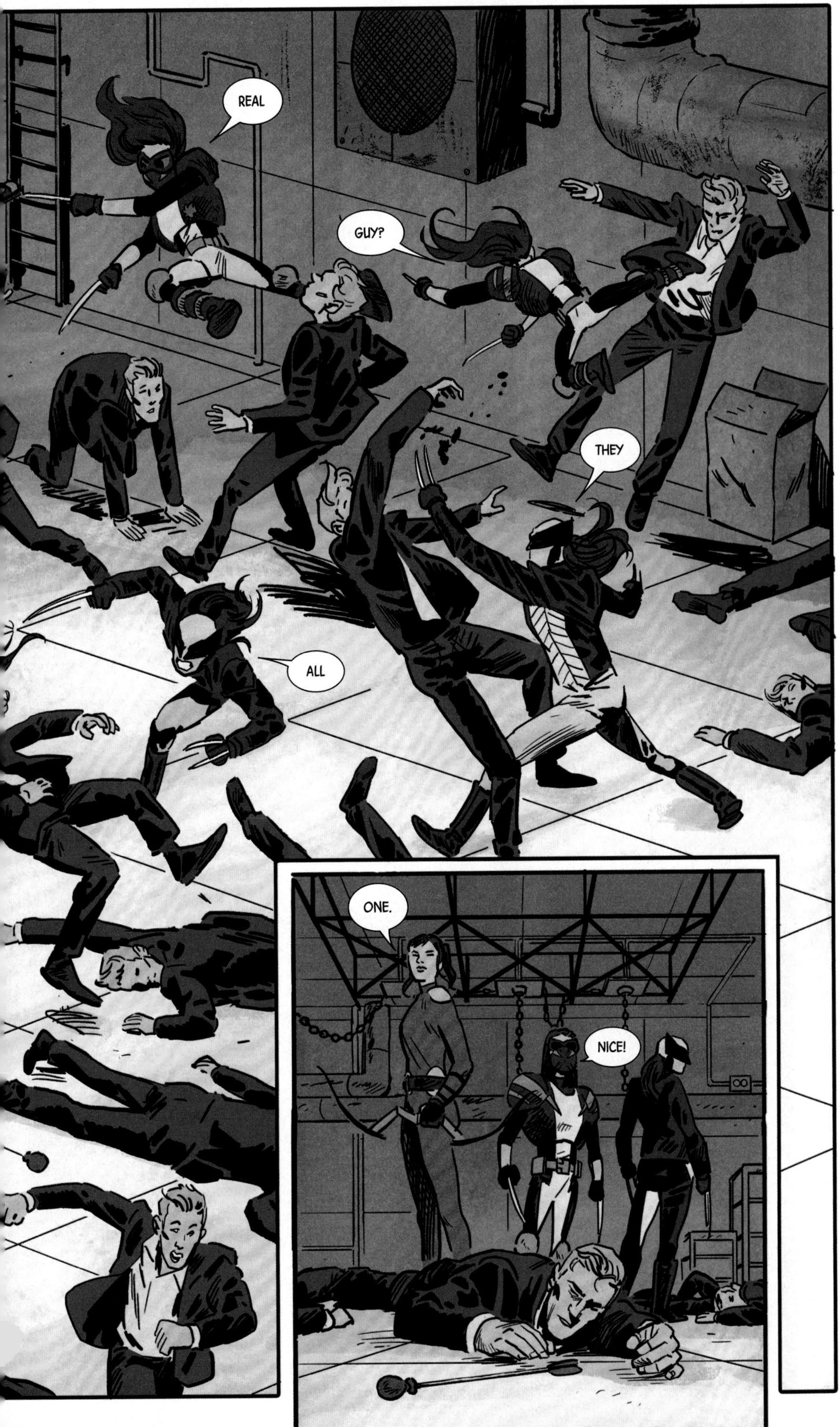
REAL
GUY?
THEY
ALL
ONE.
NICE!

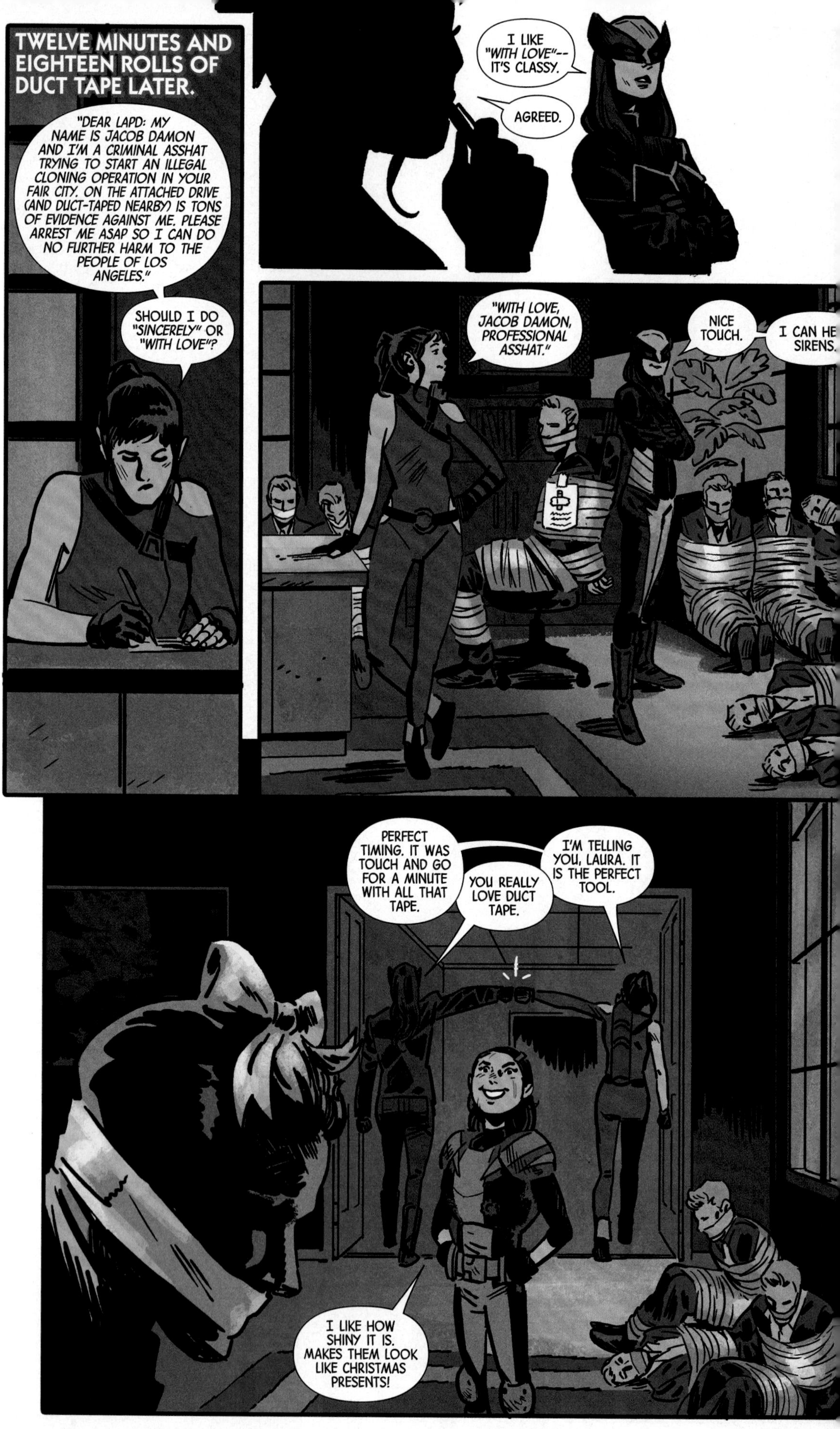

TWELVE MINUTES AND EIGHTEEN ROLLS OF DUCT TAPE LATER.
"DEAR LAPD: MY NAME IS JACOB DAMON AND I'M A CRIMINAL ASSHAT TRYING TO START AN ILLEGAL CLONING OPERATION IN YOUR FAIR CITY. ON THE ATTACHED DRIVE (AND DUCT-TAPED NEARBY) IS TONS OF EVIDENCE AGAINST ME. PLEASE ARREST ME ASAP SO I CAN DO NO FURTHER HARM TO THE PEOPLE OF LOS ANGELES."
SHOULD I DO "SINCERELY" OR "WITH LOVE"?
I LIKE "WITH LOVE"-- IT'S CLASSY.
AGREED.
"WITH LOVE, JACOB DAMON, PROFESSIONAL ASSHAT."
NICE TOUCH.
I CAN HE SIRENS.
PERFECT TIMING. IT WAS TOUCH AND GO FOR A MINUTE WITH ALL THAT TAPE.
YOU REALLY LOVE DUCT TAPE.
I'M TELLING YOU, LAURA. IT IS THE PERFECT TOOL.
I LIKE HOW SHINY IT IS. MAKES THEM LOOK LIKE CHRISTMAS PRESENTS!

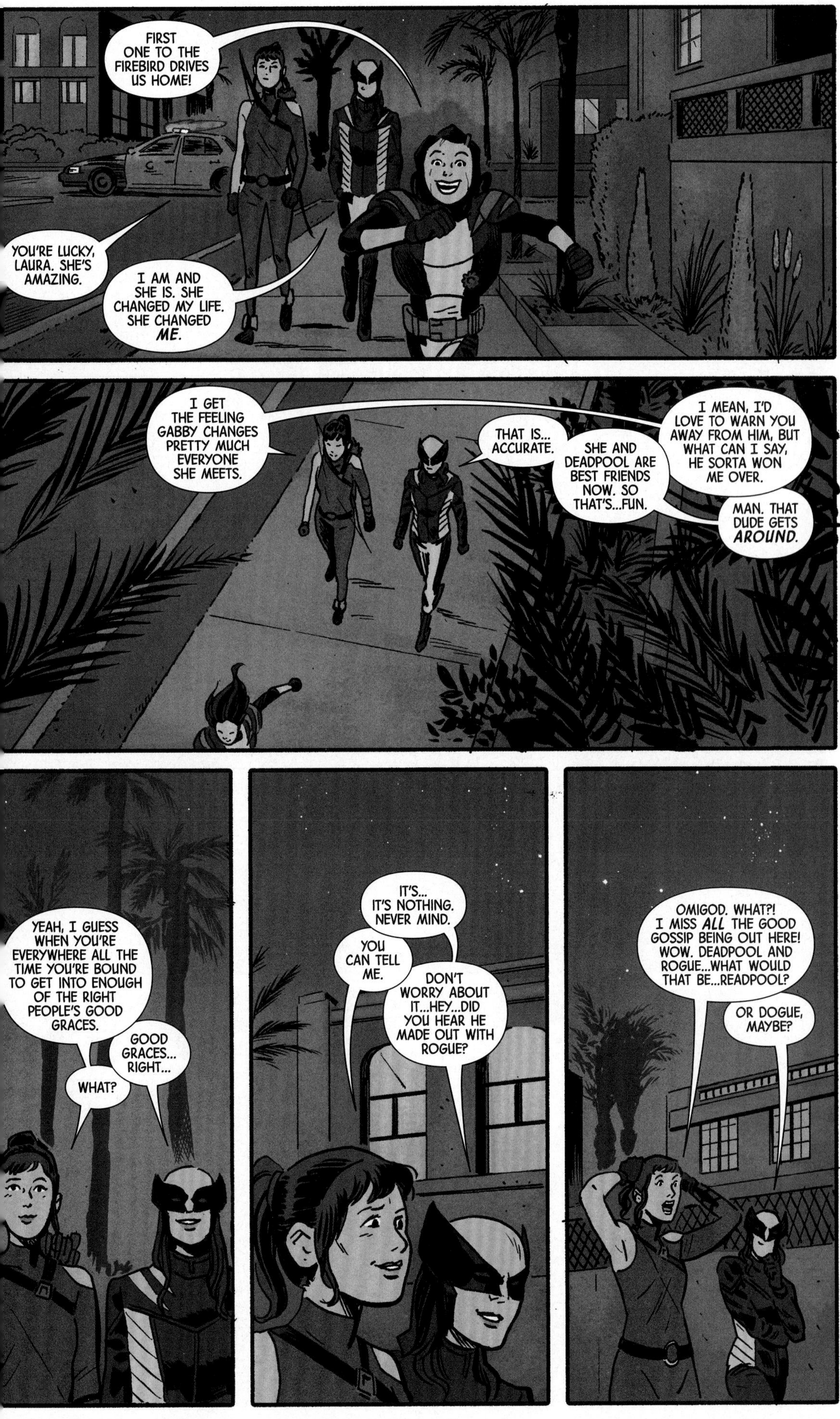
FIRST ONE TO THE FIREBIRD DRIVES US HOME!
YOU'RE LUCKY, LAURA. SHE'S AMAZING.
I AM AND SHE IS. SHE CHANGED MY LIFE. SHE CHANGED *ME*.
I GET THE FEELING GABBY CHANGES PRETTY MUCH EVERYONE SHE MEETS.
THAT IS... ACCURATE.
SHE AND DEADPOOL ARE BEST FRIENDS NOW. SO THAT'S...FUN.
I MEAN, I'D LOVE TO WARN YOU AWAY FROM HIM, BUT WHAT CAN I SAY, HE SORTA WON ME OVER.
MAN. THAT DUDE GETS *AROUND*.
YEAH, I GUESS WHEN YOU'RE EVERYWHERE ALL THE TIME YOU'RE BOUND TO GET INTO ENOUGH OF THE RIGHT PEOPLE'S GOOD GRACES.
GOOD GRACES... RIGHT...
WHAT?
IT'S... IT'S NOTHING. NEVER MIND.
YOU CAN TELL ME.
DON'T WORRY ABOUT IT...HEY...DID YOU HEAR HE MADE OUT WITH ROGUE?
OMIGOD. WHAT?! I MISS *ALL* THE GOOD GOSSIP BEING OUT HERE! WOW. DEADPOOL AND ROGUE...WHAT WOULD THAT BE...READPOOL?
OR DOGUE, MAYBE?

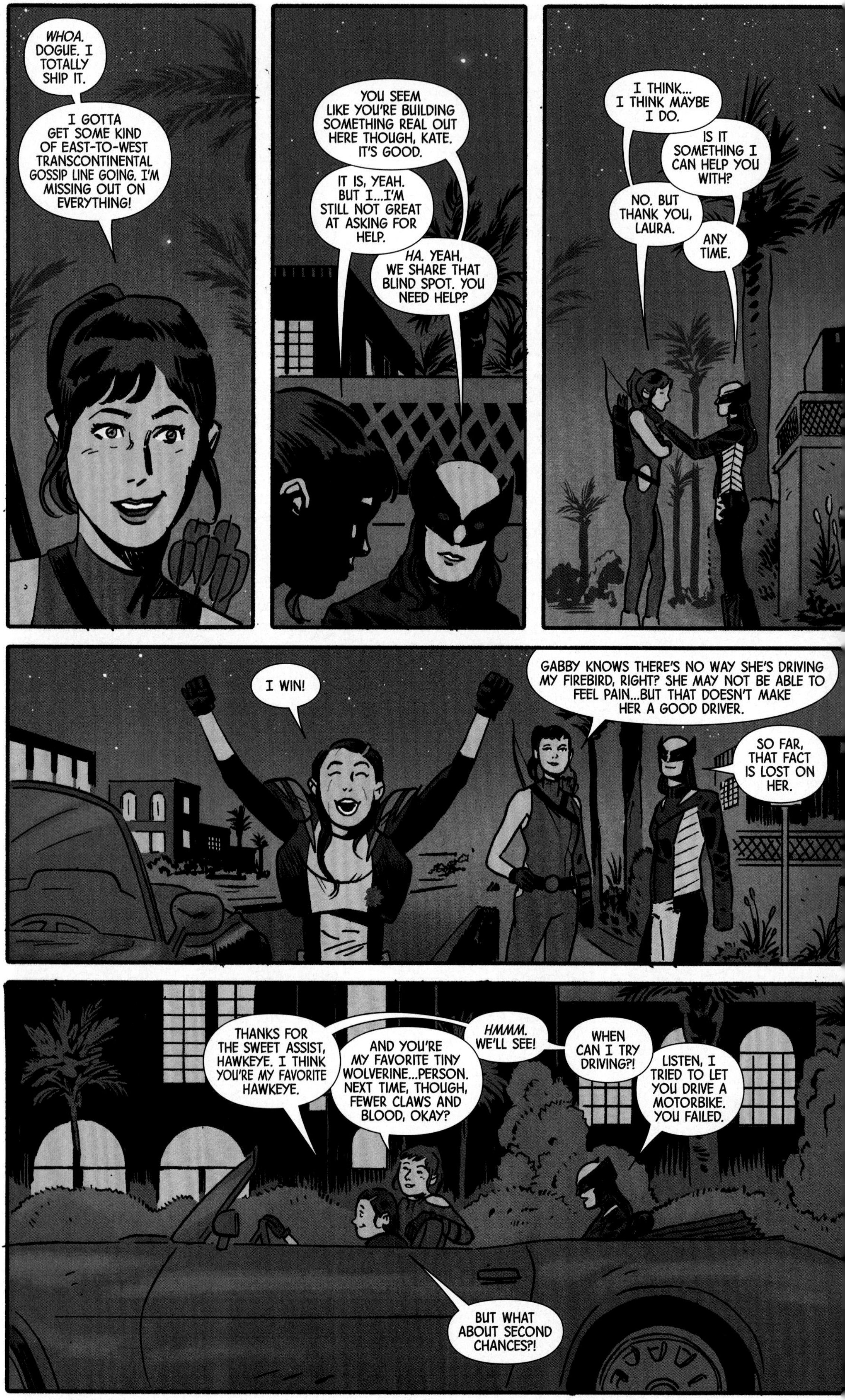
WHOA. DOGUE. I TOTALLY SHIP IT.
I GOTTA GET SOME KIND OF EAST-TO-WEST TRANSCONTINENTAL GOSSIP LINE GOING. I'M MISSING OUT ON EVERYTHING!
YOU SEEM LIKE YOU'RE BUILDING SOMETHING REAL OUT HERE THOUGH, KATE. IT'S GOOD.
IT IS, YEAH. BUT I...I'M STILL NOT GREAT AT ASKING FOR HELP.
HA. YEAH, WE SHARE THAT BLIND SPOT. YOU NEED HELP?
I THINK... I THINK MAYBE I DO.
IS IT SOMETHING I CAN HELP YOU WITH?
NO. BUT THANK YOU, LAURA.
ANY TIME.
I WIN!
GABBY KNOWS THERE'S NO WAY SHE'S DRIVING MY FIREBIRD, RIGHT? SHE MAY NOT BE ABLE TO FEEL PAIN...BUT THAT DOESN'T MAKE HER A GOOD DRIVER.
SO FAR, THAT FACT IS LOST ON HER.
THANKS FOR THE SWEET ASSIST, HAWKEYE. I THINK YOU'RE MY FAVORITE HAWKEYE.
AND YOU'RE MY FAVORITE TINY WOLVERINE...PERSON. NEXT TIME, THOUGH, FEWER CLAWS AND BLOOD, OKAY?
HMMM. WE'LL SEE!
WHEN CAN I TRY DRIVING?!
LISTEN, I TRIED TO LET YOU DRIVE A MOTORBIKE. YOU FAILED.
BUT WHAT ABOUT SECOND CHANCES?!

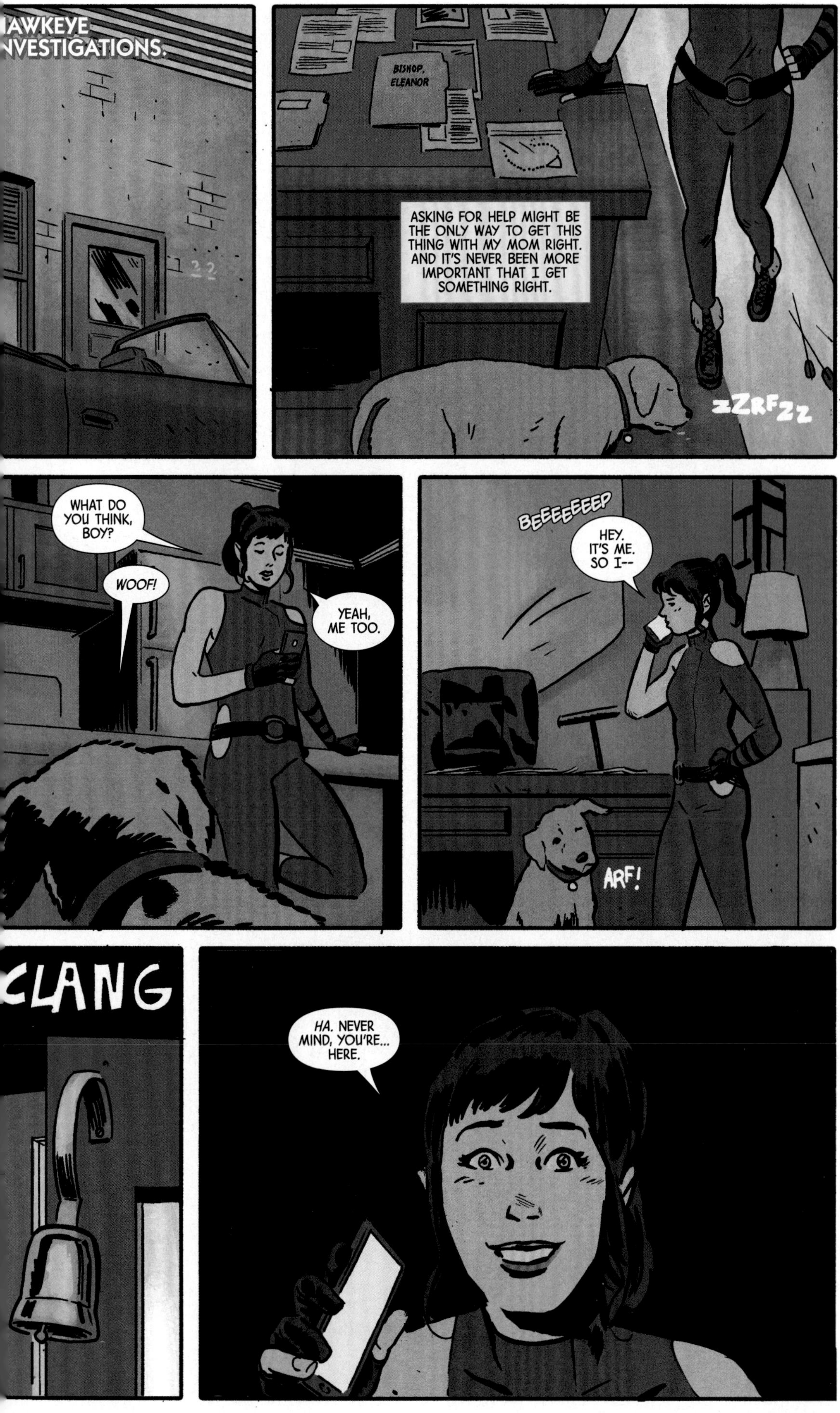

AWKEYE
NVESTIGATIONS.
BISHOP, ELEANOR
ASKING FOR HELP MIGHT BE THE ONLY WAY TO GET THIS THING WITH MY MOM RIGHT. AND IT'S NEVER BEEN MORE IMPORTANT THAT I GET SOMETHING RIGHT.
ZZRFZZ
WHAT DO YOU THINK, BOY?
WOOF!
YEAH, ME TOO.
BEEEEEEEP
HEY. IT'S ME. SO I--
ARF!
CLANG
HA. NEVER MIND, YOU'RE... HERE.

NEXT:
FAMILY REUNION

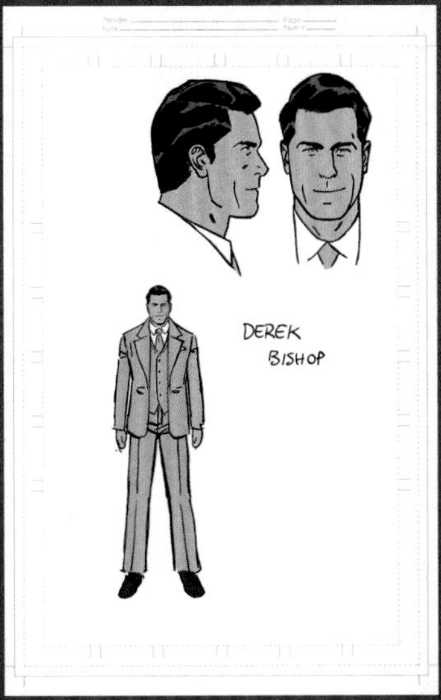
DEREK
BISHOP

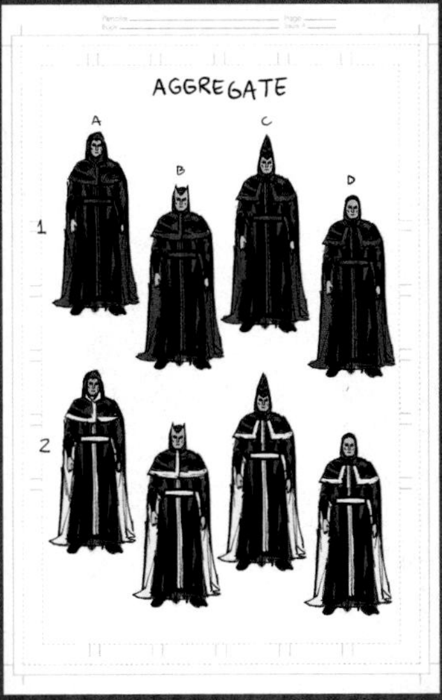
AGGREGATE
A
B
C
D
1
2

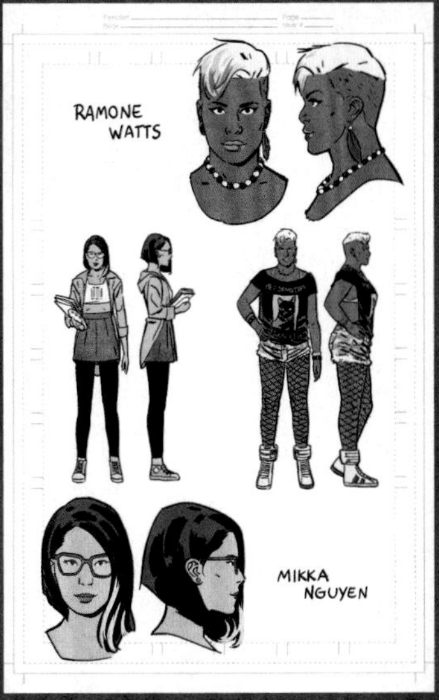
RAMONE
WATTS
MIKKA
NGUYEN

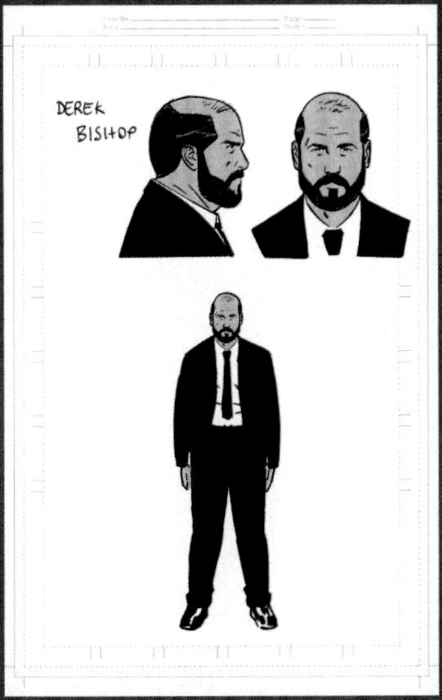
DEREK
BISHOP

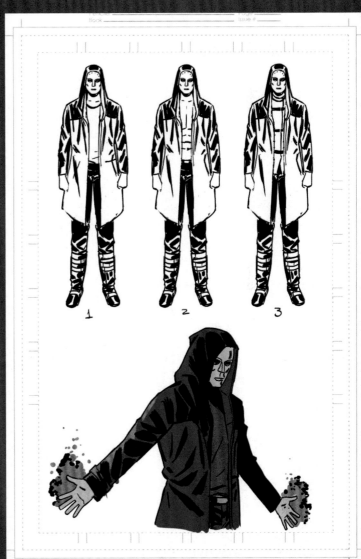

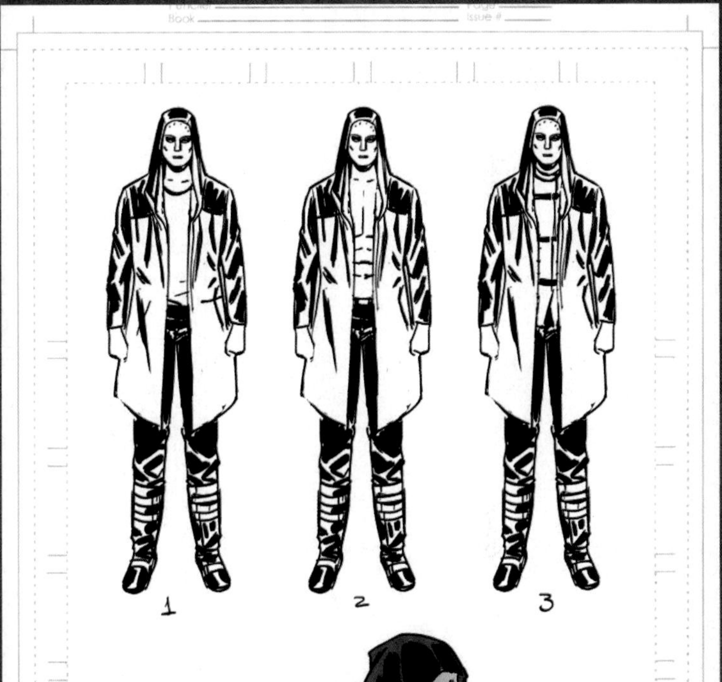
1
2
3

designs by **Leonardo Romero**

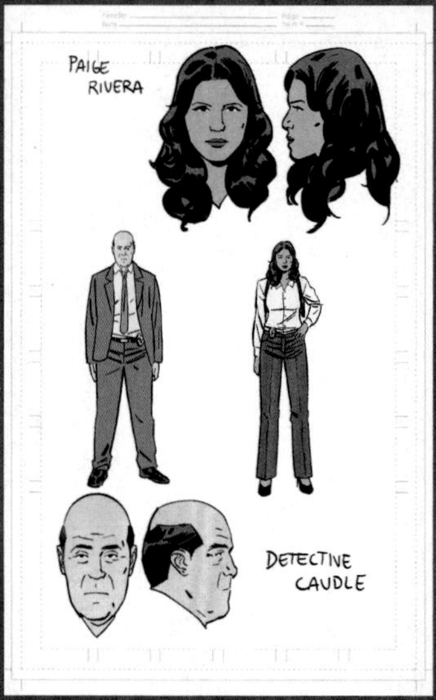
PAIGE
RIVERA
DETECTIVE
CAUDLE

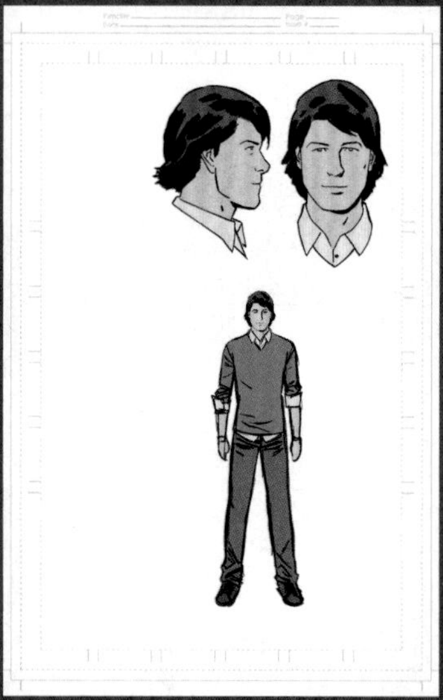

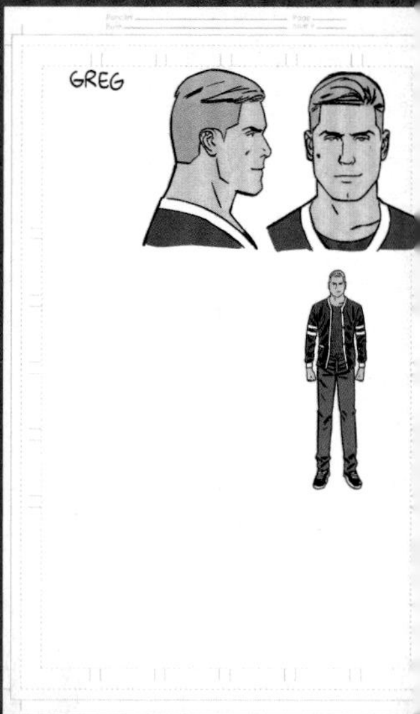
GREG

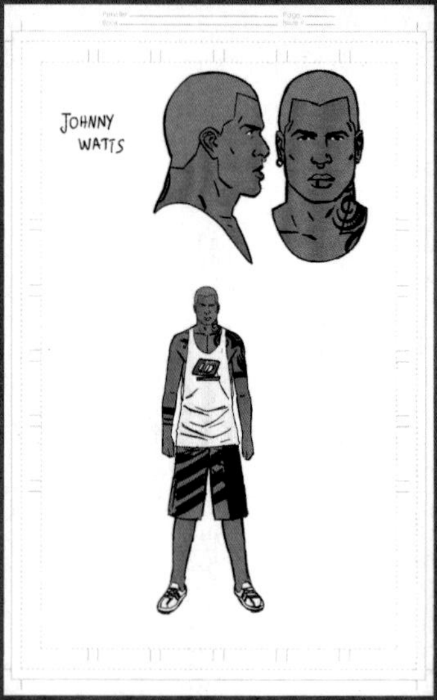
JOHNNY
WATTS

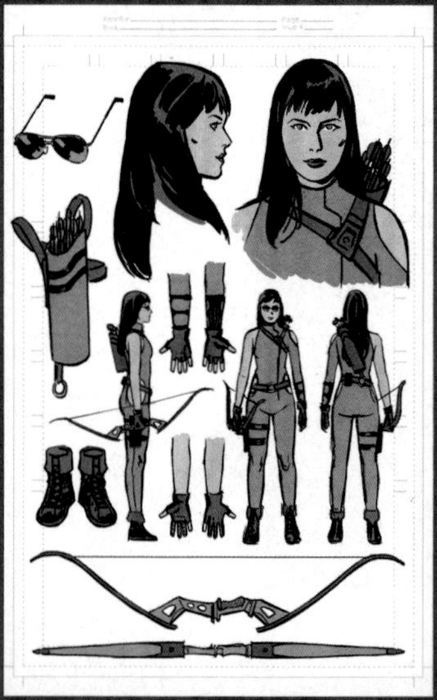

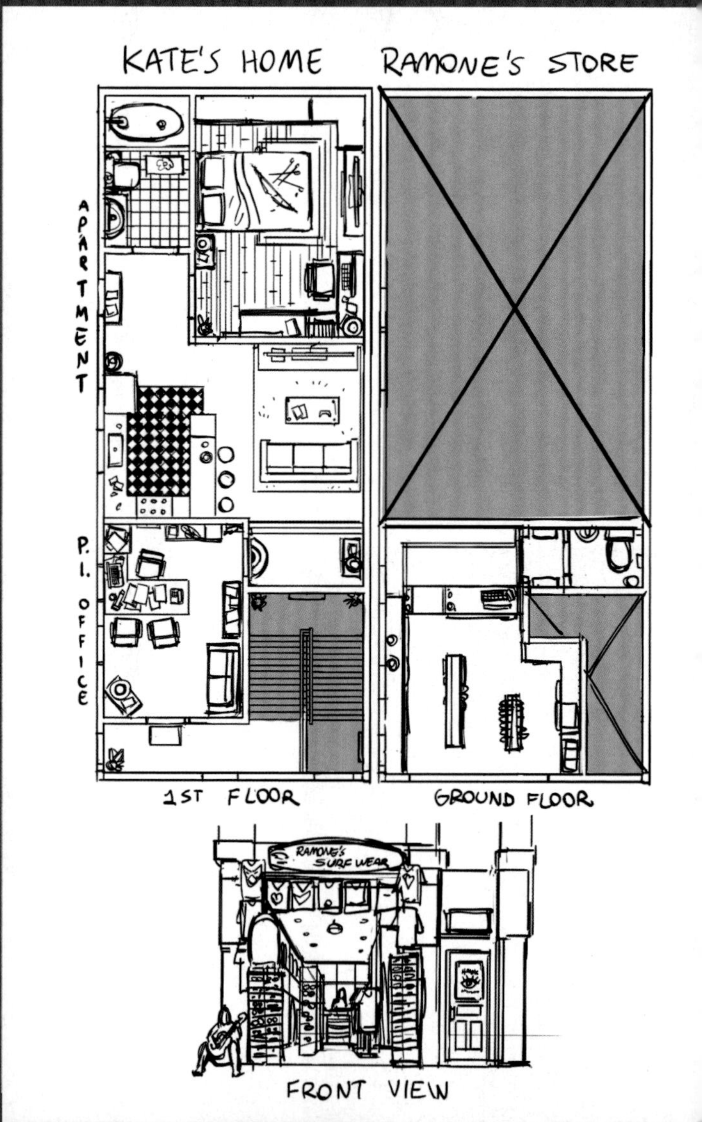
KATE'S HOME
RAMONE'S STORE
APARTMENT
P.I. OFFICE
1ST FLOOR
GROUND FLOOR
RAMONE'S SURF WEAR
FRONT VIEW

designs by **Leonardo Romero**